T0214094

Lecture Notes in Computer Science   12605

More information about this subseries at http://www.springer.com/series/7411

Samia Bouzefrane · Maryline Laurent ·
Selma Boumerdassi · Eric Renault (Eds.)

Mobile, Secure, and Programmable Networking

6th International Conference, MSPN 2020
Paris, France, October 28–29, 2020
Revised Selected Papers

 Springer

Editors
Samia Bouzefrane
Cedric Lab, Cnam
Paris, France

Maryline Laurent
Télécom SudParis
Evry, France

Selma Boumerdassi
Cedric Lab, Cnam
Paris, France

Eric Renault
LIGM, ESIEE
Noisy-le-Grand, France

ISSN 0302-9743   ISSN 1611-3349   (electronic)
Lecture Notes in Computer Science
ISBN 978-3-030-67549-3   ISBN 978-3-030-67550-9   (eBook)
https://doi.org/10.1007/978-3-030-67550-9

LNCS Sublibrary: SL5 – Computer Communication Networks and Telecommunications

This Springer imprint is published by the registered company Springer Nature Switzerland AG
The registered company address is: Gewerbestrasse 11, 6330 Cham, Switzerland

Preface

The rapid deployment of new generations of networks and the exponential increase of connected objects trigger new applications and services that in turn generate new constraints such as security and/or mobility. The International Conference on Mobile, Secure and Programmable Networking aims to provide an elicited forum for researchers and industrial practitioners to present and discuss emerging trends in networking infrastructures, distributed yet intelligent protocols, security, services and applications while focusing on machine learning and artificial intelligence, network programming and Cloud computing, Industrial Internet of Things, Digital Twins, etc.

MSPN 2020 was hosted by Cnam (Conservatoire National des Arts et Métiers), a French public institute created in 1794 and dedicated to lifelong education. Cnam is based in the heart of Paris and is associated with the Musée des Arts et Métiers.

We had 31 submissions and the program committee accepted 16 papers. Every submission was assigned to three members of the program committee for review. The accepted papers originated from Algeria, Australia, Ecuador, France, India, Ireland, Lebanon, Luxembourg, Morocco, Tunisia, United Arab Emirates, USA, and Vietnam. Three brilliant invited speakers completed the technical program. The first speaker was Dr. Edgardo Montes de Oca, the CEO of Montimage in France, who gave a vision of the industry in terms of Cyber Threat Intelligence. The second speaker was Professor Luis Almeida, from the University of Porto in Portugal, who presented the principal ideas behind synchronization using cooperating agents. The third one was Dr. Gürkan Gür, from the Zurich University of Applied Sciences (ZHAW) in Switzerland, who identified the challenges of future networks.

We would like to thank the authors for their high-quality paper contributions, the chairs and the members of the technical program committee for reviewing the submitted papers and selecting a high-quality program, and the general chairs for their support. Our special thanks go also to the Organizing Committee members for their great help and to the sponsoring institutions.

We hope that all the participants enjoyed this virtual conference despite the COVID-19 situation that did not allow them to come to Paris.

October 2020

Samia Bouzefrane
Maryline Laurent
Selma Boumerdassi
Eric Renault

Organization

MSPN 2020 was organized by CEDRIC Lab of Cnam, Paris, Télécom SudParis, the University of Limoges and the association ASELKIM with the cooperation of IFIP WG 11.2 Pervasive Systems Security.

General Chairs

Samia Bouzefrane	Cnam, France
Maryline Laurent	Télécom SudParis, France

Steering Committee

Samia Bouzefrane	Cnam, France
Eric Renault	ESIEE Paris, France
Selma Boumerdassi	Cnam, France

Program Chairs

Soumya Banerjee	Inria, France
Samia Bouzefrane	Cnam, France
Maryline Laurent	Télécom SudParis, France

Organizing Committee

Yulliwas Ameur	Cnam, France
Mamoudou Sangaré	Cnam, France
Mohamed Nafi	University of Béjaïa, Algeria

Technical Program Committee

Emad Abd-Elrahman	National Telecommunication Institute, Egypt
Amar Abane	NIST, USA
Keyvan Ansari	University of the Sunshine Coast (USC), Australia
Soumya Banerjee	Workz, Ireland
Chafika Benzaid	Aalto University, Finland
Kübra Kalkan Çakmakçı	Özyeğin University, Turkey
Miguel Elias M. Campista	Universidade Federal do Rio de Janeiro, Brazil
Luca Caviglione	Institute for Applied Mathematics and Information Technologies, Italy
Michal Choras	UTP University of Science and Technology, Poland
Emmanuel Conchon	University of Limoges, France

Julien Cordry	Teesside University, UK
Mohammed Erritali	Sultan Moulay Slimane University, Morocco
Christian Franck	University of Luxembourg, Luxembourg
Chrystel Gaber	Orange Labs, France
Bamba Gueye	Cheikh Anta Diop de Dakar (UCAD) University, Senegal
Gürkan Gür	Zurich University of Applied Sciences (ZHAW), Switzerland
Dijiang Huang	Arizona State University, USA
Nesrine Kaaniche	The University of Sheffield, UK
Thinh Le Vinh	HCMC University of Technology and Education, Vietnam
Li Li	Wuhan University, China
Wojciech Mazurczyk	Warsaw University of Technology, Poland
Aleksandra Mileva	Goce Delčev University of Štip, Republic of N. Macedonia
Hassan Noura	Arab Open University, Lebanon
Mawloud Omar	IRT SystemX, France
Karima Oukfif	Mouloud Mammeri University of Tizi Ouzou, Algeria
Assia Outamazirt	Gustave Eiffel University, France
Ola Salman	Helsinki University, Finland
Nazatul Haque Sultan	University of Newcastle, Australia
Leonardo Suriano	Universidad Politécnica de Madrid, Spain
Sabu M. Thampi	Indian Institute of Information Technology and Management, India
Patrick M. Yomsi	ISEP, Portugal
Gongxuan Zhang	Nanjing University of Science and Technology, China
Peiyi Zhao	Chapman University, USA

Sponsoring Institutions

Conservatoire National des Arts et Métiers, Paris, France
Télécom SudParis, Paris, France
University of Limoges, Limoges, France

Contents

Graph Based Subjective Matching of Trusted Strings and Blockchain Based Filtering for Connected Vehicles

Mamoudou Sangare[1,2]([⊠]), Soumya Banerjee[1], Paul Mühlethaler[1], and Thinh Le Vinh[3]

[1] Inria EVA, Centre de Recherche de Paris, 2 Rue Simone, IFF CS 42112, 75589 Paris Cedex 12, France
{mamoudou.sangare,soumya.banerjee,paul.muhlethaler}@inria.fr
[2] CEDRIC Lab, Conservatoire National des Arts et Métiers, 292 rue Saint Martin, 75141 Paris, France
[3] Ho Chi Minh City University of Technology and Education (HCMUTE), Ho Chi Minh City, Vietnam
thinhlv@hcmute.edu.vn

Abstract. Advances in technology have lead to the creation of a connected world. Due the increase in the number of smart and autonomous cars, the safety and associated comfort level of driving has led to attempts to adopt conventional vehicular access network to the world of connected vehicles. Consolidating the cooperative safety and collected mobility management from different distributed devices are of the utmost importance. However, the prime objective of connected vehicles is not only to impose security and trust measures for individual vehicles, but the strategy of connected vehicle should also concentrate on the cooperative and collective environment on fleets of vehicles. Therefore, keeping simple authentication and access control may not be efficient to evaluate trust and assurance for all the distributed stakeholders. Trust being an important entity for this entire system, the strategy for trust evaluation becomes also, crucial. In this paper we propose a broader content matching model of trusted strings and block chain based filtering for connected Vehicles. Where a content and subject headings are first matched and then the outcome of that is consolidated by a distributed block chain consensus voting mechanism for any decision taken with respect to trust evaluation.

Keywords: Content matching · Blockchain · Message disseminating protocole · Trust evaluation · Connected vehicles

1 Introduction

The safety and associated comfort level of driving motivate the development of connected vehicles. Considering the wide spectrum of connected vehicles, which can communicate in five different modes Vehicle to Vehicle (V2V), Vehicle to Infrastructure (V2I), Vehicle to Cyclist (V2C), Vehicle to Pedestrian (V2P) and

S. Bouzefrane et al. (Eds.): MSPN 2020, LNCS 12605, pp. 1–14, 2021.
https://doi.org/10.1007/978-3-030-67550-9_1

Vehicle to Everything (V2X), it is worthy to consolidate the cooperative safety and collected mobility management from different distributed devices. However, the prime objective of connected vehicles is not only to impose security and trust measures for individual vehicles, instead the strategy of connected vehicles should concentrate on the cooperative and collective environment of a fleet of vehicles. Therefore, keeping simple authentication and access control may not be efficient to evaluate trust and assurance for all the distributed stakeholders. Since trust is an important entity for this entire system, the strategy for trust evaluation also becomes crucial. There are many instances in distributed systems, where trust for multiple parties may not follow the same benchmark for the transmission and reception of messages. This phenomenon could be more prominent, when distributed users carry different mobile edge oriented devices and media. For each of those devices, the transmission and reception strategies with protocols may be different. For example, text messages sent to the mobile devices through social media may not be the same as when sending the same message through mailing or through other types of online media communication. These observations raise some challenges to synchronize distributed mobile edge devices and media from eavesdropping and intentional spam injection procedures. To establish trust for a distributed system, the system should be able to emphasise and assure from distributed users. The procedure follows a consensus mechanism for the appropriate matching of trusted entities. Dedicated Short Range Communications (DSRC) been mandatory since 2016 for light vehicles and this rule describes a defined data packet with Basic Safety Message (BSM) indicating the location of the vehicle, speed and other on-road parameters. However, DSRC is unable to specify transmitted and received messages with respect to a trusted classification. Therefore, this paper proposes a unique method to investigate the optimal trusted matching for incoming messages under connected vehicles. Interestingly, the paper does not consider key word matching (a word by word or dictionary based approach). Rather, the broader thematic content and headings for communicated messages are taken into account. This will help to establish the content categories for different untrusted behaviors like abusive behavior, forced branding of products, misleading information, blocking of safety message on road, etc. In order to achieve this matching propose for distributed mobile devices, the paper introduces a message passing procedure followed by a blockchain-based reinforcement decision (Fig. 1).

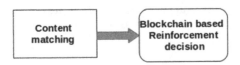

Fig. 1. System diagram

Thus, the paper comprises two parts: the first part describes content based message passing, and the second part, after matching the content and subject headings, consolidates the distributed consensus or voting mechanism for any decision with respect to the trust evaluation. The key contributions of our paper are summarized below:

- We propose a message passing scheme for connected vehicles. In this scheme, we do not consider key word matching (a word by word or dictionary-based approach). Rather, we take into account the broader thematic content and headings for messages communicated.
- We attempt to improve trust evaluation by using a voting mechanism for any decision, which is a concept based on a blockchain-based reinforcement decision.
- We aim to enhance securing and authenticating messages exchanged between vehicles by introducing the concept of content matching and trust evaluation in a connected car blockchain as a future perspective.

The remaining part of this paper is structured as follows. The preliminary work done in providing content matching protocols and trust evaluation for connected vehicles are described in Sect. 2. Section 3 presents the methodology where the entities involved in this work are describeb. The proposed solution in this study is presented in Sect. 4, and the experimental results are discussed in Sect. 5 Finally, Sect. 6 concludes the paper.

2   Related Works

Connected vehicle applications are based on both unicast and broadcast communications. However,as for all mobile and wireless networks, these communication scenarios suffer from various security issues that hinder the functionality of such communication protocols. Existing trust-based security solutions are usually classified into entity-based, data-based, and hybrid trust models, depending on the target, which can be dishonest entities, malicious messages, or both of them [6]. In addition, for message passing protocols in vehicular ad hoc networks especially between connected cars, the blockchain technology is seen as the most promising technique to provide a secured distributed networks among different frameworks[3]. In the following, we survey message content matching procedures for connected cars as well as providing soem background details on block chain technology for secure message dissemination using voting mechanism.

2.1   Message Content Matching

In general, string matching has been explored by researchers using different techniques. A technique for detecting phishing attacks was proposed by the authors in [1]. As the objective of that study, this technique was meant to specify the similarity grade between a URL with blacklisted URLs. Consequently, messages can be classified as phishing or non-phishing based on the textual properties of a URL. In their work, a well known string matching algorithm called the Longest Common Subsequence (LCS), was implemented by the authors in the hostname for comparison. With an accuracy found to be 99.1%, it is regarded as being very efficient in detecting phishing attacks. It also achieved very low false positive and false negative rates. Similarly, the same algorithm was used in [8]. The authors used it in biological files to discover sequence resemblance between genetic codes. In this test carried on a sequence of DNA that was generate randomly, the accurate DNA sequence similarity was found by the algorithm. This comparison is a path to implement codes of genetics from one DNA sequence to another. While the algorithm tested on 50 samples with two input was DNA genetic code sequences, it performed well, and showed good results.

The authors in [10] carried out an investigation on the use of string matching algorithms for spam email detection. In particular their work examined and compared the efficiency of six well-known string matching algorithms, namely Longest Common Subsequence (LCS), Levenshtein Distance (LD), Jaro, Jaro-Winkler, Bi-gram, and term frequency–inverse document frequency (TFIDF) on two various datasets, the Enron corpus and CSDMC2010 spam dataset. From observations based on the performance of each algorithm, they found that the Bi-gram algorithm performed best in spam detection in both datasets. While they claimed that all six methods gave good results in terms of efficiency, however they suffered from time performance.

The Levenshtein distance algorithm was used by K. Beijering et al. in [4]. They used it to calculate phonetic distances between every 17 Scandinavian language variation and standard Danish. When comparing phonetic transcriptions of two pronunciations, the Levenshtein distance is defined as the number of procedures necessary to convert one transcription to another. The strength of the Levenshtein distance lies in minimising the overall number of string operations when converting one pronunciation to another.

2.2   Blockchain Technology

A blockchain can be defined as a growing list of records, called blocks, that are linked using cryptography. Each block contains a cryptographic hash of the previous block, a timestamp, and transaction data. In other word, it is a distributed and decentralized public database of all transactions or digital events that have been accomplished or shared between participating nodes. Each event in the public database is validated based on the agreement of a large number of nodes in the blockchain network. The popularity of the blockchain is due to its advantages, which include decentralization, anonymity, chronological order of data, distributed security, transparency and immutability and suitability for trustless environments [9].

The block chain consists of two types of nodes. A full node is a node that stores and maintains the complete history of block chain transactions. It begins a transaction directly and independently, and it authoritatively verifies all transactions in the network. Every node in the block chain network knows the genesis block's hash. Every node in the network builds a trusted block chain based on the genesis block that acts as a secure root. The genesis block does not have the hash of a previous block. If a node is new, then it only knows the genesis

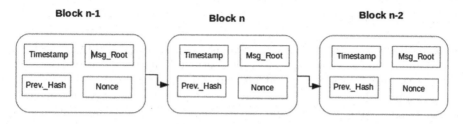

Fig. 2. Block chain diagram

block, and it will have to download all blocks starting from the genesis block to synchronize with the block chain network and is constantly updated when new blocks are found, see Fig. 2. The chaining of blocks is performed by appending hashes of the previous blocks to the current block so that the hash of the current block is in a sequential manner to the following block. Then, it is shared with other nodes in a distributed P2P network in a secure way without the need for a central authority. The sequential hashes of blocks ensure a sequential order of transactions. Therefore, previous transactions cannot be modified without modifying their blocks and all subsequent blocks. The block chain is verified by the consensus of anonymous nodes in the generation of blocks. It is considered secure if the aggregated computational power of malicious nodes is not larger than the computational power of honest nodes. In the case of Bitcoin, the concept of proof of work (PoW) makes sure that a miner is not manipulating the network to make fake blocks. A PoW is a mathematical puzzle that is very hard to solve and easy to verify so that it protects the block chain from double-spending attacks. In the research on VANETs, some of the previous studies related to secure event message dissemination are based on voting. Most voting approaches attempt to solve the issues of node security by asking the opinions of other nodes to determine the trustworthiness of a node.

However, this type of approach has the problem of whether the nodes providing the feedback can be trusted. Generally speaking, limited work has been done to study connected vehicles using the blockchain. The authors in Ref. [2] used a basic blockchain concept to simplify the distributed key management in heterogeneous vehicular networks. The authors in [7] combined the VANET and Ethereum's block chain-based application concepts and enabled a transparent, self-managed and decentralized system. They used Ethereum's smart contract system to run all types of applications on an Ethereum block chain.

In contrast, our proposed work applies a different type of block chain for secure message dissemination for connected cars. In [5], the authors proposed a block chain technology for automotive security by using an overlay network in the block chain and additional nodes called overlay block managers. The overlay network nodes are clustered by cluster heads, and these cluster heads are accountable for handling the block chain and operating its main functions. However, the introduction of additional overlay nodes might cause high latency and might be the center point of failure if the cluster head is compromised.

3   Methodology

A comprehensive analysis of message content matching improved by blockchain based reinforcement decision requires the consideration of multiple entities, e.g. mobile edge search process that allow to grab the basic concept of the architecture of mobile edge search process and graph representation of connected cars. Therefore, this study exploits multiple sources of connected vehicles in term of message content matching, builds analogous graphs of vehicles movement patterns for each entity and identifies the community structures.

3.1   Architecture of Mobile Edge Search Process

The Fig. 3 below illustrates the architecture of the mobile edge entity search process. Initially the mobile edge entity initiates the handshaking by specifying the sensor observation sequence to be queried by the terminal, and sends the search request to the the mobile edge computing (MEC) server. In return to that request, the cloud server is responsible for responding to the user's search request, and publishing the search request to the MEC server according to the requested content. The MEC server is responsible for fitting the raw data uploaded by the sensor and calculating its similarity with the search conditions published by the cloud server.

The sensor layer is responsible for collecting environmental data and uploading it to the MEC server. The steps are as follows:

1. The mobile device reports the environmental message observed to the MEC server.
2. The MEC server fits the reported message of the mobile device, and stores the processed message.
3. The connected car sends a request for an appropriate protocol to the MEC server.
4. After receiving the request for appropriate protocol, the MEC server calculates the similarity between the search condition and the mobile device message stored internally.
5. Finally, the MEC server returns matched and trusted results that match with the connected car's request to the connected cars.

3.2   Graph Representation of Connected Vehicles

A graph is a structure amounting to a set of objects in which some pairs of the objects are in some sense "related". The objects correspond to mathematical abstractions called vertices (also called nodes or points) and each of the related pairs of vertices is called an edge (also called link or line). Figure 4 illustrates graph representation of vehicles. Nodes(cars) of the graph are in a topological order. For instance in Fig. (4b) we have 1, 4, 6, 5, 2, 3, 7(visual top-to-bottom, left-to-right) or 3, 1, 5, 2, 4 (arbitrary) in fig. (4a). Each car is having an indentification number (ID).

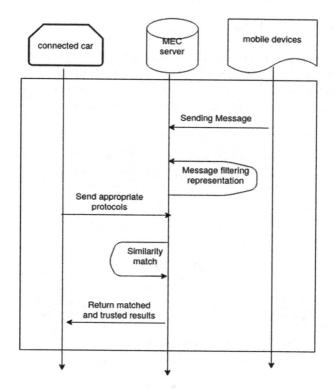

Fig. 3. Mobile edge entity search process.

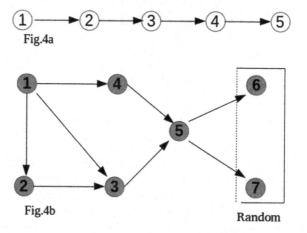

Fig. 4. Graph representation of connected cars

4   Proposed Solution

In our study, the solution proposed will perform trust enhancement among communicating nodes of connected vehicles. The operation comprises two main components, which are content matching under thematic matching operations reinforced by a graph-based blockchain mechanism, see Fig. 5.

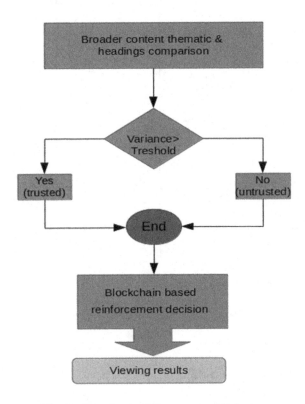

Fig. 5. Flowchart of the proposed Solution

The following themes and content are included in the proposed model.
a) **Exhaustive themes** (dangerous product or services, adult content, gambling and games,inappropriate messaging, personalized promotions, forced promotion)
b) **Non-exhaustive** (affiliating the message against the program rules, promoting the same content from multiple accounts, trying to push the brand promotion repeatedly, brand disinvestment, intentional and manipulation to switch the messages towards inappropriate content).
Under these two heads or leads, service provider of the connected car can clearly differentiate the two types of content and their thematic message strings. The dictionary is not subjected to one-to-one mapping but it defines lexical matching either in the message head (a) or in the message head (b). This is respective of

any theme or content which maybe outside these message heads. This constraint maybe a limitation for this model.

4.1 Function Matching-Trust

The function of matching-trust is described below: $(I, S_i, d_I, d_{Si}, d_{min}, \beta)$

Input :

   - I is the identifier of the priority string ("xxxx") on the trust graph edge.
- S_i is the string identifier of the moving car transmitting D_s
- d_I represents the distance I to the terminating node in case $I \neq$ None (availability steady but trusted).
- d_{Si} represents the distance I to the terminating node in case $S_i \neq$ None (not trusted)
- $d_{min} > 0$ minimum distance of connected cars to perform D_s
- $\beta > 1$ co-efficient to transmit the target string

Output:

---

   if($I \neq$ None & $S_i \neq$ None & $d_I > \beta.d_{min}$ & $d_{Si} < d_{min}$) or ($I ==$ None & $S_i \neq$ None & $d_{Si} < d_{min}$) then match_string I
else
terminate
return Match_string I // untrusted.

---

5 Experimentation and Results Analysis

Table 1. This table gives a summary of statistical parameters and values.

Data elements	0.6, 1.2, 1.8, 2.4, 3.0, 3.6, 4.2, 4.8, 6.4, 6.0
Mean	3.3
Max	6.0
Variance	2.97

5.1 Assumptions

- All connected car members are under same network service provider on their edge devices.
- Out of the total numbers of members registered in the network, only the agreement of old members (>1 1 year) could be considered.

– To avoid the physical consensus, the proposed Blockchain prototype will deploy a graph-based referencing. It implies that based on the subjective terms of untrusted message leads, service providers will predefine a maximum high-positive mutual agreement of trusted messages. This typical graph-driven direction will help to prevent latency and delay on the reply of the message block through participants and it also avoids the self-biasing to manipulate consensus, if some groups of participants are known to the victim of untrusted acts.

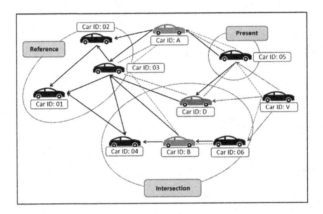

Fig. 6. Graph based referencing (Color figure online)

Intersections in Fig. 6 conceptually defines that it is the association between certain immediate past value of car with id transmitted in the message to the neighbors. This includes the values of the cars id at present participating in the message transmission. In Fig. 6 the red dotted mars indicate the length of the graph formed either by the transmitting car or its affected neighbors. Therefore they are not trusted. However, distinctly in this cluster, blue dots represent safe messages, where one of the affected cars is placed in the same cluster. In this context, graph referencing is used to investigate the variance and the degree of trust distorted by the odd entry to that cluster.

5.2   Graph-Based Referencing Towards Trusted Consensus

The concept here is designed to estimate the temporal inconsistency (ambiguity) between two messages. If two message-clusters are in the contradictory to each other, their temporal order cannot be determined. It means that the message clusters might be from isolated connected cars. However, the time discrepancy of two message-clusters is bounded by their nearest common ancestor and nearest common descendant, since the real creation time of a message-block is bounded by its ancestors and descendants. The untrusted message-clusters always intend to hide or counterfeit their real creation time in order to carry out spam message generation such as repeat occupancy (conventionally known as double spending). Therefore, the consensus agreement between the dis-trusted message block and most trusted message-cluster should be very large, otherwise the real creation time of the distrusted block would be bounded by some trusted message-cluster into a small interval. On the other hand, the agreement of two trusted message-clusters is normally much smaller. If the links between message-clusters are not artificially manipulated, the agreement of two message-clusters should only depend on the network propagation speed and the block creation rate. When the network propagation speed or the block creation rate increases, the time discrepancy between the nearest common ancestor and the nearest common descendant will decline. However, the length of shortest path between two message-cluster will increase and cancel out the decline of time discrepancy to some extent. Therefore, the agreements are not very sensitive to the network propagation speed and the block creation rate. The analysis can demonstrate that the agreements between two trusted message-clusters are mostly smaller than 10 while the agreements between the trusted block and the distrusted block might be higher by two or more orders of magnitude. Figure 7 shows the relationship between the block creation rate and the maximum agreement between trusted blocks. In each case of the block creation rate, 16 simulations are conducted. The statistical analysis is shown in Table 1. Even when the message block creation rate reaches 6 message-clusters per second, the agreement between trusted message-clusters still does not increase too greatly. Therefore, the agreements can be utilized to filter the suspect distrusted blocks. In this section, we give a proposed framework named MsgBlock_Filter for identifying the trusted message-cluster based on the agreement. Given a block DAG, we first calculate the agreements for every pair of message-clusters and get the agreement of reference matrix. Then the agreement matrix is converted into a binary matrix where each element is 1 if the corresponding element in the agreement matrix is larger than a preset threshold d, and 0 otherwise. By using the binary matrix obtained as the adjacency matrix, we can construct an undirected graph, in which each vertex represents a block. This graph is called the d-agreement graph of the given block DAG. Intuitively, if a block DAG only contains trusted blocks, the degrees in the d-agreement graph will be very small since the agreements between most trusted message-clusters are zero and the remaining non-zero agreements are also very small. Considering the trusted message-clusters to be the majority, the trusted block identification problem can be addressed by identifying the maximum subset of vertexes with small degrees.

Considering a graph $G = (V, E)$, the $k-$independent set of G refers to the vertex subset V' in which the maximum degree in the induced sub-graph does not exceed k. The maximum $k-$independent set problem is to find the k-independent set with maximum size which is a generalization of classical maximum independent set problem. The maximum k-independent set can be formulated as the following integer programming, in which xs represents whether a certain vertex s is selected and aij denotes the element of adjacency matrix of the graph G.

5.3 Direct Acyclic Graph (DAG)

considering a Direct Acyclic Graph (DAG), it is worth formulating, some statistical analysis with respect to message spreading strength (including trusted and untrusted message) precision and recall. However, due to the legacy of the consensus protocol it becomes more stringent to model the same for different participant in connected cars environment. The concept for finding the trusted messages and the untrusted or distrusted messages is to find out the interval graph from the first cycle of the message repeat, although the graph here referred to as a acyclic graph as no cycle exists for the repetition of the message. Therefore the only measure to identify the interval of the message is to find out the variance of the message repeat from one node to another with respect to time. Here we calculate primarily three values for a given message creation rate (Msg_block/second) that is $0.6, 1.2, 1.8, 2.4, 3.0, 3.6, 4.2, 4.8, 5.4, 6.0$ respectively. Under these message creation rates we find the mean to be 3.3, max to be 6 and the variance to be 2.97. The different steps to calculate the mean, max and variance are as follows. Specific points: variance of any dynamic quantity is the sum of the square difference between each data point and the mean divided by the data value. Hence sigma square should be the sum of the squared difference divided by total number of items in the given problem. This variance will help to trace the closeness of trusted and untrusted blocks assuming that the untrusted message must be repeated more than once.

– Step 1 : we find the mean of the dataset
– Step 2 : we add all the data values divided by the sample size : $\bar{x} = \frac{\sum_{i=1}^{n} x_i}{n}$
– Step3: we find the sum of the squared difference : $SS = \sum_{i=1}^{n}(x_i - \bar{x})^2$
– Step4: we calculate variance of sigma squared accordingly : $\sigma^2 = \frac{\sum_{i=1}^{n}(x_i - \bar{x})^2}{n}$

In order to identify the impression of this process, we refer to Figure 7, shows the maximum number of honest message versus the message generation rate. Here the variance gives the idea that the density of trusted messages in ideal conditions, is always higher. Therefore, even when the message block creation rate reaches 6 message_clusters/second, the variance between trusted messages and clusters become 2.97. From Fig. 6 it is also indicates that the trust level agreement cannot differ too much with respect to untrusted messages. Hence the intersection could be used as a filter for reference to create the predefined trusted and untrusted message blocks. Two measures technical specifications are considered:

a) The predefined referencing of the service provider can prevent the legitimate delay to reply the consensus or group messages.

b) self-biasing or personal manipulation is also avoided. Figure 8 provides an interesting observation with respect to the precision and the recall by which the strength of the damaging messaging can be highlighted. The left-hand side of Fig. 8 is divided almost same intervals apparently. Here also we calculate the quantiles of the given data-set from 0.6 to 6.0 to find out the exact interval of the precision and recall of trusted messages (there is no memory or learning in the recall, only topological ordering has been investigated). Statistically, quantiles are cut points, dividing the range of the data sample of the probability distribution into continuous intervals with equal probabilities. Here in Fig. 8 we started calculating message repeat strength from the median, first quarterly, third quarterly, first decile, last decile, one percentile as maximum level of 6 Msg_Block/second. The flow is to identify the median towards one percentile which is actually the maximum value of the data sample. The analysis helps to correlate the importance of the variance so that repeat messages and the variance can support it as a consensus filter.

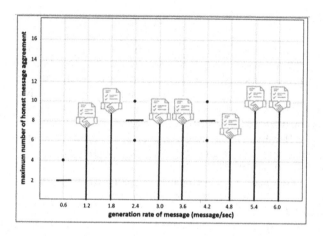

Fig. 7. Relationship between the block creation rate and the maximum agreement between trusted blocks

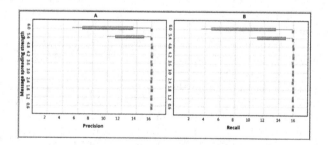

Fig. 8. Precision and recall

6   Conclusion

In this work, a message matching model and the conceptual level of graph referencing blockchain have been proposed. The model can filter the trusted and untrusted messages in connected car scenarios, analogous to a conventional blockchain mechanism. However, due to physical opinions group process for block chain which could introduce unwanted delay and self-biasing, this method can be more feasible for collective decisions. This paper has more open research problem challenging the blockchain mechanism. This is because the security is questionable due to group and collective decisions making and repeat occupancy of the message. This is equivalent to a double spending attack in normal blockchain. As a future extension therefore a DAG (Direct Acyclic Graph) and their descendants can be integrated in the block-chain consolidating its security and spoofing mechanism.

References

1. Abraham, D., Raj, N.S.: Approximate string matching algorithm for phishing detection. In 2014 International Conference on Advances in Computing, Communications and Informatics (ICACCI), pp. 2285–2290. IEEE (2014)
2. Ao, L.E.I., Ogah, C., Asuquo, P., Cruickshank, H., Zhili, S.U.N.: A secure key management scheme for heterogeneous secure vehicular communication systems. ZTE Commun. **14**(S0), 21–31 (2019)
3. Hassan, M.A., Habiba, U., Ghani, U., Shoaib, M.: A secure message-passing framework for inter-vehicular communication using blockchain. Int. J. Distrib. Sens. Netw. **15**(2), 1550147719829677 (2019)
4. Beijering, K., Gooskens, C., Heeringa, W.: Predicting intelligibility and perceived linguistic distance by means of the levenshtein algorithm. Linguist. the Netherlands **25**(1), 13–24 (2008)
5. Dorri, A., Steger, M., Kanhere, S.S., Jurdak, R.: Blockchain: a distributed solution to automotive security and privacy. IEEE Commun. Mag. **55**(12), 119–125 (2017)
6. Kerrache, C.A., Calafate, C.T., Lagraa, N., Cano, J.-C., Manzoni, P.: Rita: risk-aware trust-based architecture for collaborative multi-hop vehicular communications. Secur. Commun. Netw. **9**(17), 4428–4442 (2016)
7. Leiding, B., Memarmoshrefi, P., Hogrefe, D.: Self-managed and blockchain-based vehicular ad-hoc networks. In: Proceedings of the 2016 ACM International Joint Conference on Pervasive and Ubiquitous Computing: Adjunct, pp. 137–140 (2016)
8. Murugan, A., Udayakumar, U.: Sequence similarity between genetic codes using improved longest common subsequence algorithm. Int. J. Recent Innov. Trends Computi. Commun. (IJRITCC) **5**(7), 57–60 (2017)
9. Shrestha, R., Bajracharya, R., Shrestha, A.P., Nam, S.Y.: A new type of blockchain for secure message exchange in vanet. Digit. Commun. Netw. **6**(2), 177–186 (2020)
10. Varol, C., bdulhadi, H.M.T.: Comparision of string matching algorithms on spam email detection. In: 2018 International Congress on Big Data, Deep Learning and Fighting Cyber Terrorism (IBIGDELFT), pp. 6–11. IEEE (2018)

Secure and Internet-Less Connectivity to a Blockchain Network for Limited Connectivity Bank Users

Daniel Maldonado-Ruiz[1], Mohamad Badra[2], Nour El Madhoun[3($\boxtimes$)], and Jenny Torres[1]

[1] Departamento de Informática y Ciencias de la Computación, Facultad de Ingeniería en Sistemas Informáticos y Computación, Escuela Politécnica Nacional, Quito, Ecuador
{daniel.maldonado02,jenny.torres}@epn.edu.ec
[2] College of Technological Innovation, Zayed University, P.O. Box 19282, Dubai, UAE
mohamad.badra@zu.ac.ae
[3] Security and System Laboratory, EPITA, 14-16 Rue Voltaire, 94270 Le Kremlin-Bicêtre, France
nour.el-madhoun@epita.fr

Abstract. Over the past few years, we have seen the emergence of a wide range of banking architectures, technologies, and applications made possible by the significant improvements in hardware, software, and networking technologies. Nowadays, innovative solutions are being developed by banks to leverage the benefits of blockchain, to improve their business agility and performance, and to make their business operations more efficient and secure. However, there are still cases where regular access to Internet is impossible or unreliable due to saturated networks or harsh environments, hence limiting the deployment of typical blockchain based solutions. In this context, an approach using a new connectivity technology is needed in order to increase mobile Internet services for any device to reach nearly 95% of the world population, instantly, simply by drawing on existing mobile phone networks, with no additional infrastructure development. We aim to give the user full bank access from their device, even if the device is not a smart one, using ordinary mobile phone networks. However, providing efficient and secure communications over lossy and low bandwidth networks remains a challenge. The main objective of this paper will be to design an end-to-end and low overhead secure solution for the communications between mobile devices and their corresponding remote application servers that using blockchain via ordinary mobile networks.

Keywords: Banking transactions · Offline networks · Mobile networks · SMS · Blockchain · Ethereum · Smart contracts

© Springer Nature Switzerland AG 2021
S. Bouzefrane et al. (Eds.): MSPN 2020, LNCS 12605, pp. 15–30, 2021.
https://doi.org/10.1007/978-3-030-67550-9_2

1   Introduction

Mobile Internet access and mobile transactions have become the base of modern communications between any kind of mobile devices, be these classic ones or IoT. The users of mobile Internet can interact with their applications and systems in a variety of ways and in real time. Using mobile Internet to access banks is not worth the risk, time or costs. However, mobile banking has greater flexibility and convenience because transactions can be done anywhere, anytime, and using any mobile device. It is therefore in the interest of banks and their customers to find a way to make mobile banking safe and secure.

We are currently witnessing the adaptation of a blockchain system to explore new methods to effectively manage the security aspects of applications and services, to assure data transparency, to ensure cost efficiency when managing, and data processing. Innovative solutions are being developed by enterprises and institutions to leverage the benefits of the blockchain, to improve their business agility and performance, and to make their business operations more efficient and secure.

Blockchain is basically known as the technology behind the Bitcoin cryptocurrency [1,2]. It is a distributed/shared public ledger with a set of specific predefined rules that determine how the ledger is appended by the distributed consensus of the participants in the network. It offers a new paradigm for implementing transactions in a trust-less environment, where participants agree on the validity of the transactions that are recorded in the distributed ledger. The ledger is only updated by consensus of the participants and each transaction recorded in the ledger will be cryptographically verifiable with proof of agreement from the participants. As a result, each participant will have a copy of the same ledger with records that are immutable, so they cannot be altered or deleted later. In this way, blockchain eliminates the need for central authorities, making asset provenance and traceability more efficient and transparent than existing systems. Existing Blockchain platforms, such as Ethereum [3] or Hyperledger blockchain technologies, enable the use of smart contracts to digitalize and self-execute contractual agreements between different parties without the need for any central authority. Smart contracts are defined as self-executing contractual states automating the execution of business workflows in a fully decentralized and trust-less blockchain. However, having access to a stable Internet connection is a prerequisite to enable the deployment of blockchain based applications.

Although 95% of the world population has access to all kinds of mobile phones, in developing countries, like those in Africa or Asia for instance, 75% of people do not have access to Internet. Also, there are still cases in those countries where regular access to Internet is impossible or unreliable due to saturated networks or harsh environments, hence limiting the deployment of any Blockchain based solution. In this context, we propose a solution that aims at increasing mobile Internet services for devices that do not have access to Internet in the first place. The main idea is to reach nearly 95% of the world population, instantly, simply by drawing on existing mobile phone networks (GSM/2G), with no additional infrastructure development. The main objective of our paper will be to design an end-to-end and low overhead security solution to allow the communications between a mobile devices and their corresponding remote applications servers for GSM users not having access to mobile Internet. Our proposed solution creates a new way to extend centralized systems, such as banks and financial systems, to leverage decentralized transaction systems and decentralised identity validators. In particular, it aims to a) secure transactions between users and entities, and b) create new ways to enable these transactions for vulnerable users, which can use the system by a symplified user validation over a challenge-response validation system. It also aims to integrate the blockchain to record data that should be safe, auditable and resistant to outages.

However, providing efficient and secure communications over lossy and low bandwidth networks remains a challenge, specially in regions without a stable mobile network coverage. Addressing not only any possible delay on communication but network tampering is part of the analysis in order to find the possible solutions to build a secure transaction system for non-smart mobile devices.

The rest of this paper is organized as follows. Section 2 presents the relevant known works about banking communications using mobile networks and blockchain, focusing on systems where broadband communications are limited. We describe our privacy-preserving approach and design in Sect. 3, followed by its security analysis and performance evaluation in Sect. 4. Finally, we conclude this paper in Sect. 5.

2   Related Work

Several solutions have been proposed and deployed to enable financial transactions and financial technologies over decentralized ledgers [4]. In 2008, a Payment Application Data Security Standard (PA-DSS) was developed to standardize the security requirements of financial transactions. Applying it to Ethereum, Bello et al. [5] proved that, focusing on business operations, the ledger has a lot of security relying on the storage and implementation aspects, but fails on providing privacy of the transactions and information stored on the ledger. Xu et al. [6] propose a layered model based on Smart Contracts to ensure the access to the Open banking paradigm, where the smart contract manages the transaction but does not perform it. In cloud systems, Oktian et al. [7] describe a system where users can request information from the cloud. For that research, smart contracts are used to register an account into the cloud by the user before starting any transaction. To ensure the transaction's honesty, each user must pay a fee to maintain the subscription, so malicious subscribers can be avoided. Another approach proposed by Bhaskaran et al. [8] replaces the cloud with two blind entities (financial providers) to manage and validate the smart contracts for every user in the system. The security is defined by a double validation to create a wider network for the blockchain and to secure the information stored on the Smart Contracts. Similar approaches are used to maintain credit reporting [9] and cryptocurrency wallet management [10]. All of these solutions, however, maintain the idea of using the blockchain in a online environment, where all actors must have a broadband access. Having a broadband access allows users to use any modern device to access the system, which is not the idea proposed in this paper, where we focus on users who do not have the ability to have a running smart device that is equipped with a stable broadband connection. In opposite to the previous works, Hu et al. [11] describe a scenario where a community-run base station provides reliable local network connectivity while intermittently connecting to the broader Internet. In this scenario, users depend on smart devices to become miners or use some lightweight wallet to generate all transactions to be stored on a Ethereum blockchain with an access control that is based on tokens acting as currency intermediaries. This research incorporates the idea of using mobile devices to connect nodes to a blockchain. However, the proposal still depends on a broadband access and a smart device to perform the transactions, which is very difficult to find in harsh environments.

2.1   Blockchain Technology

Blockchain could be defined as a tamper-resistant distributed data ledger, where all the cells are linked by the hash of the previous one, turning the ledger into a "chain of blocks" [12,13]. As a tool, blockchain exists since 2008 with Nakamoto's Bitcoin, but as a technology could be tracked since 1991 [14]. The main features of blockchain are that offers a decentralized and distributed storage system that doesn't require any third party validation to assure the stored information.

Part of the current blockchain hype lies on the immutability of its structure, because all the records stored on every block cannot be tampered without alter all the blockchain itself, making the system very secure to use in all kinds of transactions.

To store the data, blockchain uses algorithms which allow to create new blocks in the system that synchronize with the entire network in a unique way: the consensus algorithms. These algorithms aimed to create an environment where only the correct block will be store in the ledger, avoiding apocryphal or malicious branches. In Bitcoin, the way to store a new block is made by a process called *mining*, where a set of nodes called *miners* try to solve a puzzle in order to find the correct new block. When the new block is found, it is broadcasted to all network, eliminating all additional possible branches. This kind of algorithms where any node could participate in the search of the new block are part of the so-called *permissionless (public) blockchain*. On the other hand, the algorithms where only a few nodes have the full copy of the ledger and could create the new blocks (with different consensus algorithms) are called *permissioned (private) blockchain*. Ethereum and Hyperledger are the best known permissioned blockchain applications.

Blockchain Applications. Besides the cryptocurrency and smart contracts applications of the ledger, there are some other implementations of blockchain, appeared in recent years. One of the main uses for blockchain is with Internet of Things (IoT) [15,16], because the ledger can store not only identities of the devices but other features that are used to analyze the behaviour of the 'things'. In that case, blockchain is a strong ally of Big Data [17–19], because can store a lots of information, either raw or through smart contracts, making the analysis easier and more trustable. Most recent applications of blockchain are a core system to implement DNS and PKI systems [20–23], where the data could be stored and accessed in a easy way. Other field where blockchain is used these days is to control e-voting systems [24–26], where the ledger offers a solution of electoral fraud and also offers all the auditory measurements that a system needs. However, this field has security and trust issues in its implementation, specially in developing countries [27].

3   System Design

Our proposed transaction model enables an Internet-less link between banking users and financial institutions and creates communication channels allowing offline users, (i.e., users with no Internet access or any broadband connection) to perform transactions.

Our proposal, unlike traditional Bitcoin/Ethereum transactions, requires an origin and a destination bank account instead of a user identification, since the entire transactional management will be purely virtual due to the obvious impossibility of transmitting physical money via SMS (Short Message Service). Consequently, every user identity will be managed by the bank, using the registered user account and the identity information related to it.

To better explain the features of our proposal, we first describe the communication system structure, then we discuss our proposal's communication features and specifications.

3.1   Communication System Structure

Figure 1 illustrates the structure of our proposed approach. First, each user should register to the offline system using his bank account credentials. Hence, the users' identity will always be managed by the bank. The registration allows the system to create a smart contract, which contains the user ID (some identification related to the user's bank data), the balance account of the user and a transaction log. Next, a specific mnemonic ASCII PIN will be generated for each registered user, by using both the smart contract and the user ID. The mnemonic ASCII PIN will be used to validate the user to the mobile network. The generation of this PIN emulates the creation of a wallet address on a Bitcoin wallet [1]. Even though transactions are made in a cellphone, the phone number is not an important component here. With the mnemonic ASCII PIN, users can access to the transaction system from any cellphone, because the validation is always made through that PIN. In our model, all messages exchanged between the user and the system are transported by SMS.

We define a node called Gateway Node to manage the communication between the blockchain network and the end-user device over the mobile network. The Gateway Node acts as a buffer for transactions before being mined.

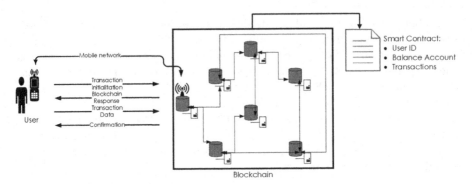

Fig. 1. Offline system structure

The Gateway node also acts as an enabler of the consensus protocol (in this case the Proof of Stake (PoS) as the new consensus protocol for Ethereum 2.0 network) for the buffered transactions. To maintain the neutrality of the transaction, the Gateway Node starts the consensus but never engages on it. The other nodes, however, execute the PoS when the Gateway Node starts the process.

Every node of the blockchain network must be associated with a bank or a group of banks, that will handle the financial transactions for every user. In particular, the banks will ensure the communications established with its users and create a link between the classical user bank account and the Smart Contract created for the offline transactions model, in a way that is similar to the model described in [28]. Hence, users undergo transactions in both ways (standard face-to-face bank transaction and via SMS) and all operations made to the user's account will be updated on the Smart Contract and vice versa.

3.2 Smart Contract Features

To store the information of every user in the Ethereum blockchain, it is important to design a specific Smart Contract, which will also be used to store the balance of the user, and act as a ledger of every transaction made or received by the user. Figure 2 illustrates the different fields needed by our proposed Smart Contract required to secure and manage all transactions. Each user must be identified by their own Ehtereum direction, based on the account number of their bank accounts, the related PIN and other identification information (such as names). The name will be used to search for the user, as described in the Name search process (Fig. 5a). Besides keeping the balance for the account and an array of transactions made by the users, the Smart Contract will also perform several other functions and operations, such as generating PIN or encrypting the balance and the user's transactions. In Ethereum technology, when the data type address is used in a Smart Contract, it is possible to use embedded balance and transaction functions and to modify them in order to accomplish, not only the security storage, but also the privacy of every user's data within the network.

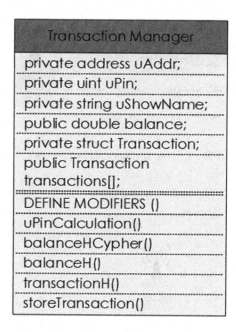

Fig. 2. Basic smart contract structure

3.3   Communication Features

Without a broadband communication, each transaction exchanged between the user (a cellphone) and the ledger (the Gateway Node) should have two fundamental features:

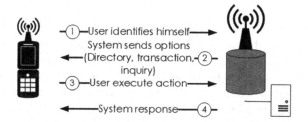

Fig. 3. Offline transactions general scheme

- A maximum of 140 ASCII characters
- Identifiers and commands that will be easily remembered and entered by a user having a device equipped with a non-QWERTY keyboard.

Taking the two features mentioned above, we define several specific message structures used for the transaction between the users and the Gateway Node, as follows:

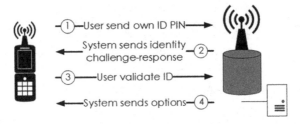

Fig. 4. User authentication process

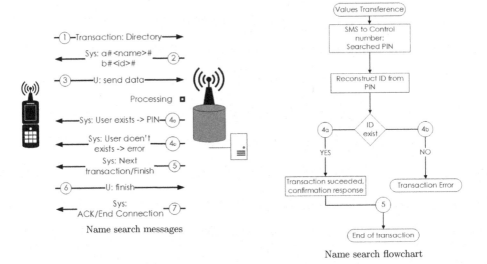

Fig. 5. Name search process

– **Initialization and Authentication:** Figure 3 illustrates how, in general terms, the transaction scheme is performed. The user usually starts the session by sending an SMS to authenticate himself to the Gateway Node, as the initialization message. This initalization message triggers the authentication phase, explained hereinafter. When authentication is complete (1), the system asks the user to select the operation he wishes to perform (2) with a message to the user as a response for a successful authentication. As an answer to the operation message sent by the gateway, the user send one with the transaction he need to perform (3). Once the transaction/operation is complete, the system ends the connection with the user (4).

Figure 4 specifies how the authentication process is achieved. As an initialization message, the user sends a HELLO-type message, which conveys the user's identity, also known as the PIN to the Gateway Node (1). The blockchain network, which receives the message through the Gateway Node, verifies the existence of the user's PIN and initiates a challenge-response handshake with

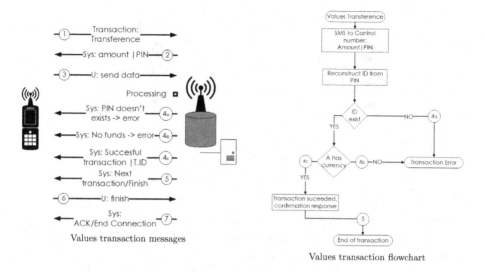

Fig. 6. Values transaction process

the user to verify the user's identity, this before starting any subsequent transaction process (2). After the network successfully identifies the user, the Gateway Node will: a) block all initialization attempts from any other device until the transaction ends or is considered as lost (due to delay, fail of authentication, lost of connection, etc.), and b) send back an ASCII passcode or a random number to the user to authenticate the current connection. As part of the challenge-response handshake, the user must identify himself to the network, by transmitting some personal information, such as a portion of the user's identity number or personal/biometrical validation data in a form of ASCII mnemonic code defined by the Smart Contract (3). This information is unique for every user and work as a passcode/password against the system. As a result, the network will be able to validate the user's identity and start the transactions. When the identification/authentication process is performed successfully, the network, through the Gateway Node, will ask the user to determine the transaction/operation he wishes to perform (4).

– **Transaction Items:** Our system defines three types of transaction operations between the users and the blockchain:

• Name search: It may happen that the users do not know or remember the PIN of the receiver of the transaction initiated by a particular user. In this optic, Fig. 5a illustrates how the blockchain network will implement a Name Search System. Users need to make a request to the blockchain network to start a search for a specific user that will be the destinatary of the transaction (1), and the network will reply by asking for an identifier (e.g., User ID number, User account or User name) for the requested user (2). In (3), the user sends the identifier to the system, that determines whatever the queried user exists (4a) or not (4b) as illustrated in Fig. 5b.

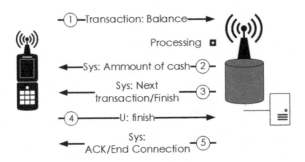

Fig. 7. Inquiry messages

The query/response process will continue as long as the user has further transactions; otherwise, the system will close the communication (5, 6, 7).

- Values Transaction: Once the user has confirmed the transaction recipient's PIN, he will start the transfer of values, as illustrated in Fig. 6a. When the user starts the transaction (1) and receives the confirmation from the system (2), the user shall specify the amount of currency to be transferred, along with the PIN of the receiver. The network will therefore verify and check the transaction before performing it (3). Fig. 6b illustrates how the network will validate the received transaction based on the data transmitted by the user. Particularly, it will validate if the ID associated with the requested PIN exists (4a). Then, it will verify if the user has sufficient amount of currency in his/her account to perform the transaction (4b). If both verification processes are achieved successfully, the transaction is then performed and stored using homomorphic encryption [29](4c). Finally, the network will close the connection in case no further transactions are received from the user (5, 6, 7).
- Inquiry Balance: All the transactions will be supported by Ethereum capabilities to generate balances from the information stored in every Smart Contract. Figure 7 illustrates how the system will act when it receives a request from the user to ask for the available currency amount in his/her account. When the user asks for the available balance (1), the system will check the user's Smart Contract and return the balance information (2). After that, the network will close the session in case no further transactions are received from the user (3, 4, 5).

4   Analysis

In this section, we present a security analysis of our proposed solution and we evaluate it versus the aforementioned solutions. We also demonstrate its effectiveness in preserving the user's privacy and in maintaining the integrity and confidentiality of data.

4.1   Blockchain Security Analysis

The first and most important consideration relies on how transactions are stored in the blockchain. It is obvious that transactions are securely stored in the blockchain. However, it is not possible to manipulate them in their encrypted format and the system needs to decrypt them first, which may cause several security risks. Even with the idea that only the bank which manages the user's bank account can access the ledger records, it is still a security issue. Consequently, our proposed system applies an additive homomorphic cryptosystem on user's transactions to enable computations and financial related functions to be carried out on the encrypted transactions, without revealing the transaction plain text [29]. Consequently, Smart Contracts could execute the programmed operations over the encrypted transactions that are stored in the blockchain without having to individually decrypt each transaction. With this, we intend to solve one of the main security issues of blockchain: privacy on stored data.

4.2   Identity Management

Part of our proposal is to break any link between the user's account and the mobile device (or a phone number) that the user might use to connect to the system. Our proposal intends to give the users the flexibility to interact with the system without a specific device. We considered that it is as difficult to have a stable broadband connection as to have a specific device to interact with the system. To have access to the transaction system, every user must connect to the Gateway node through a specific service number (similar to 911 or other short communication numbers) and validate their identity, no matter what phone number the message originates from. In this context, the identity management will be completely managed by our proposed system. The latter provides an easy-to-remember ASCII PIN to identify the user and the PIN is generated based on both the user identity already stored by the financial institutions and the address stored in the Smart Contract.

That identity management paradigm is used because it is hard and insecure for the user to create identity credentials from their mobile phone by using SMSs. Moreover, this paradigm makes it easier for the network to validate and confirm the user identity through a challenge-response mechanism, instead of a password that could be lost or stolen from the user.

4.3   Offline and Delayed Transactions

The main difference between a classical online transaction system and our proposed system is that the transactions will not be executed in broadband real time, but mobile network time as an offline communication. This offline feature may include a variety of delays, both in transit and in message processing on the Gateway. In fact, the transaction that is received from the user and that is to be executed must first of all be stored in its corresponding Smart Contract. Hence, the transaction should first be mined before updating both the user account and the Smart Contract to consolidate the information. Once the user transaction is executed by the system, the user will receive a confirmation of the transaction. In other words, and to avoid any double-spending, the system is designed to lock the current session and consolidate the legder before any transaction confirmation is sent to the user.

Some delay may depend on the time needed by the mobile network to transmit all messages related to a transaction. Although this delay cannot be considered as a security breach, it should be taken into account to find ways to handle it, so global transaction time will be reduced and the involved parties (users and the network) can improve their response times for every transaction.

The delay between the time a user sends a transaction message and the time the same user receives a confirmation could be critical and needs to be short enough to emulate an online transaction performance. But, even with all the possible improvements, all the proposed transactions are still in mobile band time; which means that the whole system needs to take into account different keep-alive session times rather than the broadband ones. Consequently, a specific time window is defined for our proposed system to keep the session alive in harsh connection conditions. That window window considers all the delays in the classical mobile network communications to define the border times in order to receive a message during the established session. In other words, the time needed to consider a session lost or expired is larger than in other transaction over a broadband connection. For as long as a session can last, the user PIN will be blocked to start a new session. That way, the user does not need to re establish a new session or lose transactions because of mobile network delays or coverage issues.

4.4   Mobile Operator Role

In the context of our proposed system, the mobile network will be only used as a communication channel, so the mobile network is not involved in the creation or processing of the user information. However, the system must ensure that the network supports the message format and character codification for all mobile devices. The main idea of this proposal is to run bank transactions in harsh environments, where SMS is the only available way to exchange data between the user and the system.

4.5   Comparison

Table 1 provides a theoretically comparison between our proposed solution and the solution proposed in [11] in terms of the following features:

- Network Access (1, 3, 7): how users interact with the blockchain network and the compared connection capabilities.
- Security (2, 4, 6): This includes features offered by the network to ensure secure data storage, authentication and privacy of all user information and interactions.

Table 1. Comparison table between existent solutions and this proposal

Parameters/ Works	Offline access (1)	Secure storage (2)	Transmission media (3)	Identity privacy (4)	Identity generation (5)	Secure transaction (6)	Broadband connection (7)	Users as nodes (8)	App requirement (9)	Tokens as Money (10)
[11]	No	No	Open wireless	No	Via app	Yes	Mandatory	Yes	Yes	Yes
Our proposal	Yes	Yes	Mobile network	Yes	Via bank account	Yes	Not needed	No	No	No

- Identity Management (5): How users can access to an identity to use and manipulate the network and their own stored information.
- Users Interaction (8, 9): How users can communicate with the network and what types of devices they need to start the transactions.
- Representation of currency (10): How the network understands the units of currency and manages them for every transaction.

The above features guide us to compare our proposed solution to the solution described in [11]. It is worth noting that the features (1)(3)(7) in Table 1 show that users using our proposal don't need a broadband connection to interact with the network, which is not the case of the solution in [11].

The features (2)(4)(6) in Table 1 demonstrate that our proposal intends to manage the information stored in the Smart Contract, by cypher the user transactions as well as the user's identity information, so that the user's data is stored in a secure and private way. Feature (5) shows how the users' identities are managed in both works. In our proposal, the identity is created by the bank and the interaction between the bank account and the information in the Smart Contract will create the user PIN. Instead, the other solution relies on the user's device to create the user's identity through and defined app. As we discussed in Sect. 4.2, it is more secure to let the banks manage their users' identities, rather than assigning this to any third party. Features (8) and (9) compare the interaction between the users and the network, and illustrate that our proposal does not need any app to communicate with the users. Consequently, the users can not be network nodes, where in the solution discussed in [11], a user can be a network node. Finally, feature (10) shows how both proposals manage the currency. In fact, our proposal uses the same currency used by the bank for transactions and balances, and hence, the transparency of transactions between the network, the bank and the users is guaranteed. However, the solution in [11] converts currency into token and consequently, its use is limited to few banks supporting these type of tokens.

5   Conclusion and Future Work

In this paper, we present and analyse an end-to-end and low overhead secure solution for the communications between limited connectivity mobile devices and their corresponding remote applications servers using blockchain. Our system incorporates the deployment of Ethereum network and its Smart Contracts and extends it with internal encryption to make the information not only secure and tamper-resistant but also private for every user. Financial information is considered very sensitive for all the regulation authorities in the world and keeping that information secure is not enough to have a whole secure banking system. With our proposal, we not only intend to create a way to transact with banks offline but also to map between the Smart Contract and the classical bank accounts to improve banking management and services. Our proposed solution intends to create and accessible system for every bank user and to keep their transactions accessible, transparent and secure. Our future work consists in implementing our proposed solution using Solidity, which is an object-oriented, high-level language for implementing smart contracts. In addition, we are planning to implement the infrastructure that allows the Gateway Node to manage transactions between mobile users and their banking systems through the blockchain in a way that mobile transaction delays can be reduced to improve the speed of all transactions.

References

1. Nakamoto, S.: Bitcoin: A peer-to-peer electronic cash system (2008). https://bitcoin.org/bitcoin.pdf
2. Maldonado-Ruiz, D., Torres, J., El Madhoun, N.: 3BI-ECC: a decentralized identity framework based on blockchain technology and elliptic curve cryptography. In: 2020 2nd Conference on Blockchain Research & Applications for Innovative Networks and Services (BRAINS), pp. 45–46 (2020)
3. Wood, G.: Ehtereum: a secure decentralized generalized transaction ledger. Ethereum Proj. Yellow Pap. **151**, 1–32 (2018). https://www.cryptopapers.info/eth_yellow
4. Eyal, I.: Blockchain technology: transforming libertarian cryptocurrencydreams to finance and banking realities. Computer **50**(9), 38–49 (2017). https://doi.org/10.1109/MC.2017.3571042. http://ieeexplore.ieee.org/document/8048646/
5. Bello, G., Perez, A.J.: Adapting financial technology standards to blockchain platforms. In: Proceedings of the 2019 ACM Southeast Conference on ZZZ - ACM SE 2019, pp. 109–116. ACM Press, New York (2019). https://doi.org/10.1145/3299815.3314434, http://dl.acm.org/citation.cfm?doid=3299815.3314434
6. Xu, Z., Wang, Q., Wang, Z., Liu, D., Xiang, Y., Wen, S.: PPM: a provenance-provided data sharing model for open banking via blockchain. In: Proceedings of the Australasian Computer Science Week Multiconference, pp. 1–8. ACM, New York, February 2020. https://doi.org/10.1145/3373017.3373022, https://dl.acm.org/doi/10.1145/3373017.3373022
7. Oktian, Y.E., Witanto, E.N., Kumi, S., Lee, S.G.: BlockSubPay - a blockchain framework for subscription-based payment in cloud service. In: International Conference on Advanced Communication Technology, ICACT 2019-February, pp. 153–158 (2019). https://doi.org/10.23919/ICACT.2019.8702008
8. Bhaskaran, K., et al.: Double-blind consent-driven data sharing on blockchain. In: 2018 IEEE International Conference on Cloud Engineering (IC2E), pp. 385–391. IEEE, April 2018. https://doi.org/10.1109/IC2E.2018.00073, https://ieeexplore.ieee.org/document/8360358/

9. Kafshdar Goharshady, A., Behrouz, A., Chatteriee, K.: Secure credit reporting on the blockchain. In: 2018 IEEE International Conference on Internet of Things (iThings) and IEEE Green Computing and Communications (GreenCom) and IEEE Cyber, Physical and Social Computing (CPSCom) and IEEE Smart Data (SmartData), pp. 1343–1348. IEEE, July 2018. https://doi.org/10.1109/Cybermatics_2018.2018.00231, https://ieeexplore.ieee.org/document/8726769/

10. Selvaraj, P., Prabakaran, S., Krishnateja, V.: Novel payment wallet management with blockchain based cryptocurrency. Int. J. Recent Technol. Eng. **8**(2S4), 228–233 (2019). https://doi.org/10.35940/ijrte.B1042.0782S419. https://www.ijrte.org/wp-content/uploads/papers/v8i2S4/B10420782S419.pdf

11. Hu, Y., et al.: A delay-tolerant payment scheme based on the ethereum blockchain. IEEE Access **7**, 33159–33172 (2019). https://doi.org/10.1109/ACCESS.2019.2903271

12. Zhang, R., Xue, R., Liu, L.: Security and privacy on blockchain. ACM Comput. Surv. **52**(3), 1–34 (2019). https://doi.org/10.1145/3316481. http://dl.acm.org/citation.cfm?doid=3341324.3316481

13. Ahmed, M., Elahi, I., Abrar, M., Aslam, U., Khalid, I., Habib, M.A.: Understanding blockchain. In: Proceedings of the 3rd International Conference on Future Networks and Distributed Systems - ICFNDS 2019, pp. 1–8. ACM Press, New York (2019). https://doi.org/10.1145/3341325.3342033, http://dl.acm.org/citation.cfm?doid=3341325.3342033

14. Narayanan, A., Clark, J.: Bitcoin's academic pedigree. Commun. ACM **60**(12), 36–45 (2017). https://doi.org/10.1145/3132259. http://dl.acm.org/citation.cfm?doid=3167461.3132259

15. Dorri, A., Kanhere, S.S., Jurdak, R., Gauravaram, P.: Blockchain for IoT security and privacy: the case study of a smart home. In: 2017 IEEE International Conference on Pervasive Computing and Communications Workshops (PerCom Workshops), pp. 618–623. IEEE, March 2017. https://doi.org/10.1109/PERCOMW.2017.7917634, https://ieeexplore.ieee.org/document/7917634/

16. Kravitz, D.W., Cooper, J.: Securing user identity and transactions symbiotically: IoT meets blockchain. In: 2017 Global Internet of Things Summit (GIoTS), pp. 1–6. IEEE, Geneva, June 2017. https://doi.org/10.1109/GIOTS.2017.8016280, http://ieeexplore.ieee.org/document/8016280/

17. Bragagnolo, S., Marra, M., Polito, G., Gonzalez Boix, E.: Towards scalable blockchain analysis. In: 2019 IEEE/ACM 2nd International Workshop on Emerging Trends in Software Engineering for Blockchain (WETSEB), pp. 1–7, May 2019. https://doi.org/10.1109/WETSEB.2019.00007

18. Yue, L., Junqin, H., Shengzhi, Q., Ruijin, W.: Big data model of security sharing based on blockchain. In: 2017 3rd International Conference on Big Data Computing and Communications (BIGCOM), pp. 117–121, August 2017. https://doi.org/10.1109/BIGCOM.2017.31

19. Bandara, E., et al.: Mystiko-blockchain meets big data. In: 2018 IEEE International Conference on Big Data (Big Data), pp. 3024–3032, December 2018. https://doi.org/10.1109/BigData.2018.8622341

20. Tewari, H., Hughes, A., Weber, S., Barry, T.: X509Cloud - framework for a ubiquitous PKI. In: MILCOM 2017–2017 IEEE Military Communications Conference (MILCOM), vol. 2017-Octob, pp. 225–230. IEEE, Baltimore, October 2017. https://doi.org/10.1109/MILCOM.2017.8170796, http://ieeexplore.ieee.org/document/8170796/

21. Karaarslan, E., Adiguzel, E.: Blockchain based DNS and PKI solutions. IEEE Commun. Stand. Mag. **2**(3), 52–57 (2018). https://doi.org/10.1109/MCOMSTD. 2018.1800023. https://ieeexplore.ieee.org/document/8515149/

22. Axon, L., Goldsmith, M.: PB-PKI : a privacy-aware blockchain-based PKI. In: Proceedings of the 14th International Joint Conference on e-Business and Telecommunications (ICETE 2017), vol. 4, pp. 311–318. SciTePress, Madrid (2017). https://www.scopus.com/inward/record.uri?eid=2-s2. 0-85029461108&partnerID=40&md5=a3c5bd3c1f35085a047453ad1c386c9c

23. Won, J., Singla, A., Bertino, E., Bollella, G.: Decentralized public key infrastructure for Internet-of-Things. In: MILCOM 2018–2018 IEEE Military Communications Conference (MILCOM), pp. 907–913. IEEE, Los Angeles, October 2018. https://doi.org/10.1109/MILCOM.2018.8599710, https://ieeexplore. ieee.org/document/8599710/

24. Shahzad, B., Crowcroft, J.: Trustworthy electronic voting using adjusted blockchain technology. IEEE Access **7**, 24477–24488 (2019). https://doi.org/10. 1109/ACCESS.2019.2895670. https://ieeexplore.ieee.org/document/8651451/

25. Carr, L., Newtson, A.J., Joshi, J.: Towards modernizing the future of American voting. In: 2018 IEEE 4th International Conference on Collaboration and Internet Computing (CIC), pp. 130–135. IEEE, October 2018. https://doi.org/10.1109/ CIC.2018.00028, https://ieeexplore.ieee.org/document/8537826/

26. Hanifatunnisa, R., Rahardjo, B.: Blockchain based e-voting recording system design. In: 2017 11th International Conference on Telecommunication Systems Services and Applications (TSSA), pp. 1–6. IEEE, October 2017. https://doi.org/10. 1109/TSSA.2017.8272896, http://ieeexplore.ieee.org/document/8272896/

27. Harris, C.G.: The risks and dangers of relying on blockchain technology in underdeveloped countries. In: NOMS 2018–2018 IEEE/IFIP Network Operations and Management Symposium, pp. 1–4. IEEE, Taipei, April 2018. https://doi.org/10. 1109/NOMS.2018.8406330, https://ieeexplore.ieee.org/document/8406330/

28. Peters, G.W., Panayi, E.: Understanding modern banking ledgers through blockchain technologies: future of transaction processing and smart contracts on the internet of money. In: Tasca, P., Aste, T., Pelizzon, L., Perony, N. (eds.) Banking Beyond Banks and Money. NEW, pp. 239–278. Springer, Cham (2016). https:// doi.org/10.1007/978-3-319-42448-4_13

29. Fontaine, C., Galand, F.: A survey of homomorphic encryption for nonspecialists. EURASIP J. Inf. Secur. **2007**, 1–10 (2007)

Developing Customized and Secure Blockchains with Deep Federation Learning to Prevent Successive Attacks

Soumya Banerjee[1,3], Soham Chakraborty[2], and Paul Mühlethaler[3(✉)]

[1] Trasna-Solutions, Dublin, Ireland
soumya.banerjee@trasna-solutions.com
[2] KIIT, Bhubaneshwar, India
sohamchakrabortty@gmail.com
[3] EVA Project, Inria - Paris, Paris, France
Paul.Muhlethaler@inria.fr

Abstract. Recently, blockchain technology has been one of the most promising fields of research aiming to enhance the security and privacy of systems. It follows a distributed mechanism to make the storage system fault-tolerant. However, even after adopting all the security measures, there are some risks for cyberattacks in the blockchain. From a statistical point of view, attacks can be compared to anomalous transactions compared to normal transactions. In this paper, these anomalous transactions can be detected using machine learning algorithms, thus making the framework much more secure. Several machine learning algorithms can detect anomalous observations. Due to the typical nature of the transactions dataset (time-series), we choose to apply a sequence to the sequence model. In this paper, we present our approach, where we use federated learning embedded with an LSTM-based auto-encoder to detect anomalous transactions.

Keywords: Blockchain · Anomaly detection · Intelligent algorithm · Auto-encoders · Sequence-to-sequence models · Federated learning

1 Introduction

Blockchain is a peer-to-peer, distributed ledger technology (DLT), which stores data/transactions in a distributed data-structure. Anyone on the network can explore and participate in the transactions on the blockchain in a secure manner. Several techniques are involved, such as a consensus mechanism and block mining. Although certain techniques make it more secure and fault tolerant (e.g. Byzantine fault tolerance), certain malicious and untrusted nodes/users still can persist. They can severely affect the transactions and interrupt the security of the system [1]. The two main challenging security

© Springer Nature Switzerland AG 2021
S. Bouzefrane et al. (Eds.): MSPN 2020, LNCS 12605, pp. 31–43, 2021.
https://doi.org/10.1007/978-3-030-67550-9_3

issues are double spending [2] and record hacking (or record manipulating). There are several non-intelligent algorithms for checking whether a transaction involves double spending or a transaction is being hacked (e.g. maintaining transaction id, hashing and cryptographic encryption). However, they seldom fail to investigate the nature of malicious nodes and may lead to blocks getting hacked/affected. Therefore, we can switch to using machine learning driven intelligent algorithms [3] to detect the possibility of whether a particular node is malicious or not. Predicting this phenomenon will clearly be advantageous, as any malicious transactions can be halted at that instant without the possibility of a spoofing attack. The remaining part of this paper is as follows:

Section 2 briefly describes recent research breakthroughs in the field of machine learning (ML) algorithms. The proposed model is presented in Sect. 3, with while Sect. 3.1 giving the high level description of the algorithm with the relevant mathematical parameters. Section 4 discusses the experimental results yielded through the proposed model and finally Sect. 5 summarizes the contribution as conclusion with future possibilities of extension of research in this regard.

2 Related Work

This paper is motivated by the ideas and implementations of reinforcement learning towards enhancing the security of blockchains [4, 5]. However, most studies tend to offer consolidated reviews of blockchain, irrespective of blockchain implementations. Thus, the authors in [5] point out that the principal of optimization in the context of blockchains enabled the Internet of Vehicles (IoV). In contrast, this present work sets out to achieve two main goals: a) to represent a distributed training algorithm that applies an autoencoder to detect anomalies in the chain of transactions in different nodes. The autoencoder uses LSTM for sequence-to-sequence learning and the Adam optimization algorithm to optimize the parameters. This choice was made since Adam optimizers usually work better than RMSprop and SGD. b) to analyse the complexity of blockchain processes.

In parallel, the proposed model also executes the ML algorithm to investigate suspicious spikes that appear during the process of creating the blocks (it is known as the Growth model). Let α and β be positive and non-negative probability distributions.

Let t_k represent the (absolute) time at which block k is created, h_k the length of the local blockchain after being extended with block k, and z_k the cumulative maximum given by $z_k := \max \{hi \mid i \leq k\}$. The overall complexity of conventional O(mn) is due to the computation of any functional matrix d and its time complexity is O $(nm + n^2)$. It should be noted that there are n iterations for any blockchain process, each requiring O(n) and O(m) time to compute h_k and d_k, respectively. However, if a single fast algorithm is used to compute h_k, the average overall complexity is reduced. In the worst-case scenario, the complexity is $O(k)$. Here, the experimental evaluations suggest an average below $O(\beta/\alpha)$ (constant with respect to k). Thus, the average runtime complexity is bounded by $[O\ nm + \min\{n^2, n + n\beta/\alpha\}]$, and this corresponds to $O(nm)$, unless the blockchain system is extremely fast $(\beta \gg \alpha)$.

This paper subjects a challenging proposition over this typical complexity evaluation of blockchain processes. In fact, the proposed model considers the total process, including the complexity of ML with this present blockchain complexity in parallel mode. Therefore, the objective is to synchronize the process of intelligent algorithm in parallel mode with the master blockchain algorithm.

3 Proposed Model

As a primary step, a minimum number of transactions are collected as data to train the designated neural model on these transactions. We can arrange the transactions in time window frames - a set of temporal transaction vectors will be considered as a single observation point. As the data mostly contains a balanced mixture of proper and non-malicious transactions without relevant labels, we need to deploy an unsupervised learning technique. The malicious transactions can be found by using the encoder-decoder model. Here, the n-dimensional transactions will be cast into a latent space. As the malicious activities will comprise different patterns/trends than normal transactions (it is assumed that the number of normal transactions is probably greater in number), therefore they will be considered as outliers in the latent space. Once the decoder has been applied we will again retrieve the n-dimensional search space containing the non-malicious transactions. By comparing the previous search space with the generated one, we can identify the malicious transactions. Once the basic auto-encoder model is trained, it is put into the distributed setting. Here, we incorporate deep federated learning [9] for the purpose of real-time distributed learning. The transaction data generated at every connected client/node participating in the blockchain will be used to train the federated model. Finally, the weights of the client models will be updated and aggregated in the master model. Initially the pre-trained encoder decoder model is set as the master model in the federated learning setup. At every remotely connected nodes, a client model will be responsible and prepared, which will use the weights of the master model at the beginning. With time, transactions occur at nodes and the corresponding client node updates it weights. After a particular interval the aggregate of all the client node model's weights is sent to the master model for a final update.

There are certain basic features that have a correlation with the type of transactions whether they are malicious or not. These are:

- time of transaction,
- frequency of transaction,
- sending transaction id,
- receiving transaction id.

A holistic view of functional flow is presented in Fig. 1.

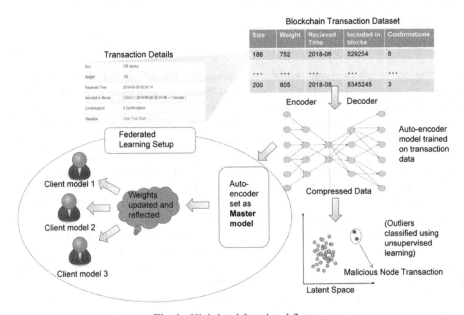

Fig. 1. High-level functional flow

The algorithm has the following input and output.

Input Data: The training dataset contains NF features and NO number of observations. We take NW number of temporally consecutive observations as a single observation window. So the input matrix $X \in R^{N_O*N_F*N_W}$.

Output: Trained encoder parameters (θ) and decoder parameters (φ) (Tables 1 and 2).

Algorithm: Training Algorithm(X, θ, ϕ)

1: Initialize number of training loops as N_T

2: for i $\in$ { 1, 2, ..., N_T } do

3:     Select a window from training set; $X^W \subset X : X^W := [X_S, X_{S+1}, ..., X_{S+Nw}]$

4:     s:= s+1

5:     Initialize encoder LSTM loop : $h_{j\theta}^{2} := f_{LSTM} \theta (h_{j\theta}^{1})$ for j $\in$ {1,2,3,... N_W}

6:     for n $\in$ { 2, 3, ..., N_W } do

7:         $h_{j\theta}^{n+1} := f_{LSTM} \theta (h_{j\theta}^{n})$; for j $\in$ {1,2,3,... N_W}

8:     Initialize decoder LSTM loop: $h_{j\phi}^{2} := f_{LSTM} \phi (h_{j\phi}^{1})$ for j $\in$ {1,2,3,... N_W}

9: for n $\in$ { 2, 3, ..., N_W } do

10:         $h_{j\phi}^{n+1} := f_{LSTM} \phi (h_{j\phi}^{n})$; for j $\in$ {1,2,3,... N_W}

11:   Objective Function: $J(\theta, \phi) := -\sum_{w=1}^{|N_W|} \sum_{f=1}^{|N_F|} \| X_{w,f}^{W} - X_{w,f}'^{W} \|_2$

12:   Calculate gradient: G $\dfrac{dJ(\theta, \phi)}{d(\theta, \phi)}$ $\leftarrow$

13:   Update parameters: $\theta, \phi := $ ADAM(G)

14: end for

Table 1. Descriptions of Notations used in training algorithm

Notation	Interpretation
N_T	Number of training loops
X^W	Window frame vector
N_W	Number of transactions in a window frame
$h_j \theta$	hidden parameters for encoder
$h_j \varphi$	hidden parameters for decoder
N_F	Number of features
J	Objective function
G	Gradient

Algorithm: Federated Learning algorithm

Local window frame size N_W, the number of participants m per iteration, the number of local epochs E.

Randomly initialize the parameters θ_G, ϕ_G

1: [Participant i]

2: LocalTraining(i, θ, ϕ):

3:     Split local dataset Di to consecutive temporal window frame of size N_W

4:     Training Algorithm (Di, θ, ϕ)

6: [Master Node]

7: Initialize $\theta^0{}_G, \phi^0{}_G$

8: for each iteration t from 1 to T do

9:     Randomly choose a subset St of m participants from N

10:     for each participant i ∈ St do in parallel

11:          $\theta^{t+1}{}_i, \phi^{t+1}{}_i$ ← LocalTraining(i, $\theta^t{}_G, \phi^t{}_G$)

12:     end for

13:     $\theta^t{}_G, \phi^t{}_G = \frac{1}{\sum_{i \in \mathcal{N}} D_i} \sum_{i=1}^{N} D_i * (\theta_i^t, \phi_i^t)$

14: end for

Table 2. Notations used in the Federated Learning algorithm

Notation	Interpretation
M	Number of participants considered for weight aggregation
θ_G, φ_G	Global parameters
E	Number of local epoch
θ, φ	Local parameters

In the original dataset, every individual transaction event is counted in several window frames. So the degree of outliers in each of them can be calculated by calculating the mean error between the predicted output vector and the input vector that contains the particular transaction event.

$$score\left(\vec{X_t}\right) = \frac{1}{N_W} \sum_{i=1}^{N_W} \left\| X^W - X'^W \right\|^2 \tag{1}$$

where i represents the index of all the window frames that contain transaction X_t, where X^W is the actual frame and X'^W is the predicted frame.

4 Results and Discussion

In this proposed methodology, a distributed autoencoder model is set that can summarize the state of the ledger on a latent space and can itself recreate the actual information from the latent space. The underlying idea of this methodology is that whenever the state of the transactions is consistent, the autoencoder preserves the original information from the space. On the other hand, anomalous situations contain inconsistent properties and values that result in unsuccessful reconstruction of the original information. Let's consider an instance where the amount of transactions is too high compared to all other attributes of the transaction. The autoencoder will represent this value as a noise and will automatically ignore this at the time of reconstruction. In such cases, the differences between the actual values and the recreated values depict the score of outliers, which in turn depicts the degree of anomalous issues over the transaction. Therefore, the transactions that have abnormally high outlier scores will be considered as suspicious transactions.

The dataset was collected from github [10]. This dataset was created on historical transactions of BitCoin. The dataset contains 2906 samples with 24 attributes. The attributes of the dataset are listed in the table below (Table 3).

Table 3. Features of the dataset

Date
btc_market_price
btc_total_bitcoins
btc_market_cap
btc_trade_volume
btc_blocks_size
btc_avg_block_size
btc_n_orphaned_blocks
btc_n_transactions_per_block
btc_median_confirmation_time
btc_hash_rate
btc_difficulty
btc_miners_revenue
btc_transaction_fees
btc_cost_per_transaction_percent
btc_cost_per_transaction
btc_n_unique_addresses
btc_n_transactions
btc_n_transactions_total
btc_n_transactions_excluding_popular
btc_n_transactions_excluding_chains_longer_than_100
btc_output_volume

(continued)

Table 3. (*continued*)

Date
btc_estimated_transaction_volume
btc_estimated_transaction_volume_usd

Some of the previously studied trends/patterns of certain attributes are shown in Fig. 2. In the dataset, some of the features had missing values. To get an idea of the trend for interpolation, those features are plotted, the missing data being replaced by forward filling method.

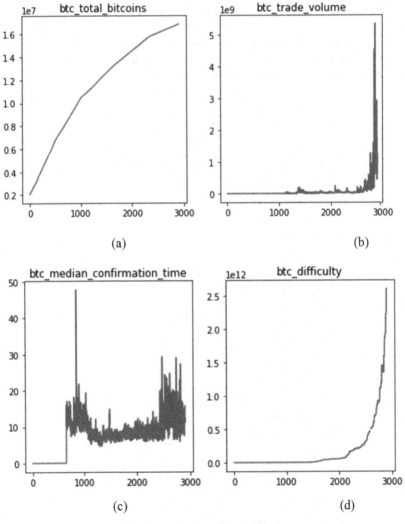

Fig. 2. Exploratory Data Analysis

As discussed in the previous section, we have divided the data into several time frames consisting of time-based transaction events. These individual time frames were trained in the model, and an illustration of the training loss curve is given represented in Fig. 3.

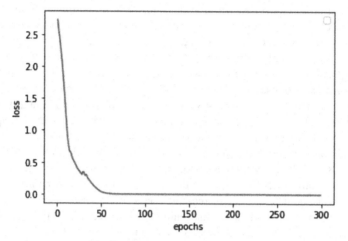

Fig. 3. Loss Curve on training data

Finally, after the model has been trained we try to analyse the score of the outliers. Here we analysed on the first 91 transaction events. Every temporal window considered consisted of three transactions. Once the autoencoder generated a new set of values for every window frame, it was compared with the original timeframe values and the score was calculated using Eq. 1. The scores are graphically displayed in Fig. 4. It can be clearly understood from the pictorial view that some of the transactions have an abnormally high outlier score. These transactions can be considered as suspicious transactions.

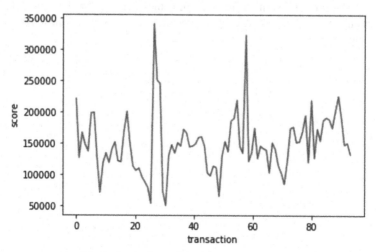

Fig.4. Score for outliers in transaction events

5   Conclusion

The main objective of this work was to detect an attack in a blockchain network using federated learning embedded with a sequential autoencoder model. As attacks are very rare among many transactions, it is very difficult for anyone to label them manually. We considered an unsupervised learning mechanism in a distributed framework. The proposed model can be used to detect successive attacks beforehand with the master-client mechanism of the federated learning system. In a distributed manner, the model is trained on several client machines and after every interval, the weights of the master model are updated. As soon as any transaction falls as an outlier, it is predicted to be an attack or a suspicious transaction. Using LSTM instead of generic RNN for our training algorithm, we reduce the possibility of vanishing and exploding gradient as the amount of data is large. The sequence-to-sequence deep learning model helps to capture the underlying probability distribution for normal consistent transactions.

The work has manifold future possibilities to integrate ML algorithms in blockchain processes [6–8, 11]. It is worth investigating deep learning deployment for energy perspectives blockchain. Therefore, the parallel mode and optimized approach of block mining time with the detection of suspicious blocks might lead to sound synchronization of blockchain process and such distributed machine learning interfaces. The node is in the free state (1). The node leaves this state upon reception (2) or emission (6) of a message on the channel. If a new message arrives, the delay is defined based on the related SINR value, which is distributed according to the exponential law (3).

This setting of the delay interval gives priority to messages with lowest SINR levels, because the source of these messages is either far away or are located in the deepest fading zone. If no duplicate message is received during the delay interval, the current message is sent (4). Otherwise (i.e. if a duplicate message is received), then the original message is deleted. In the following cases of duplicate messages, they are all deleted immediately (10).

Once the deletion interval is elapsed, the message is removed from the delay buffer (7). If the delay buffer is empty, the node switches to the "free" state (8). Otherwise, the node expects the timer to expire to treat the next message (9). After all messages have been sent using the transmit queue (11), the node returns to the free state (5) or switches to the waiting state (12).

Appendix

source code:

```
# import libraries
import pandas as pd
import numpy as np
import matplotlib.pyplot as plt

# import the dataset
data = pd.read_csv('bitcoin_dataset.csv')
test = pd.read_csv('test_set.csv')

# plotting some of the features with missing value
%matplotlib inline
fig, axes = plt.subplots(1, 3, figsize=(12, 4))

axes[0].plot(data['btc_total_bitcoins'])
axes[0].set_title("btc_total_bitcoins")

axes[1].plot(data['btc_trade_volume'])
axes[1].set_title("btc_trade_volume")

axes[2].plot(data['btc_blocks_size'])
axes[2].set_title("btc_blocks_size")

fig, axes = plt.subplots(1, 3, figsize=(12, 4))

axes[0].plot(data['btc_median_confirmation_time'])
axes[0].set_title("btc_median_confirmation_time")

axes[1].plot(data['btc_difficulty'])
axes[1].set_title("btc_difficulty")

axes[2].plot(data['btc_transaction_fees'])
axes[2].set_title("btc_transaction_fees")

# filling the missing data with forward fill method
X = data.fillna(method='ffill')

#creating window frames from the temporally consecutive transactions

ll=[]
for i in range(2,93):
    l = []
    l.append(list(X.iloc[i-2]))
    l.append(list(X.iloc[i-1]))
    l.append(list(X.iloc[i]))
    ll.append(l)

sequence = np.array(ll)
n_in = len(sequence)
#resahping the flattened array
sequence = sequence.reshape((n_in, 3, 22))
```

```
# define model
model = Sequential()
model.add(LSTM(100, activation='relu', input_shape=(3,22)))
model.add(RepeatVector(3))
model.add(LSTM(100, activation='relu', return_sequences=True))
model.add(TimeDistributed(Dense(22)))
model.compile(optimizer='adam', loss='mse', metrics=['accuracy'])

# fit model
history = model.fit(sequence, sequence, epochs=300, verbose=0)

t = model.predict(sequence)

# plotting the loss curve of the model
plt.plot(history.history['loss'])
plt.legend()
xlabel('epochs')
ylabel('loss')

# storing the actual transactions
actual=[]
actual.append(list(sequence[0][0]))
actual.append(list(sequence[0][1]))
actual.append(list(sequence[0][2]))

for i in range(1,len(sequence)):
    actual.append(list(sequence[i][2]))

# storing the predicted transactions
pred=[]
pred.append(list(t[0][0]))
pred.append(list(t[0][1]))
pred.append(list(t[0][2]))

for i in range(1,len(t)):
    pred.append(list(t[i][2]))

# finding the error between the actual and the predicted transactions
error=[]
for i in range(len(pred)):
    e = 0
    for j in range(22):
        e = e + pow(abs(pred[i][j]*pred[i][j] - actual[i][j]*actual[i][j]),(1/2))
    error.append(e)

# plotting the outlier score vs transaction curve
import matplotlib.pyplot as plt
x = np.linspace(0,93,93)
plot(x,error)
xlabel('transaction')
ylabel('score')
```

References

1. Ye, C., Li, G., Cai, H., Gu, Y., Fukuda, A.: Analysis of security in blockchain: case study in 51%-attack detecting. In: 2018 5th International Conference on Dependable Systems and Their Applications (DSA), pp. 15–24 (2018).
2. Chohan, W.: The double spending problem and cryptocurrencies.SSRN Electronic Journal (2017).
3. Buczak, A.L., Guven, E.: A survey of data mining and machine learning methods for cyber security intrusion detection. IEEE Commun. Surv. Tutorials **18**(2), 1153–1176 (2016)
4. Reinforcement Learning in Blockchain- Enabled IIoT Networks: A Survey of Recent Advances and Open Challenges, MDPI Sustainability, 24 June 2020.
5. Liu, M., Teng, Y., Yu, F.R., Leung, V.C., Song, M.: Deep reinforcement learning based performance optimization in blockchain-enabled internet of vehicle. In: Proceedings of the ICC 2019. 2019 IEEE International Conference on Communications (ICC), Shanghai, China.
6. Dinh, T.N., Thai, M.T.: AI and blockchain: a disruptive integration. Computer, **51**(9), 48–53 (2018). ISSN: 0018- 9162
7. Juneja, A., Marefat, M.: Leveraging blockchain for retraining deep learning architecture in patient-specific arrhythmia classification. In: 2018 IEEE EMBS International Conference on Biomedical Health Informatics (BHI), pp. 393–397, March 2018. https://doi.org/10.1109/BHI.2018.8333451
8. Shen, M., et al.: Privacy-preserving support vector machine training over blockchain-based encrypted IoT data in smart cities. IEEE Internet Things J. **6**(5), pp. 7702–7712 (2019). ISSN: 2372–2541.
9. Li, Y., Chen, C., Liu, N., Huang, H.: Zibin Zheng. Qiang Yan, A Blockchain-based Decentralized Federated Learning Framework with Committee Consensus (2020)
10. https://github.com/Yrzxiong/Bitcoin-Dataset
11. Ferrag, M.A., Maglaras, L.: Deepcoin: a novel deep learning and blockchain-based energy exchange framework for smart grids. IEEE Trans. Eng. Manag., p. 13 (2019). ISSN: 1558–0040. https://doi.org/10.1109/TEM.2019.2922936.

Toward a Blockchain-Based Technology in Dealing with Emergencies in Patient-Centered Healthcare Systems

Ha Xuan Son[1], Trieu Hai Le[2(✉)], Nga Tang Thi Quynh[3],
Hung Nguyen Duc Huy[1], Nghia Duong-Trung[1], and Huong Hoang Luong[1]

[1] FPT University, Can Tho City, Vietnam
`sha@uninsubria.it`, `ndhhung1011@gmail.com`, `duong-trung@ismll.de`,
`huonglh3@fe.edu.vn`
[2] Tho University of Technology, Can Tho City, Vietnam
`lhtrieu.0127@gmail.com`
[3] National Taiwan University of Science and Technology, Taipei, Taiwan
`tangnga2695@gmail.com`

Abstract. Nowadays, medical healthcare always plays a vital role for humans in society, especially problems related to personal health records due to its security and sensitivity. For each patient, personal health records are critical and vital assets, so how to manage them effectively is becoming exciting research to solve. Many types of research in aspects of managing and operating personal health records have been introduced; however, dealing with patients' data in emergency cases remains an uncertain issue. When emergencies happen in reality, using a traditional access system is very hard for patients to give consent to staff to access their data. Besides, there is no secured record management of patient' data, which reveals highly confidential personal information, such as what happened, when, and who has access to such information. Therefore, in this paper, an emergency access control management system is proposed to protect the patients' data. This system is built based on permissioned Blockchain Hyperledger fabric. The proposed system will define several rules and regulations by using smart contracts and time duration to deal with emergencies. The patients also restrict the time to access the data in such urgent cases. Several algorithms that represent how the system works are also provided to make readers understand about the proposed management system.

Keywords: Emergency access · Blockchain · Hyperledger fabric · Privacy and security · Patients' data · Personal health record

1 Introduction

Various emerging technologies such as cloud computing and Blockchain have been employed in modern health care to cultivating patient safety, health outcomes,

ⓒ Springer Nature Switzerland AG 2021
S. Bouzefrane et al. (Eds.): MSPN 2020, LNCS 12605, pp. 44–56, 2021.
https://doi.org/10.1007/978-3-030-67550-9_4

service efficiency, and delivery models. The aim of such efforts is dedicated to guaranteeing patients' health situation, continuity of care in all services, including diagnostic, primary, and emergency care. Nowadays, due to the transference of healthcare industry to volume-based care or healthcare-centered service (fee-for-service), the model of patient-centered care is becoming more and more important and it is necessary to implement a platform to manage the security of data insides. However, dealing with such problems in emergency cases still leaves a space for researchers to fill in. Patient-centered care is a system that puts patients at the heart of health care services based on shared, informed decision-making [10]. Patients are given several rights to access their medical records with a comprehensive view of their entire health history. The rights should be easy to access so that it could potentially reduce information fragmentation and inaccuracy caused by communication delays or coordinator errors.

The health care data (such as healthcare history, medication procedures, and significant diseases as well as allergy information etc.) are integrated and stored in the personal account [1,8,23,28]. These data are compassionate, so it is necessary for patients to control whom and when their personal data is shared and choose which other participants can access data area. Secure data sharing is critical to present sufficient collaborative treatment and care choices for patients [30]. Hence, in the patient-centered healthcare system, doctors and nurses are given rights to access patients' personal health records including modifying and querying, but all the activities are recorded. In the emergency situations, the medical staff needs some essential and valuable health information about the patients for cumulating the chance to supply an appropriate cure to save the patient's life or assuage in perilous conditions. Because of the sensitivity and confidentiality of the data, accessing to the patients' health record is restricted for everyone included his/her physician. However, in such situations, such predefined access control [11,17,19] becomes less because there are still no policies defined that would allow an emergency medical team to access the patients' health records. Also, patients at that time can operate and control their health account [24,25]. In another aspect, the patients' care is necessary and their health accounts record such a very essential aspect of their security and privacy. Therefore, after accessing the patients' health account, misuse of personal information can be exploited illegally. Compared to the traditional emergency cases, the system does not verify the identification of the object, either a people or organization sends a request. When the staff has done some activities on their personal health records, the malicious could try to obtain the patients' information. There is no audit and transaction log where the patient can trace all the accesses of their information because, in this emergency situation, the patients cannot participate in the emergency access authorization.

To alleviate these problems and ensure secure access handling in emergency situations and maintain a secure ledger, a framework is proposed to leverage the distributed and immutable shared ledger called Blockchain technology. The Blockchain is a decentralized architecture that features a distributed immutable ledger in which all sections are recorded. In the system, there are five main types of users group: patients, doctors, medical men, nurses, and insurance men. Our system is a Hyperledger Fabric that alleviates these problems with an architecture that allows our system to be extensible and scalable. In order to maintain high application performance and economic viability, all of the patients' data, such as personal data, diagnostic images, lab test results, prescriptions, treatment drug plans, etc., are stored in our client account. Each user is identified by a user id and collection of their users' group. In this private blockchain platform, as mentioned in [26], normal situations happen as each participant creates and has the right to access the data that he/she created. With smart contracts, personal health record data owners (patient) set the condition for an emergency staff or team member who can set access permissions to any of their data items flexibility and securely with the time limitation.

The central part of the paper is organized as follows: Sect. 2 gives more details about the background on the Blockchain technology, Hyperledger Fabric (HF). Section 3 delivers a brief literature review of emergency access control. In the fourth section, the proposed system and its design are clarified. The system implementation is illustrated in Sect. 4. Section 5 provides the analysis of the framework and conclusion of the paper with a summary of the research contribution.

2   Background

The detailed description of the technical underpinnings of the blockchain technology is out of scope in this research. Nevertheless, for the purpose of our discussion going forward, it is vital to shed light on some blockchain concepts, features, and terminologies that will cultivate the understanding of how Blockchain is applied to solve healthcare problems in emergency cases. This section reviews the background on the blockchain technology network and Hyperledger Fabric. In this paper, the system is built based on private Blockchain integrated with Hyperledger Fabric.

2.1   Blockchain Technology Network

Blockchain technology is a shared and distributed database, a digital data structure that consists of a continuously expanding log of transactions with chronological order. It is a decentralized network known as a peer-to-peer platform that features a distributed immutable ledger in which all transactions are recorded. Participants in Blockchain has its own distributed ledger because it is a technique for frauds, errors, and ineptitudes. This action is devoted to record a transaction peer-to-peer and reduce those vulnerabilities. There are three main types of Blockchain: consortium, public Blockchain, or private Blockchain. In the current area [12], Blockchain has extended to produce both inside and outside the industry, not only the financial system. Blockchain has promising solutions for different applications in various fields, such as the healthcare domain or medical study. Several forms in the healthcare industry have provided financial supports for this new technology in order to build a protected podium for maintaining and assessing confidential healthcare information.

2.2   Permissioned Blockchain

The permissioned Blockchain (known as private Blockchain) is built to permit a person, an organization of a group to transfer information and record transactions efficiently. It adds a layer to decide who can participate in the network system, with the identity of each participant known to all participants. In the permissioned blockchain network system, each participant does not have a chance to fraud as their identity is exposed to the management server.

2.3   Hyperledger Fabric

Hyperledger Fabric is an implementation of a private (permissioned) blockchain system [21]. It is one of the primary permissioned blockchain structure at present. It allows only concerned stakeholders as participant members to meet the network, invokes in the transactions, and temper the ledger. The Hyperledger Fabric consists of several kinds of nodes that are related to various organizations. Each node's identity presents for a member service provider. This platform is used in several approaches to solve the Cash-on-delivery problems [5,14,15,17,22]. In the Hyperledger Fabric network, all nodes have distinctness to the identities of all parties. Besides, it provides the opportunity to utilize a consensus mechanism that is much lighter computationally than the Proof of Work mechanism. The fabric has smart contracts, which are the main parts of our system. Smart contracts enable participants to execute complex transactions per defined permissions.

3   Related Work

3.1   Emergency Access Control for Personal Healthcare Records

Zhang et al. [31] proposed an online system for polling to provide available access for urgent control to a personal health record. For every request of emergency access, the system controls the right access based on the collected views of the patient's predefined emergency contact information and additional online enrolled physicians. Because the operation of the system is determined according to the demographic amount of the healthcare provider association nationwide, it presents a constant emergency access control at all times. In another research published by Thummavet and Vasupongayya [24], they proposed a framework to deal with personal health record data in emergency cases. The main challenge in such emergency conditions is how emergency staff and doctors obtain their patients' personal data when they are incapable of providing information. Thus, in the paper, a recommended system is proposed to solve this problem. It permitted each personal health record to classify into three categories. In this work, a threshold cryptosystem was adopted to measure the number of grant permissions from the delegated members which are selected by the patients. Another system that used fingerprints of patients is proposed in Guan et al. [9]. This system allows doctors to obtain quick access permission of personal health records by using patients' fingerprints. In this system, patients' fingerprints played as a role of permission key for the doctor to access and obtain the necessary information. The server administers compared the presented data and the original data saved on the database. If the data are sanctioned, the doctor is allowed to have quick access to personal health records. With the aim to reduce the space absorbed by the fingerprint and update the authentication performance, the principal components analysis (PCA) method is further proposed to collect and meet the fingerprint.

In the research of Rabieh et al. [16], a secure medical records access plan was designed to provide emergency access for the patients using a cloud server. In this case, an emergency center could decrypt a patient's medical records without exposing the secret key used to encrypt them with the guidance of the patients' smartphone and the cloud server. An advanced model for the emergency access control system was suggested by Chen et al. [3]. The system was built by using an automatic add token and identifier scheme. When the final token had been removed, the patient could update to define the token and identifier by himself.

3.2   Blockchain-Based Technology Application in Health Care System

Ichikawa et al. [13] developed a mHealth scheme for cognitive-behavioral treatment for sleeplessness practicing a smartphone application. The volunteer's data information obtained by the application was saved in JSON format and forwarded to the blockchain HF system. They confirmed the data update process under circumstances where all the validating peers were working routinely. Azaria et al. [2], until now, the MedRec functioning prototype was the first and only prototype that had been proposed.

An implementation that utilized smart contracts as mediators were proposed by [4] to access electronic health records in a largescale information system. In this paper, the problem of accessibility and data privacy issues in healthcare was emphasized. The current version of the Ethereum platform was the base idea of the suggested architecture, which smart contracts played as the core role in the system. Smart contracts were implemented to register all access to data, process access requests, and store new transactions in the ledger. In this system, the data were owned by the user, not by health institutions. The system used a distributed ledger to execute smart contracts and recorded references to health transactions, store health records, and users' public and private cryptographic keys. One of the apparent advantages of this system was the delegation of data management to patients. Patients had full control over their medical records. However, of a user lost his private key, this became a huge challenge. Thus, this proposed design system is still in the early stage of conceptualization.

MeDShare [27] was another efficient blockchain-based management system to handle medical records. This system was implemented to use cloud repositories that manage shared medical records and data among medical big data entities. This proposed system guaranteed data provenance, security, auditing, and user verification via cryptographic keys. The mechanism of MedShare was divided into four main layers, including user, data query, data structuring and provenance, and an existing database infrastructure layer. When users intended to access the database, a private key was generated and signed digitally by the user. The query system then forwarded the request to data structuring and the provenance layer. After that, a smart contract was executed to share data among cloud service providers.

In the research of Duong-Trung et al. [6,7], a patient-centric care system was built based on a smart contract mechanism. It is also introduced in [20]. The system consisted of five main parties: doctor, medical man, nurse, insurance man, and patients. Patients were the heart of the system. They were the only group of users who can access data to store information about update activities, query data of the other user group. Doctors had the rights to initialize the medical record information, drug information, and were able to update and query data to track information from the data domain. The group of nurse users had the responsibility to generate and update the information in two domains, such as medical records and drug information. Medical men can only query the medical record data while insurance men only query the patient's hospital fee information. Thus, in case of an emergency when the patients are incapable of accessing their health record, the health system need to design an automatic control to deal with this problem. This paper has not solved this problem yet. Thus, in our paper, we will continue to develop blockchain-based technology to deal with urgent situations when patients need their information for medical reasons but cannot access their data by themselves.

4 The Proposed System

In an emergency case, accessing personal health records can provide the necessary medical treatment for patients. Nevertheless, when the patient is in a situation of being unconscious, it is complicated for them to operate the control access to their personal health record and provide their information to doctor or nurse. Therefore, it requires an automatic system control to manage the medical record and to be able to access or share the health record data during the medication or post-treatment monitoring. Due to the sensitivity of the data, it is compulsory to keep the data complete, securely saved, and can be accessed just only based on the patient's approval quickly and expediently. Hence, in this paper, we apply private Blockchain. Hyperledger Fabric technology network to create a framework of a personal health record. By operating permissioned blockchain technology, this paper provides emergency access for expediting the consent management and speeding up PHR data fetc.h from the PHR system. A smart contract is developed to enable patients to impose permission access control policy [18,29] for their data efficiently and allow personal health record data for sharing to emergency doctors during emergency situations.

4.1 Blockchain-Based Technology Application in Health Care System

Our proposed system will define some permission access rules through Hyperledger Fabric. In this paper framework, the doctor or nurses can initiate an emergency request at the medical center equipment, sent directly to the data management service center. This request is sent under the restrictions of the patient's rules through the framework. Personal health data is saved via the blockchain network or, in other words, is kept in their personal health record. There may be multiple accesses from different participants; however, the authority is only given to staff who have the granular access rights from the database according to the permissions. The data requests are also updated frequently by the blockchain network. Thus, the patients, after recovering, can see who already accessed and took their data.

In our system, a smart contract plays a crucial role. All the transactions are concerned with authorization, and data fetching from the ledger are executed through the smart contracts (a business, logic). The proposed framework operates based on the smart contracts of the ledger, which makes the system-protected, effective, and auditable. Figure 1 shows the proposed design of the system for emergency control in healthcare using Blockchain. This system consists of five actors, including patients, doctors, nurses, medical men, and insurance men. The detailed explanation of the entities is as follows.

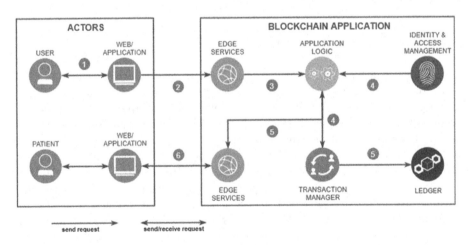

Fig. 1. A proposed system for emergency access for personal health record using Blockchain

As can be seen from Fig. 1, six steps are performed. In the first step, the user, who is the nurse or doctor, initiates an emergency request at the medical center equipment, sent to the edge service to process data. Then, in the second step, the edge services will check the validity of the data sent from the requests to avoid missing data when the user makes the request. The data, after being checked, will be sent to the compute module at the APPLICATION LOGIC. Next, in the third step, these modules conduct data format before storing into the system, id user is also collected to store to identify the person making the transaction; in addition to the immutability of data, transparency is also a strong point of the blockchain system when it allows to identify which user made a transaction and when it was made. Then, in the fourth step, when an emergency request is initiated, the system will send request information to the Transaction Manager for storage with the waiting state. At the same time, Application Logic will also send an emergency case message to the patient with a preset timeout. If the patient has no problem, they will reject the request. Application Logic will update the request again with the reject status. Conversely, if the system does not receive the message within the waiting time, Application Logic will update the request with approval status and grant access to the patient's database to the doctor and nurse. Finally, TRANSACTION MANAGER includes the api tasked with storing or querying data. When an emergency request is sent, the Transaction Manager will store emergency information with a waiting status, which can be updated to change to reject or approve depending on whether the patient has a response to the system or not. In many cases, individuals may attempt to gain unauthorized access to patient data, so the confirmation or denial of a patient's emergency request is essential in this model.

4.2   System Implementation

Our system consists of three functions, including registering accounts for patients (if they have not registered any personal health record in emergency cases), initializing emergency access control for doctors or nurses in urgent situations, and get_patient_data from Hyperledger blockchain. These functions can be regarded as Hyperledger Fabric transactions triggered by the main actors such as doctors, nurses, and patients. The role of each participant is controlled under the access control policy. It shows (who) participants should access which role and under which condition, the right to access should be given to participants. Three algorithms belows are representing for each function in the proposed system

---

Algorithm 1: Create an account for patients in emergency situation (who does not have an account)

1: Input: staff ID, patient ID, First Name, Last Name, emergency, date-time
2: Output: emergency data storing to the ledger
3: **for** emergency case **do**
4:    **if** staff ID valid **then**
5:       storing data of emergency case
6:    **else**
7:       **return** error
8:    **end if**
9: **end for**

Patient account registration: Generally, patients already have an account before emergency cases happen. Nevertheless, if they have not registered the system, the system supports them to register accounts quickly. Registration enters the (staff ID, patient ID, First Name, Last Name, emergency, date-time) as input and submits the request to the system. After registering the patients' accounts, it creates an identity card for the patient and stored in the identity wallet. Algorithm 1 summarizes the patient registration function in detail.

Algorithm 2: Initialize Emergency Access Control to Personal Health Record

---
1: Input: staff ID, patient ID, patient name, emergency, date-time
2: Output: Init and store emergency data to the ledger
3: **for** Emergency case created **do**
4:     send a request to patient
5:     **if** no denial response from the patient **then**
6:         create emergency data
7:         storing data to the ledger
8:     **else**
9:         reject an initial emergency request
10:    **end if**
11: **end for**

Initialize emergency access control: for initialization of emergency access control, the emergency doctor enters staff ID, patient ID, patient name, emergency, date-time as input, and submits the request in the system. Then, the emergency access is created and continues without stopping in a limited time until it receives the response from the system to access the personal health record. Algorithm 2 summarizes the emergency access control initialization function in detail.

Algorithm 3: Get patients' data

1: Input: staff ID, patient ID, date-time
2: Output: data of an emergency situation
3: **for** patient ID **do**
4:     **if** staff ID valid **then**
5:         data ¡- get data to depend on patient ID
6:         **if** data!= null **then**
7:             **return** data
8:         **else**
9:             **return** error
10:        **end if**
11:    **else**
12:        **return** error
13:    **end if**
14: **end for**

Get patients' data: For the access of the patient data in the emergency condition, `get_patient_data` function enters (the staff ID, patient ID, date-time) as input. After obtaining the requirement to access the data, the system will automatically check the defined rules to allow emergency doctors or nurses to access the data or not. The smart contract assign duration based on the time limitation as defined by the patient. Besides, the system also creates "Time constraints" for emergency cases. During the emergency time, the current doctor can see the patient's data. Algorithm 3 summarizes the `get_patient_data` function in details.

The system operation process starts when an emergency situation occurs. At this point, the doctor or nurse will initiate an emergency request, the data of this request is described in detailed in the source code bellows.

The data recorded in emergency cases consists of ID of emergency cases, creators, emergency staff (doctors, nurses), patients' ID, date, time, description and status of that case. In the beginning, the status of request is "waiting". It means the system is starting to react to the response from patient. In the waiting period, if the system receives the patient's denial response, there will exist an automatic emergency request status and the system will reject the request from doctors or nurses to access patients; data. At which point, the status of the system attribute will change to "reject". Conversely, if the system does not receive any response during the timeout period, the system will update the status of the emergency request and allow the doctor and nurse to access patient information, at this point the emergency status. The emergency request will present the "approved" status.

```json
{ "ID":"emergency001",
  "creater":"user001",
  "staff":[
   "doctor1":"doctor001",
   "doctor2":"doctor002",
   "nuse1":"nuse001",
   "nuse2":"nuse002",
   ...
  ]
  "patientID":"patient001",
  "date":"09/20/2020",
  "time":"11:45",
  "description":"emergency situation",
  "state":"waiting"
}
```

The process also creates data for patients in case they do not have any account, which shows in the source description bellows.

```json
{ "ID":"emergency001",
  "creater":"user001",
```

```
"staff":[
 "doctor1":"doctor001",
 "doctor2":"doctor002",
 "nuse1":"nuse001",
 "nuse2":"nuse002",
  ...
]
"patientID":"patient001",
"date":"09/20/2020",
"time":"11:45",
"description":"emergency situation",
"state":""
}
```

In case the patient still has no data at the health authority, an emergency request will be initialized with the state as an empty field. The data needed in this process includes ID of patients, creator, staff (nurses and doctors), patients' ID, date, time (to create data), description, and status of the emergency cases. The most important information in the process is patients' ID and the status of the emergency cases because this information is used to classify specific patients in which situations with other patients and emergency cases.

Moreover, the authors provide the sources codes for the proof of concept, instruction of installation. Interesting readers might refer to our GitHub repository[1].

5   Conclusion

The proposed system in this paper provides privacy protection and security policy to manage patients' data in urgent situations. Technically, the system is built based on Hyperledger Fabric and Smart Contract, which is a permissioned based blockchain technology. The proposed framework deals with the problems of how to get access to a patients' data when emergency situations arise, also consider the problems of setting suitable rules for accessing the emergency control management of personal health records. The system is implemented through Hyperledger Fabric to evaluate the efficiency of our framework. Our experimental results also confirm that this system can ensure the privacy and security of sensitive patient data.

References

1. Adida, B., Kohane, I.S.: Geneping: secure, scalable management of personal genomic data. BMC Genom. **7**(1), 1–10 (2006)

---

[1] https://github.com/Masquerade0127/emergency-blockchain.

2. Azaria, A., Ekblaw, A., Vieira, T., Lippman, A.: Medrec: Using blockchain for medical data access and permission management. In: 2016 2nd International Conference on Open and Big Data (OBD), pp. 25–30. IEEE (2016)
3. Chen, Y.Y., Huang, C.C., Jan, J.K.: The design of aatis emergency access authorization for personally controlled online health records. J. Med. Biolog. Eng. **35**(6), 765–774 (2015)
4. da Conceição, A.F., da Silva, F.S.C., Rocha, V., Locoro, A., Barguil, J.M.: Eletronic health records using blockchain technology. arXiv preprint arXiv:1804.10078 (2018)
5. Duong-Trung, N., et al.: Multi-sessions mechanism for decentralized cash on delivery system. Int. J. Adv. Comput. Sci. Appl. **10**(9)
6. Duong-Trung, N., Son, H.X., Le, H.T., Phan, T.T.: On components of a patient-centered healthcare system using smart contract. In: Proceedings of the 2020 4th International Conference on Cryptography, Security and Privacy. pp. 31–35 (2020)
7. Duong-Trung, N., Son, H.X., Le, H.T., Phan, T.T.: Smart care: integrating blockchain technology into the design of patient-centered healthcare systems. In: Proceedings of the 2020 4th International Conference on Cryptography, Security and Privacy, pp. 105–109 (2020)
8. Gao, Z., Wang, D., Wan, S., Zhang, H., Wang, Y.: Cognitive-inspired class-statistic matching with triple-constrain for camera free 3d object retrieval. Future Generation Computer Systems **94**, 641–653 (2019)
9. Guan, S., Wang, Y., Shen, J.: Fingerprint-based access to personally controlled health records in emergency situations. Sci. China Inf. Sci. **61**(5), 059103 (2018)
10. The U.S. Department of Health and Human Services (HHS): Personal health records and the hipaa privacy rule. Washington, DC. https://www.hhs.gov/sites/default/files/ocr/privacy/hipaa/understanding/special/healthit/phrs.pdf [accessed 2016-06-20][WebCite Cache] (2008)
11. Hoang, N.M., Son, H.X.: A dynamic solution for fine-grained policy conflict resolution. In: Proceedings of the 3rd International Conference on Cryptography, Security and Privacy, pp. 116–120 (2019)
12. Hölbl, M., Kompara, M., Kamišalić, A., Nemec Zlatolas, L.: A systematic review of the use of blockchain in healthcare. Symmetry **10**(10), 470 (2018)
13. Ichikawa, D., Kashiyama, M., Ueno, T.: Tamper-resistant mobile health using blockchain technology. JMIR mHealth uHealth **5**(7), e111 (2017)
14. Le, H.T., et al.: Introducing multi shippers mechanism for decentralized cash on delivery system. Int. J. Adv. Comput. Sci. Appl. **10**(6) (2019)
15. Le, N.T.T., et al.: Assuring non-fraudulent transactions in cash on delivery by introducing double smart contracts. Int. J. Adv. Comput. Sci. Appl. **10**(5), 677–684 (2019)
16. Rabieh, K., Akkaya, K., Karabiyik, U., Qamruddin, J.: A secure and cloud-based medical records access scheme for on-road emergencies. In: 2018 15th IEEE Annual Consumer Communications & Networking Conference (CCNC), pp. 1–8. IEEE (2018)
17. Son, H.X., Chen, E.: Towards a fine-grained access control mechanism for privacy protection and policy conflict resolution. Int. J. Adv. Comput. Sci. Appl. **10**(2) (2019)
18. Son, H.X., Dang, T.K., Massacci, F.: Rew-smt: A new approach for rewriting xacml request with dynamic big data security policies. In: International Conference on Security, Privacy and Anonymity in Computation, Communication and Storage. pp. 501–515. Springer (2017)

19. Son, H.X., Hoang, N.M.: A novel attribute-based access control system for fine-grained privacy protection. In: Proceedings of the 3rd International Conference on Cryptography, Security and Privacy, pp. 76–80 (2019)
20. Son, H.X., Nguyen, M.H., Vo, H.K., et al.: Toward an privacy protection based on access control model in hybrid cloud for healthcare systems. In: International Joint Conference: 12th International Conference on Computational Intelligence in Security for Information Systems (CISIS 2019) and 10th International Conference on EUropean Transnational Education (ICEUTE 2019). pp. 77–86. Springer (2019)
21. Son, H.X., et al.: Dem-cod: Novel access-control-based cash on delivery mechanism for decentralized marketplace. In: 2020 19th IEEE International Conference On Trust, Security And Privacy In Computing And Communications(TrustCom). IEEE (2020)
22. Son, H.X., et al.: Scrutinizing trust and transparency in cash on delivery systems. In: International Conference on Security, Privacy and Anonymity in Computation, Communication and Storage. Springer (2020)
23. Tang, P.C., Ash, J.S., Bates, D.W., Overhage, J.M., Sands, D.Z.: Personal health records: definitions, benefits, and strategies for overcoming barriers to adoption. J. Am. Med. Inform. Assoc. **13**(2), 121–126 (2006)
24. Thummavet, P., Vasupongayya, S.: A novel personal health record system for handling emergency situations. In: 2013 International Computer Science and Engineering Conference (ICSEC), pp. 266–271. IEEE (2013)
25. Thummavet, P., Vasupongayya, S.: Privacy-preserving emergency access control for personal health records. Maejo Int. J. Sci. Technol. **9**(1), 108–120 (2015)
26. Wang, S., Zhang, Y., Zhang, Y.: A blockchain-based framework for data sharing with fine-grained access control in decentralized storage systems. IEEE Access **6**, 38437–38450 (2018)
27. Xia, Q., Sifah, E.B., Asamoah, K.O., Gao, J., Du, X., Guizani, M.: Medshare: trust-less medical data sharing among cloud service providers via blockchain. IEEE Access **5**, 14757–14767 (2017)
28. Xia, Y., Qu, S., Wan, S.: Scene guided colorization using neural networks. Neural Computing and Applications, pp. 1–14 (2018)
29. Xuan, S.H., Tran, L.K., Dang, T.K., Pham, Y.N.: Rew-xac: an approach to rewriting request for elastic abac enforcement with dynamic policies. In: 2016 International Conference on Advanced Computing and Applications (ACOMP), pp. 25–31. IEEE (2016)
30. Zhang, P., White, J., Schmidt, D.C., Lenz, G., Rosenbloom, S.T.: Fhirchain: applying blockchain to securely and scalably share clinical data. Computational and structural biotechnology journal **16**, 267–278 (2018)
31. Zhang, Y., Dhileepan, S., Schmidt, M., Zhong, S.: Emergency access for online personally controlled health records system. Informat. Health Social Care **37**(3), 190–202 (2012)

Using Process Mining to Identify File System Metrics Impacted by Ransomware Execution

Arash Mahboubi[1]([⊠])(iD), Keyvan Ansari[2]([⊠])(iD), and Seyit Camtepe[3]([⊠])(iD)

[1] Charles Sturt University, 7 Major Innes Road,
Port Macquarie, NSW 2444, Australia
amahboubi@csu.edu.au
[2] University of the Sunshine Coast, 90 Sippy Downs Dr,
Sippy Downs, QLD 4556, Australia
kansari@usc.edu.au
[3] CSIRO Data61, Corner Vimiera and Pembroke Rd, Marsfield, NSW 2122, Australia
Seyit.Camtepe@data61.csiro.au

Abstract. Malware authors leverage strong cryptographic primitives to hold user files as a hostage in their own devices until a ransom is paid. Indeed, victims not protected against ransomware are forced to pay the ransom or lose the files if ignoring the extortion. Devices are by no means immune from ransomware attacks. The reality is that there is a limited study on how to protect end-user devices against ransomware while there is hardly any protection available. Ransomware uses legitimate operating system processes that even state-of-the-art and advanced anti-malware products are ineffective against them. The results of our static and dynamic analysis illustrate that a local file system plays a critical role in the operation of all ransomware engines. Therefore, this study investigates the correlation existed between the file system operations to identify metrics such as the absolute occurrence frequency of a system file to identify a ransomware attack from within the kernel. We employ business process mining techniques to analyze collected log files from samples of seven recent live ransomware families and use the Naive discovery algorithm to study the absolute occurrence frequency of system files. The findings are visualized by state charts and sequence diagrams. Finally, the study identifies eight common system files that ransomware calls on in order to encrypt a victim's files on their device.

Keywords: Ransomware · Business process mining · File system · Attack analysis · Attack mining · Malware

1 Introduction

Malicious software, aka malware [16], has posed severe threats to the security of Information and Communication Technology (ICT) systems with a wide variety

© Springer Nature Switzerland AG 2021
S. Bouzefrane et al. (Eds.): MSPN 2020, LNCS 12605, pp. 57–71, 2021.
https://doi.org/10.1007/978-3-030-67550-9_5

of attack vectors impacting the cyber security landscape, i.e., confidentiality, integrity, and availability. Results of malware attacks may vary depending on the degree of malicious payload drops on victims' devices, including personal computers or smart devices, which may result in not only financial losses but also significant information breaches such as data theft, sabotage, or espionage [21]. One wide-spread type of malware that has a trend in the history of malware developments targeting both individuals and organizations is ransomware. Ransomware takes complete control of information on servers, desktop computers or smart devices while allowing limited access for victim's interactions with their machine to pay a ransom amount. Ransomware releases data to victims only when a successful payment is received, and if a victim refuses to pay, ransomware may extend payment periods and ransom amounts or destroy files from the systems altogether.

Ransomware is based on the cryptovirology concept, which uses cryptographic algorithms to demonstrate offensive extortion based attacks that result in compromising the confidentiality of data and data leakage, and causing loss of access to information [22]. Earlier versions of ransomware attacks would encrypt two hard disk cylinders of victims' machines. To this end, hard disks may however be decrypted temporarily when accessed by victims so to ensure that the victim does not realize that the hard disk was encrypted and allows the encryption process to continue. Today, ransomware developers use commercial and non-commercial packers that prevent automated unpacking routines used by the endpoint security software, making it much more difficult to identify and determine the intent of the packaged executable, as well as more difficult for malware analysts to reverse engineer the malicious package. Polymorphic, stealth, mutation, and tunnelling methods have been heavily utilized by ransomware authors for evading malware detection. Using these methods allows ransomware to gain "high survivability", which is defined as maintaining control over a system's resource X in such a way that an access to X is granted as needed. Based on survivability, ransomware can be categorized into three groups, Cryptoworm that is replicated to other devices for highest possible infection and impact, Ransomware-as-a-Service (RaaS) that is sold on the dark web as a distribution package, and Automated Active Adversary that uses tools to automatically search the Internet for weakly protected devices [15].

After initial infections and survivals, the encryption engine of ransomware plays a critical role in generating cryptographic keys to encrypt victims' data within a minimum period of time. For example, Aids Info Disk (AIDS), the first-ever ransomware, generates random encryption keys using the bitwise XOR operation in order to hide directories and encrypt names of all files on a victim's hard disk. Contemporary ransomware is developed to make a cost-effective use of computationally advanced central processing units (CPU), and parallelizes individual jobs to guarantee more agile and, consequently, more severe impacts before even victims realize that they are under attack. Ransomware may be locally deployed in-memory such that ransomware becomes very difficult to detect as it would entirely exist inside a legitimate process. These types of ransomware attacks initiated from within the memory of a victim's device fetch all instructions to the memory to increase performance and lower latency of data encryption as opposed to traditional ransomware that retrieved instructions from an external device, i.e., storage, which was a slower process. Since ransomware would use a legitimate process, detecting and preventing cryptographic operations become extremely challenging. To add to the complexity of dealing with ransomware, developers sign their ransomware codes with authentic code certificates to minimize detection by antivirus software or other defence mechanisms in place. This means anti-malware or anti-ransomware software might not be able to detect attacks by code-signed ransomware and prevent file from being encrypted as it has a valid digital signature.

There are currently limited anti-ransomware mechanisms available due to computational costs associated with the detection of such malware and changing traits of malware that are unknown to the information security community. This paper argues that business process mining techniques can be utilized to identify in-memory process call activities performed by a ransomware can be detected from collected event logs. Business process mining techniques are used for analysis of process performance, detection of anomalies, inspection of patterns and the like. To date, most of the studies on process mining have focused on data extraction from the data control-flow and organizational points of view. In this paper, business process mining techniques are employed to understand the impact of ransomware on critical file system metrics while a system is under attack. Understanding file system behavior during the in-memory execution of ransomware will enable the information security community to combat the crypto-malware family permeated in critical infrastructures. The Naive discovery algorithm is used to identify the absolute occurrence of file system processes and to visualize the collected log files from live ransomware samples in statechart and sequence diagrams.

The rest of the paper is organized as follows. Section 2 presents related work in process mining and security. Section 3 investigates ransomware behaviors at micro and macro levels. Section 4 provides the details of experiment setup and the process mining approach used in this study. Section 5 presents the results obtained from the evaluation of the proposed approach. Finally, Sect. 6 contains a summary of the article and our future work.

2   Related Work

There is a limited number of studies which investigated the feasibility of using business process mining techniques to enable security auditing. Among them, few studies such as those presented in [3,12,18,19] attempted to use process mining for auditing and detection of security violations in business processes. In [19], the authors used α-algorithm to support security efforts at various levels ranging from low-level intrusion detection to high-level fraud prevention. They explored the detection of anomalous process executions in mined Petri-nets by playing the "token game" for particular cases. They claimed that the similarity of the process could be checked by examining the parts of the process to the Petri-net discovered.

In [4], authors combined process data mining methods and high-level visually detailed descriptions of an attacker's behavior to help the network administrator analyze the alerts, i.e., the number of malicious events included in the trace, created by the intrusion detection system at the University of Maryland. If this volume is significantly higher than the predefined threshold, the alert shall be recorded. Process discovery methods have also been used to investigate and categorize malicious software and codes in [6]. This study created a classification of malware families by retrieving a methodological framework from the system logs of infected devices and comparing it to the normal execution of non-infected similar devices.

Bernardi et al. [6] investigated malware detection and studied dynamic phylogeny analysis using process mining. Their approach included using process mining methods to identify relationships and recurring patterns of executions in the operating system traces collected from a mobile app in order to define its behavior. Recovered characterization is demonstrated in terms of a set of declarative limitations between system calls and is a kind of run-time fingerprint of the application. The comparison between the so defined fingerprints of a given application and those of known malware was used to verify: (1) if the application is malware or trusted software; (2) in the case of being malware, (2.1) which family it belongs to, and (2.2) how it differs from other known variants of the same malware family. Similarly, [7] investigated how an attack can be triaged using process mining techniques to support IoT systems. The authors analyzed the logs of commands issued by IoT botnets, including Mirai, Bashlite and LightAidra, against IoT devices during the fingerprinting phase 2 and discovered a process model that represents an up-to-date image of the behaviour of the botnet.

3   Investigating Ransomware Behaviors at Micro and Macro Levels

3.1   Ransomware Working Mechanisms

While researchers are improving the detection and defence schemes against ransomware, ransomware developers are also continually developing stealthier bots. A recent review of ransomware literature solutions indicates, similar to conventional anti-malware solutions, most anti-ransomware solutions are developed based on a blacklist that includes code signatures of known ransomware [10]. However, blacklist-based anti-malware approaches can not prevent ransomware from being spread because of either zero-day payloads or improved variations of known ransomware. Ransomware authors are very aware that network or endpoint security checks pose a fatal threat to any process, so they have developed a logic detection fix. New ransomware spends an incredible amount of time to sabotage security mechanisms, making a digital ecosystem ready for future harvesting. It's a lot easier to change a malware's appearance (obfuscate its code) than to change its purpose or behavior, and ransomware always shows its tell when it strikes. The increasing frequency with which we hear of large ransomware attacks indicates the code obfuscation techniques that ransomware now routinely employs, such as the use of runtime packers, must continue to be fairly effective against some security tools, otherwise ransomware developers wouldn't use them. A different approach to the prevention of ransomware is to continuously observe the abnormal behavior of a process running on a victim's device. Several researchers have focused on monitoring the operating system process that access to files stored on device storage. However, these inspections and monitoring of operating system processes can significantly degrade the performances of devices [11,13].

We have divided ransomware actives into four (4) phases that are illustrated in Fig. 1. In Phase 1, different approaches are employed by ransomware developers to make their victims trigger an initial malware drop and grant it administrator rights to exploit vulnerabilities for privilege escalation. Common ransomware infection vectors include phishing, exploit packs, botnets and downloader, as well as social engineering methods and traffic distribution systems [17]. After a successful initial ransomware drop, ransomware may receive several updates from the command and control (C&C) servers. Ransomware may also function well where no package from C&C servers is required. In Phase 2, ransomware generally uses embedded or cryptographic libraries available in the operating system to generate unique user ID, cryptography keys, and symmetric or asymmetric cryptography algorithms to encrypt files on a victim's device. Normally, the victim's user ID will be used for the generation of symmetric keys. Next step is to encrypt it with a hard-coded public RSA key. This method is the same for known ransomware variants. The encrypted user ID is stored in a file, or the ransom note that appears on the user's desktop. The symmetric key used to encrypt files is generated from, or part of, the user ID. Generally, the hash function (MD5) is used to generate a key in all known ransomware variants. Also, to identify a symmetric algorithm for key generation, ransomware usually calls ALG_ID to identify key specifications. The values for the ALG_ID function, which are different depending on the cryptographic service provider used, determine the key that is generated. In Phase 3, ransomware uses the file system to copy, rename and delete victims' files. After ransomware evades security countermeasures, it uses an exhaustive search to find and encrypt a victim's files on device storage. During the encryption process, ransomware usually uses overwriting or copying methods to write data to the storage again. Table 1 illustrates the differences between file overwriting and file copying methods in different ransomware variants. In Phase 4, ransomware asks the victim to contact the attacker using an email address provided on the ransom note in return for the decryption key. Figure 1 shows a general overview of ransomware transitions between the four phases identified above.

3.2 Ransomware and File System

A file system is a crucial part of every operating system (OS) which manages how and where data should be stored on the storage. Although it has been in making and refinement for decades utilising numerous data protection techniques such as access control and sanity checking, ransomware traditionally engage file systems to read, write, and rename a victim's files on the device storage. Suppose Ransomware R contains the malicious payload $R(M_p)$ that consists of a subset of malicious packages such as $R_P = \{M_{P_1}, M_{P_2}, M_{P_3}, \dots, M_{P_l}\}$. This allows R to

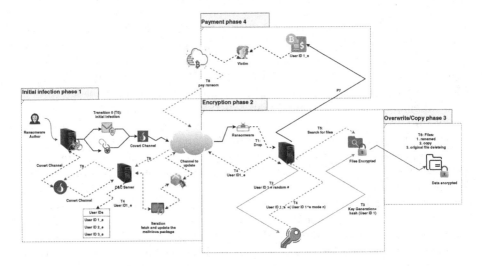

Fig. 1. General overview of ransomware transitions between four phases.

Table 1. Overwriting and copying methods used in different ransomware variants.

	Ransomware file encryption methods	
#	**File Overwriting:** Encrypted files are kept on same hard disk sectors as original files	**Files copying:** Encrypted files are kept on available free hard disk
1	Read the victim's files as a Read/Write	Read the victim's files as a Read only
2	Write encrypted file over original file	Encrypt (write) file and copy encrypted file with a different file extension
3	Rename file after encryption	Delete file after encryption
#	Comments	
1	Unable to recover original files.	File names of encrypted copies are the same as original files.
2	LockerGoga ransomware renames original files prior to actually encrypting them prior to actually encrypting it	Without further deletion actions thereafter, it is possible to recover some original files with forensic tools
3	Files are overwritten, and not deleted after encryption	WannaCry ransomware deletes original files from another tool or process

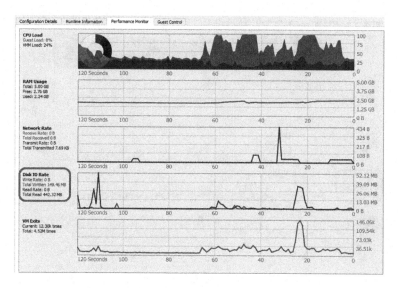

Fig. 2. Under a normal operation of OS, disk IO performance is about 591 MB (see the Disk IO Rate enclosed in a red rectangle) (Color figure online)

engage the file system using its search engine S that performs exhaustive linear searches to locate the Information I on the compromised device D. Assuming I consists of a subset of different types of data, $I_D = \{I_{D_1}, I_{D_2}, I_{D_3}, \dots, I_{D_n}\}$ is identified based on the search list $I_e = \{I_{e_1}, I_{e_2}, I_{e_3}, \dots, I_{e_m}\}$. After I_D is located, R's encryption engine (denoted as the $f_k()$ function) sequentially encrypts $I_{D_1}, I_{D_2}, I_{D_3}, \dots, I_{D_n}$. Therefore, we denote the search engine and encryption in R as $\sum_{i=0}^{m} I_{e_{[i]}} \sum_{j=0}^{n} e = \{f_k(I_{D_{[j]}})\}$. This function is utilized by the $T5$ transition of Phase 2 shown in Fig. 1 for encrypting files. The search is based on I_e that is the ransomware's list of file extensions. After, locating and encrypting data, ransomware overwrites or copies original data to a temporary directory on the victim's storage. Figure 2 illustrates basic user operations that performed 591 MB of disk IO. Figure 3 and Fig. 4 illustrate LockerGoga and WannaCry (two of the seven families of ransomware considered in this study) heavily engaged computational resources and in both ransomware cases, disk IO performance, i.e., read and write, increased significantly. Therefore, in this paper, we focus on the file system and specifically Disk IO to identify file system metrics impacted by ransomware.

3.3   Use of Process Mining to Visualize Ransomware Behavior

Process mining aims to investigate, monitor and improve business processes by knowledge discovery from event logs available in today's information systems [1]. Using process mining methods, business processes can be explored and investigated in a semi-auto manner [20]. Process mining techniques have been defined

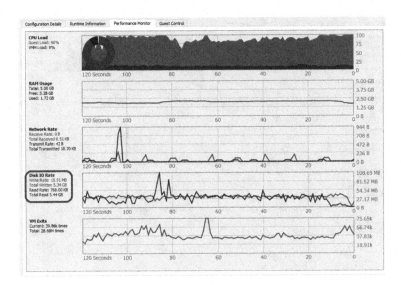

Fig. 3. Under a LockerGoga ransomware attack, disk IO performance has significantly increased to 10.78 GB (see the Disk IO Rate enclosed in a blue rectangle) (Color figure online)

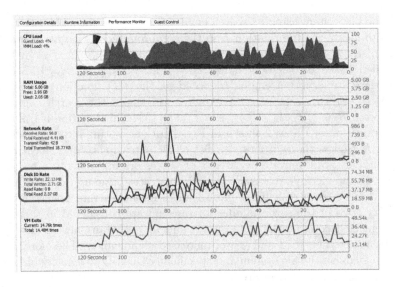

Fig. 4. Under a WannCry ransomware attack, disk IO performance has increased to 5.08 GB (see the Disk IO Rate enclosed in a red rectangle) (Color figure online)

based on process discovery, conformance checking, and model enhancement. Process discovery [2] is a technique to discover a pattern from original traces in an event log file. The process discovery technique [5] automatically constructs a reproduction of complicated processes based on their original performances found in an event log file, without utilizing any prior knowledge. Conformance checking is a technique that compares the mined behaviour in an event log file with a given traced behavior so to discover behaviors from the log file and create a trace based on occurring events within the log. Model enhancement is a technique extending models based on additional information in an event logs file to detect bottlenecks of a business model.

In this paper, we focus on the process discovery of ransomware using live capturing events. This technique helps to deal with significant amounts of data obtained from ransomware attacks. Events are captured on-the-fly, as they occur, and only information about the most relevant events is stored in a limited budget of memory. We execute live ransomware samples to obtain the event logs of its operations and encrypting files in the victim's storage. Our approach aims to identify metrics on which ransomware utilizes a file system and compares it to known file system metrics. This information can be used to classify similar malware attack patterns. Classification of attacks is well-known to the Information security industry which enables the identification of critical threat activities. Nevertheless, it enables security administrators to distinguish well-known properties of a variety of attack patterns while identifying unique metrics can help with predicting the derivation of attacks. For this reason, we examined seven recent ransomware instances from different families that run on 64 bit architecture to collect their file system activities. The process models discovered in the study are represented using Petri nets that grow over time, as new events are created.

4   Methodology

4.1   Ransomware and File System Activities

Our preliminary investigation was to analyze ransomware and emulate basic user activities, e.g., opening folders, reading and writing documents, moving mouse pointer and launching different applications, to collect normal user activities as per the suggestions in [8]. After collecting a set of normal behavior of the system, we executed ransomware packages from seven different ransomware families and collected live logs of their activities. We let the ransomware packages to run and encrypt all user files that included 250 different types of files, such as docx, pptx, exe, rar and zip, which were located on different partitions of the disk. We also let the Process Monitor tool to collect all the activities of the file systems until ransomware has encrypted the files and issued an invoice to the victim. We also emulated network connections to deny communication with C&C servers and avoid receiving harmful traffic, e.g., spam, during the live experiments. We deployed specific file system filters when collecting the logs mainly because our preliminary analysis showed that normal file system operations can create more than 100,000 operations per process, which significantly increase the size of operations log. We applied the following filters, Table 2, when collecting ransomware activities and logs for analysis with the ProM framework [9].

Table 2. File system filters to collect normal and abnormal operations within the system.

File System Filters	Descriptions
QueryAllInformationFile	Query all information files
QueryBasicInformationFile	Record timestamps on original document.
QueryCompressionInformationFile	Query compressed information file
QuerySizeInformationVolume	Query size information volume
QueryStandardInformationFile	Determine file size of original document on disk
SetRenameInformationFile	Change file extension of encrypted file/ Rename file
SetSecurityFile	Modify discretionary access control list (DACL) of original document to Full for group Everyone,

ProM (Process Mining framework) is open source and licensed under GNU Public License (GPL) with an extensible framework that maintains an extensive collection of process mining algorithms and techniques as Java plug-ins. The first step of analysis and process mining included converting the collected CSV log file for ransomware to an OpenXES Xlog object (XES). Converting the CSV log file to XES creates traces that represent executions of the same kind of process. The traces from both normal file system behaviour and ransomware behaviour contain time stamp, process name, process ID, operations, path, result and details of events among which we focused on the process names and operations to create traces.

Let Æ be the set of all events occurring when a process access the file system, which is called the universe set that can define the set of all possible process calls. Let ρ be the set of all possible process instances that are called by a particular process, and ϱ be the set of all activity names during the ransomware execution. We also assume events may be characterized by various attributes. Therefore, let Θ be a set of attribute names for each event. For example, for one event e that accesses read file which has different attributes (n), where $n \in \Theta$, $n(e)$ represents the attribute name n for the event e. Based on the universe set, we can define a trace as a finite set of non-empty sequence of all events $\tau = [e_1, e_2, e_3..., e_n]$ from the universe set Æ where τ does not contain an event $e \in$ Æ greater than one. This can be shown as Equation (1):

$$\forall\, e_x, e_y \ \in Æ \wedge x, y \in [1, n]\,, x \neq y : e_x \neq e_y. \tag{1}$$

4.2   Discovery and Analysis

We used Statechart Workbench [14], which is a plug-in of the ProM tool, for exploring file system event frequencies and conformance checking within the normalized model, i.e., normal operations illustrates in Fig. 5. We selected file system event processes because of the structure of ransomware, i.e., multi-threadedness. The absolute frequency identifies how often a process is called or events occur, while the case frequency identifies how many traces are left from a

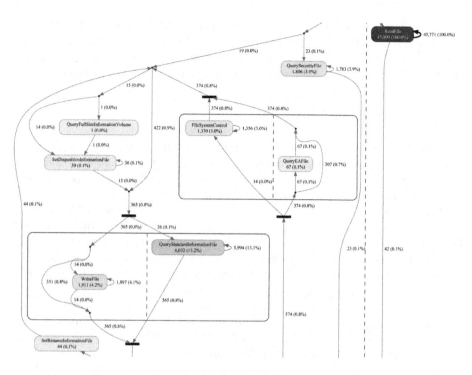

Fig. 5. Discovered process within a normal file system behaviors

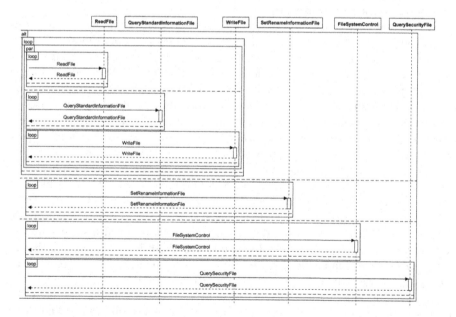

Fig. 6. Matrix ransomware engaging file system in aggressive iterations represented in sequence diagram.

process call or events during the execution of ransomware. The analysis settings to calculate the metrics can be set up using either a *fast approximation algorithm* or the *accurate alignment-based algorithms*. In this study, we used a fast approximation algorithm to calculate the absolute and case frequencies.

5   Evaluation and Results

Our aim is to find a ratio between normal and abnormal activities when a type of ransomware attacks a system. To address our aim, we have setup a ransomware analysis lab that consists of two Linux and one Windows 10 (64-bit) professional virtual machines on a high permanence computer. We used several software such as Procmon64, Process Explorer, Fakenet, Wireshark, TCPview and PEview to emulate and obtain normal and abnormal logs. To obtain abnormal behavior logs, we have collected seven live ransomware packages and reverse engineered them to understand their encryption mechanisms and their differences. Based on operation filters illustrated in Table 2, 83000 normal events collected from the freshly installed Windows operating system with normal applications available on this system. During data collection, operations and processes which are not related to the file system operations were excluded. In addition, because the file system can create a large quantity of read and write activities, in some instances, the read and write operations were disregarded. We applied the same filters to all collected ransomware packages and executed each ransomware package within the same host and snapshotted back to the uninfected state each time a ransomware package was executed.

We compare the collected logs from ransomware and normal user operations to find out about the absolute frequencies of file system operations. The proposed framework and metrics are implemented in the Statechart plugin of the ProM tool. We imported a normal log to ProM, applied the Naive algorithm on it for pattern searching, and visualized the processed log using the Statechart diagram. The visualization setup allows us to easily describe different states of events and file system calls captured in the log. Figure 5 illustrates the process discovery from a control-flow point of view of the file system in normal operations without any malicious intervention. Our collected ransomware encrypts 10 GB of files in two different partitions. To be precise for capturing all the events related to the file systems when ransomware encrypts a victim's files, we filtered the directory that contained different types of files to capture the correlation between the disk traffic and the file system. Table 3 illustrates absolute occurrences of file system events during the execution of seven live ransomware packages. It is noted that the SetRenameInformationFile operation was significantly engaged to rename files during the ransomware encryption phase, whereas this operation was trivial under normal operations. The Read and Write file system operations were remarkably engaged in all scenarios and hence held the highest frequency of occurrences among the other file system events. The Read and Write file system operations cannot be considered to be critical metrics as a majority of legitimate operating system operations create, read and write files during their process. Figure 6 illustrates engagements of the file system operation during the execution of ransomware in a sequence diagram. Considering the formalization of sequential executions of file encryption discussed in Sect. 4.1, the sequence diagram in Fig. 6 shows that ReadFile, QueryStandardInformationFile, and WriteFile operations are performed together in a nested loop. This is because the file system uses disk buffer or buffer cache in for read and write operations of the loop. However, setRenameInformationFile, FileSystemControl and QueryFile operations are each performed in a single loop after the WriteFile sequence has completed. In this case, each individual loop can be a potential metric to identify if ransomware is present in the file system. Figure 7 shows how heavily ransomware engaged the SetRenameInformationFile operation for either overwriting or copying a victim's files.

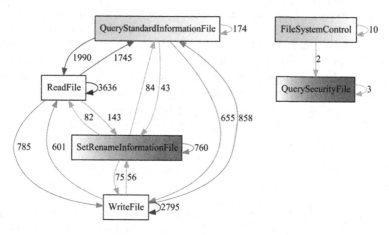

Fig. 7. Matrix ransomware in the flow diagram illustrates 760 files were renamed during execution.

Table 3. File system operations utilized during ransomware executions, highlighting the SetRenameInformationFile was significantly engaged compared with the normal activity log.

Ransomware	MD5 Signature	Abs:Freq FileSystemControl	Abs:Freq QuerySecurityFile	Abs:Freq QueryStandard InformationFile	Abs:Freq SetRename InformationFile	Abs:Freq WriteFile	Abs:Freq ReadFile	SetDisposition InformationFile	QueryEAFile
Normal Log	NA	2.398%	3.161%	10.57%	0.077%	3.345%	80.18%	0.151%	0.117%
GandCrab	2b60d1b89c9ae1bb 5c92e6fcb9c7048e	0.02%	0.466%	10.318%	10.318%	41.281%	37.595%	0.0%	0.0%
Matrix-A	907635b28d162f71 0b067a8178fa38c	0.221%	1.376%	19.826%	6.927%	29.794%	41.857%	0.0%	0.0%
RaaS	843911f67cf9f70ab 708372a8d30de30	0%	0%	0%	24.524%	50.952%	24.524%	0.0%	0.0%
ROGER	7bf2f1187fb0f748 93de4d4f54591af4	0.0%	0.0%	25.216%	2.414%	25.752%	38.896%	.7.722%	0.0%
Sodinokibi B	da703b96b936c71 e749debec6818ec3c	0.0%	0.058%	14.244%	14.563%	30.256%	40.878%	0.0%	0.0%
WannaCryptor	84c82833a5d21b bcf75a61706d8ab549	0.0%	0.0%	6.004%	6.004%	47.747%	33.763%	6.483%	0.0%
WastedLocker	f67ea8e471e827 e4b7b65b65647d1d46	0.086%	0.618%	17.223%	8.611%	17.223%	56.24%	0.0%	0.0%

6   Conclusion

While the development of ransomware is not new, this type of malware has currently experienced a revival of popularity. In reality, a wide variety of high-profile ransomware attacks have been recorded in recent years. In this paper, we extensively reverse engineered seven live ransomware packages to understand their components. Due to the failure of traditional security protection mechanisms, we focused on the file system of operating system to identify ransomware activities in a local machine. Our analyses showed ransomware takes two approaches of file overwriting or file copying when encrypting a victim's files on device storage. We setup a malware lab to execute seven well-known ransomware packages and capture the file system logs during their live executions. We employed process mining to analyze collected logs under normal and infected operations to identify critical file system metrics that are impacted during the execution of ransomware. We identified eight operations of the file system are impacted during the execution of ransomware. These include FileSystemControl, QuerySecurityFile, QueryStandardInformationFile, SetRenameInformationFile, WriteFile, ReadFile, SetDispositionInformationFile and QueryEAFile. It was however observed that SetRenameInformationFile was impacted repeatedly by all seven ransomware families, which makes this file system operation a good candidate for security observation. Our future work will include developing a kernel level protection to stop ransomware from in-memory execution within the file system.

References

1. Van Der Aalst, W.: Service mining: using process mining to discover, check, and improve service behavior. IEEE Trans. Serv. Comput. **6**(4), 525–535 (2013). https://doi.org/10.1109/TSC.2012.25
2. Van der Aalst, W.: Data Science in Action, pp. 3–23. Springer, Heidelberg (2016). https://doi.org/10.1007/978-3-662-49851-4
3. Accorsi, R., Stocker, T., Müller, G.: On the exploitation of process mining for security audits: The process discovery case. In: Proceedings of the 28th Annual ACM Symposium on Applied Computing, pp. 1462–1468. SAC 2013. Association for Computing Machinery, New York, NY, USA (2013). https://doi.org/10.1145/2480362.2480634, https://doi.org/10.1145/2480362.2480634
4. de Alvarenga, S.C., Zarpel, B., Miani, R.: Discovering attack strategies using process mining. In: Proceedings of the 11th Advanced International Conference on Telecommunications, pp. 119–125 (2015)
5. Augusto, A., et al.: Automated discovery of process models from event logs: review and benchmark. IEEE Trans. Knowl. Data Eng. **31**(4), 686–705 (2019). https://doi.org/10.1109/TKDE.2018.2841877
6. Bernardi, M.L., Cimitile, M., Distante, D., Martinelli, F., Mercaldo, F.: Dynamic malware detection and phylogeny analysis using process mining. Int. J. Inf. Secur. **18**(3), 257–284 (2018). https://doi.org/10.1007/s10207-018-0415-3
7. Coltellese, S., Maggi, F.M., Marrella, A., Massarelli, L., Querzoni, L.: Triage of iot attacks through process mining. In: OTM Confederated International Conferences" On the Move to Meaningful Internet Systems". pp. 326–344. Springer (2019)

8. Continella, A., et al.: Shieldfs: a self-healing, ransomware-aware filesystem. In: Proceedings of the 32nd Annual Conference on Computer Security Applications, pp. 336–347. ACSAC 2016, Association for Computing Machinery, New York, NY, USA (2016). https://doi.org/10.1145/2991079.2991110

9. van Dongen, B.F., de Medeiros, A.K.A., Verbeek, H.M.W., Weijters, A.J.M.M., van der Aalst, W.M.P.: The prom framework: A new era in process mining tool support. In: Ciardo, G., Darondeau, P. (eds.) Applications and Theory of Petri Nets 2005, pp. 444–454. Springer, Berlin Heidelberg, Berlin, Heidelberg (2005)

10. Hassan, N.A.: Ransomware Families, pp. 47–68. Apress, Berkeley (2019)

11. Honda, T., Mukaiyama, K., Shirai, T., Ohki, T., Nishigaki, M.: Ransomware detection considering user's document editing. In: 2018 IEEE 32nd International Conference on Advanced Information Networking and Applications (AINA), pp. 907–914 (2018). https://doi.org/10.1109/AINA.2018.00133

12. Jans, M., Alles, M., Vasarhelyi, M.: The case for process mining in auditing: sources of value added and areas of application. Int. J. Account. Inf. Syst. 14(1), 1–20 (2013). https://doi.org/10.1016/j.accinf.2012.06.015, http://www.sciencedirect.com/science/article/pii/S1467089512000462

13. Kim, D., Lee, J.: Blacklist vs. whitelist-based ransomware solutions. IEEE Consumer Electr. Mag. 9(3), 22–28 (2020). https://doi.org/10.1109/MCE.2019.2956192

14. Leemans, M.: Statechart prom plugin : statechart workbench (2017)

15. Loman, M.: How ransomware attacks. Sophos (2019), https://www.sophos.com/en-us/medialibrary/PDFs/technical-papers/sophoslabs-ransomware-behavior-report.pdf

16. Mahboubi, A., Camtepe, S., Morarji, H.: A study on formal methods to generalize heterogeneous mobile malware propagation and their impacts. IEEE Access 5, 27740–27756 (2017). https://doi.org/10.1109/ACCESS.2017.2772787

17. Sgandurra, D., Muñoz-González, L., Mohsen, R., Lupu, E.C.: Automated dynamic analysis of ransomware: Benefits, limitations and use for detection. arXiv preprint arXiv:1609.03020 (2016)

18. Van Der Aalst, W.M.P., Van Hee, K.M., Van der Werf, J.M., Verdonk, M.: Auditing 2.0: using process mining to support tomorrow's auditor. Computer 43(3), 90–93 (2010). https://doi.org/10.1109/MC.2010.61

19. Van Der Aalst, W., de Medeiros, A.: Process mining and security: Detecting anomalous process executions and checking process conformance. Electr. Notes Theoret. Comput. Sci. 121, 3–21 (2005). https://doi.org/10.1016/j.entcs.2004.10.013, http://www.sciencedirect.com/science/article/pii/S1571066105000228. Proceedings of the 2nd International Workshop on Security Issues with Petri Nets and other Computational Models (WISP 2004)

20. Wakup, C., Desel, J.: Analyzing a TCP/IP-protocol with process mining techniques. In: Fournier, F., Mendling, J. (eds.) BPM 2014. LNBIP, vol. 202, pp. 353–364. Springer, Cham (2015). https://doi.org/10.1007/978-3-319-15895-2_30

21. Yaqoob, I., et al.: The rise of ransomware and emerging security challenges in the internet of things. Comput. Networks 129, 444–458 (2017). https://doi.org/10.1016/j.comnet.2017.09.003, http://www.sciencedirect.com/science/article/pii/S1389128617303468. Special Issue on 5G Wireless Networks for IoT and Body Sensors

22. Young, A., Yung, M.: Cryptovirology: extortion-based security threats and countermeasures. In: Proceedings 1996 IEEE Symposium on Security and Privacy, pp. 129–140 (1996). https://doi.org/10.1109/SECPRI.1996.502676

Efficient and Secure Statistical Port Scan Detection Scheme

Hussein Majed[1], Hassan N. Noura[1], Ola Salman[2], Ali Chehab[2],
and Raphaël Couturier[3(✉)]

[1] Department of Computer Sciences, Arab Open University, Beirut, Lebanon
[2] Department of Electrical and Computer Engineering,
American University of Beirut, Beirut 1107 2020, Lebanon
[3] Univ. Bourgogne Franche-Comté, FEMTO-ST Institute, CNRS, Belfort, France
`raphael.couturier@univ-fcomte.fr`

Abstract. One of the most challenging problems in Cybersecurity is the identification and prevention of port scanning, which is the primary phase of further system or data exploitation. This paper proposes a new statistical method for port scan detection, in addition to preventive and corrective counter-measures. The suggested solution is intended to be implemented at the Internet Service Provider (ISP) side. The proposed solution consists of aggregating NetFlow statistics and using the Z-score and co-variance measures to detect port scan traffic as a deviation from normal traffic. The experimental results show that the proposed method achieves a high detection rate (up to 100%) within a time frame of 60 s.

Keywords: Port scan · Intrusion detection · Traffic aggregation · Network security

1 Introduction

The Internet is drastically expanding in terms of number of users, number of applications, and number of connected devices [1]. This will result in a huge amount of generated data to be digitally stored and available online. Having a heterogeneous set of connected devices with different capabilities presents new security challenges and vulnerabilities. This will attract cyber criminals to exploit and control vulnerable Internet connected devices. Cyber attacks go through multiple phases before achieving a successful exploitation. The first phase is the reconnaissance of the target, which can be either active or passive reconnaissance. Port scanning is one active reconnaissance technique to probe a server or host for open ports. Ports are usually numbered from 0 to 65535. The "Well Known" ports are within the range of 0 to 1023 and have been assigned by the Internet Assigned Numbers Authority (IANA) to well-known protocols and applications [2].

During a port scan, attackers send a message to each port, one at a time. The received response from each port determines whether this port is opened or

S. Bouzefrane et al. (Eds.): MSPN 2020, LNCS 12605, pp. 72–88, 2021.
https://doi.org/10.1007/978-3-030-67550-9_6

closed. The scan can be conducted on Transmission Control Protocol (TCP) or User Datagram Protocol (UDP). According to SANS, port scanning is the most popular technique used by attackers to discover vulnerable services/devices and to exploit them [3].

The most common tool used for port scanning is NMAP [4]. The attacker can perform scan on a single Internet Protocol (IP) address (host) or a subnet of IPs (hosts). The attacker can also choose to scan a specific port or a range of ports. NMAP can be used to perform many types of scanning (See Fig. 1). The major types are mainly known as follows:

- TCP Syn Scan: connects quickly to thousand of ports without completing TCP handshake.
- TCP Connect Scan: a full connect scan that completes the three-way hand-shake to the target.
- TCP ACK Scan: sends packets with ACK flag set. If the port is open, the target will send an RST packet in the reply. If the port is closed, the target will ignore the packet.
- Xmas Scan: sends a set of flags to create a nonsensical interaction. If an RST packet is received, it means the port is closed, otherwise, the port is considered open.
- UDP Scan: sends an empty UDP packet to every targeted port. If no response is received the port is considered open, otherwise, if ICMP type 3 (destination unreachable message) is received, it means the port is closed.

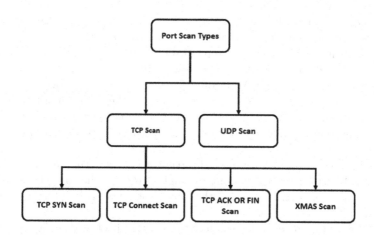

Fig. 1. Port scan taxonomy

In this paper, we propose a new port scan detection method based on Net-Flow statistics. NetFlow is a network protocol developed by Cisco for collecting and monitoring IP network traffic. New measures are proposed based on flows statistics to differentiate between port scan and normal traffic based on the count of unique contacted port numbers and IP addresses. The experimental results conducted on an ISP collected data-set, containing port scan attack traffic, show that the proposed method achieves a high detection rate with low false positive rate.

This paper is organized as follows. In Sect. 2, we review the existing port scan detection techniques. In Sect. 3, we present our proposed detection solution. The experimental results are presented and discussed in Sect. 4. Finally, we conclude in Sect. 5.

2   Related Work

In this section, we review the most recent port scanning detection techniques. In [5], a mathematical model for detecting anomalies caused by port scan attacks has been proposed. The proposed solution relies on constructing a set of vectors based on the IP-address of the sender, and the packets' TCP flags. Based on assumption that normal traffic patterns are known, the model calculates the frequency of occurrence of TCP flags. The negative likelihood logarithm is used to define the anomaly packets index. In [6], Balram et al. considered the count of TCP control packets to detect TCP SYN scan by training a Neural Network model. The counts of TCP SYN, SYN-ACK, and FIN packets were used to train the model to differentiate between attack and normal behaviors. The authors simulated the TCP SYN scan with multiple probe delays from 5 to 300 s. They found out that they cannot rely on the RST flag for detection, instead the calculation of the difference between incoming SYN and outgoing SYN-ACK were the key features for detection.

An adaptive threshold for detecting various types of port scans based on using time independent features set was proposed in [7]. The approach consists of updating the threshold by relying on a fuzzy-based detector. Tested on DARPA 98/99, the proposed solution presented a high false positive rate when traffic is destined to servers. Additional features should be added to the solution in order to address this issue. Another study relied also on the fuzzy logic to analyze various traffic parameters in order to detect port scan. The solution in [8] relied on the time average between received packets by destination/victim, the number of sent packets by source, and the number of received packets by the destination/victim. The results showed the effectiveness of the proposed method when multiple attackers are scanning a single target at the same time. Also, a recent port scan detection method that used the fuzzy rule interpolation was presented in [9].

In [10], a new port scan detection approach was proposed using time-based flow size distribution sequential hypothesis testing (TFDS). This solution can be applied in transit networks, where only unidirectional flows' information is available. The authors realized that the scanners produce small flows with equal byte size and thus, they adopted the Flow Size Distribution (FSD) in bytes for modeling the scanning activity to build the FSD entropy metric. The FSD for each source IP is used to build and update the likelihood ratio table. Repetitive likelihood measures were used to detect scanning activity. Profiling of IP addresses is another technique that was proposed for detecting TCP SYN scan in [11]. IP profiling consists of constructing profiles for each IP address participating in TCP connections. The whole theory is built on the assumption that a scanner leaves more initialised TCP handshakes half-open. If the attacker does not send ACK request within 30 s of receiving the SYN ACK, it will be flagged as an attacker, otherwise the traffic will be considered normal. Although this detection method can be easily bypassed by using full connection scanning techniques, yet it showed promising results when applied on several data-sets. Moreover, deep learning and Support Vector Machine (SVM) algorithms were used in [12] for detecting scan attempts. In the deep learning case, the features were extracted automatically while in SVM, a supervised machine learning, the researchers selected all fields as features. Deep learning performed much better than SVM, where 97.80%, and 69.79% detection rates were achieved, respectively. Also, a set of recent solutions that are based on deep learning were presented such as [13–19].

However, in this paper, we consider a lightweight scan detection technique built on top of NetFlow protocol. NetFlow is a network protocol introduced by Cisco to collect traffic/flows statistics at the router interfaces. Handling huge amount of traffic at the network core or the ISP side, NetFlow is a good candidate for extracting flows statistics without burdening the network with new APIs or add-ons to extract measures for port scan detection. In this context, this work considers the Z-score and co-variance measures derived from NetFlow statistics. Moreover, this work considers the combination of different features such as the count of destination IP addresses, the count of source and destination port numbers, and the packet size distribution. Thus, the contributions of this paper can be summarized as follows:

- Proposing a customized NetFlow aggregation targeting the two main scan strategies (single host port scan and sub-net port scan).
- Presenting a fast and reliable statistical approach to detect different types of port scan based on Z-score, co-variance and mean values.
- Proposing a mitigation process to block further communication between the attacker and victims, at the ISP level (Table 1).

3   Proposed Port Scanning Detection

The proposed port scan detection method consists of 5 main steps as illustrated in Fig. 2, and detailed below.

Fig. 2. Proposed port scan detection scheme

Table 1. Table of notations

Symbol	Definition
μ	Mean
σ	Standard deviation
CV_{SP}	Coefficient variation of the number of source ports per group of source and destination IPs
CV_{DP}	Coefficient variation of the number of destination ports per group of source and destination IPs
CV_{DA}	Coefficient variation of the number of destination addresses per group of source addresses and destination sub-nets
ZSC_{SP}	Z-score of the number of source ports per group of source and destination IPs
ZSC_{DP}	Z-score of the number of destination ports per group of source and destination IPs
ZSC_{DA}	Z-score of the number of destination addresses per group of source addresses and destination sub-nets

3.1 Data Collection

At this stage, the incoming traffic statistics are collected for a regular interval of time such as one minute. This is possible by configuring the NetFlow exporter on the edge router to send all the NetFlow statistics to an external surveillance device (i.e. NetFlow collector). The port scan was performed on several targets from different sources and a time table was updated each time a scan is performed, with the type of attack, source IP and target. Based on the time table, the data-sets were manually labeled.

3.2 Data Aggregation and Features Extraction

In this step, the collected traffic NetFlow statistics are aggregated. Port scanning can target a single address or an IP sub-net. For this reason, we propose two data aggregation methods as follows:

- For sub-net scanning, we focus on knowing if a source IP communicated with different destination IPs in the same sub-net on different destination ports; that is why the traffic is grouped by source address, destination subnet, destination port, and transport protocol. After grouping the flows, the number of distinct destination IPs is counted.
- For single device scanning, we focus on knowing if a source IP communicated with a single destination IP on multiple distinct ports; that is why the traffic is grouped by source and destination IP addresses, and the count of unique source and destination port numbers is calculated for each group.

3.3   Filtering Process

Filtering is a very essential phase to obtain correct results. In normal conditions, the flow of traffic contains hundreds or thousands of connections from one single IP address to another single IP address. If we keep these records, it will definitely affect the standard deviation and mean values during the statistical analysis. Thus, we keep only the flows that serve the purpose of each conducted test. Concerning the sub-net scan, the filtering process should eliminate all the flow records, if the source IP address communicates with less than 4 destination IP addresses, and also filter and remove packets that do not share the same size. During sub-net scan, the attacker communicates with multiple IP addresses within the same sub-net. In this case, eliminating traffic from one source IP address to less than 4 destination IP addresses will only keep potential sub-net scan flows. While in case of single host port scan, the filtering process should eliminate all the flow records if the source IP address communicates with less than 4 port numbers on the same destination IP address. During single host port scan, the attacker communicates with a range of port numbers on a single host. In this case, eliminating traffic from one source IP to destination IP, if the number of distinct destination port numbers is less than 4 will only keep the potential single host port scan traffic.

3.4   Statistical Analysis

At this phase, the aggregated filtered statistics are analyzed using the Z-score metric (see Algorithm 1. The basic Z-score formula for a feature x is:

$$z = \frac{x - \mu}{\sigma} \tag{1}$$

where μ and σ represent the mean and the standard deviation of each feature in the aggregated traffic, respectively.

Sub-net Port Scan. The NetFlow is grouped per source address, destination sub-net, destination port number, and protocol. For each group, the count of unique destination addresses is calculated. During TCP scan, the attacker tries to probe the open ports by sending packets containing TCP flags and making assumption based on the response. These packets have the same size and are destined to different IPs within the same sub-net. The count of distinct TCP packets sizes is also computed. The Z-score of the count of unique destination IP addresses for each group is calculated.

Single Host Port Scan. The NetFlow statistics are grouped per source and destination IP addresses. For each group, the count of unique destination port numbers is calculated. In addition, the count of unique source port numbers is calculated for TCP packets to avoid false positive alarms in case of communication between a client and a server. While the count of source ports is calculated for UDP, because for example, NMAP uses the same source port for scanning. The Z-score of the count of unique destination ports and the Z-score of the count of source ports for each group are calculated.

These values are used as input to the next step. The aggregation can be seen as a form of non-reversible compression. The advantage of this step is to reduce the required processing complexity and storage overhead. Thus, the following detection features are selected and used for each scan method:

- TCP based sub-net port scan: the count of unique destination addresses and the count of distinct packet sizes.
- UDP based sub-net port scan: the count of unique destination addresses.
- TCP based host port scan: the count of unique source port numbers and the count of unique destination port numbers.
- UDP based host port scan: the count of source port numbers and the count of unique destination port numbers.

3.5   Detection Process

For each aggregated filtered flow, the obtained Z-scores of the selected features are compared to the corresponding threshold values that are based on the coefficient of variation (CV). CV represents a statistical indicator for the dispersion of data points in a data set (series) around the mean. It is the ratio of the standard deviation to the mean, and it is a useful statistical metric for comparing the degree of variation from one data series to another, even if the means are different. CV is computed as illustrated in the following equation:

$$CV = \frac{\sigma}{\mu} \tag{2}$$

Accordingly, a port scan is detected if the obtained Z-score values of these features are greater or equal to the corresponding thresholds (see lines 7, or 10 of Algorithm 1 & line 9 of Algorithm 2). These thresholds are set based on a training step (initial step), and depend on the ISP profile (traffic and network characteristics). Using static thresholds is not practical because they need to be updated manually each time a bandwidth upgrade takes place. In addition, they might lead to false positives and false negatives. To make the proposed solution based on a dynamic threshold, the Z-score value of each feature is compared to its CV.

Sub-net Port Scan. In case of sub-net port scan, the attacker tries to connect to a single or multiple ports for each destination address in the same sub-net. The scan will increase the mean value and standard deviation of the count of unique destination IPs for the same sub-net in the data-set, which leads to a high CV of the count of unique destination IPs. By Calculating the Z-score of each feature for each group, the group of source IP address, destination sub-net, and protocol will have a high Z-score value in relation to the count of unique destination address. Since we have the CV value of the count of unique destination IP addresses, we can compare it to the Z-score of count of unique destination IP addresses of each data point; there is a slight difference between the behavior of TCP scan and UDP scan. While studying the results of the approach, we realized that the TCP scan traffic always produces a CV of the count of unique destination addresses higher than 1, while UDP scan always produce Z-score higher than the mean value of the count of unique destination addresses.

- In case of TCP, If the Z-score of unique destination addresses is higher than the CV, and the CV of the count of unique destination addresses is higher than 1, the flow is considered an outlier compared to the rest of the flows (see line 7 of Algorithm 1).
- In case of UDP, If the Z-score of unique destination addresses is higher than the CV, and the count of unique destination addresses is higher than the mean, the flow is also considered an outlier compared to the rest of the flows (see line 10 of Algorithm 1).

Host Port Scan. In case of host port scan, the attacker will try to connect to multiple ports on the scanned host. The scan will increase the mean value and standard deviation of the count of source ports and the count of unique destination ports of the affected group of communication between one IP and another in the data-set, which leads to a high CV for each affected feature. By Calculating the Z-score of each feature for each group, the group of source addresses, destination addresses, and protocol will have a high Z-score value for each selected feature (count of source ports and destination ports). Since we have the CV value of each feature, we can compare it to the Z-score of each corresponding feature. If the Z-score of source port count and Z-score of destination port count are higher than the CV of the corresponding feature, it is considered an outlier compared to the rest of the flows (see line 9 of Algorithm 2).

It should be indicated that the Z-score is a well known method for the detection of outliers. Applying the Z-score on each feature for the aggregated flows clearly reveals the outliers, but each type of scan has its own characteristics.

4   Experimental Setup and Results

In this section, we explain the implementation of the proposed port scan detection scheme in details.

4.1   NetFlow Collection

For data collection, the set up was implemented in an ISP network taking into consideration the full traffic visibility. NetFlow is a network protocol introduced by Cisco which collects IP network traffic statistics as the packets flow in or out of an interface. A virtual machine based on Centos 7.0 was deployed on Vmware

---

Algorithm 1. Subnet port scan detection algorithm

    Input: Aggregated Flow AF
    Output: R
1: **procedure** $R = \mathsf{Detection}(AF)$
2:    $NIP \leftarrow Number of Rows(AF)$
3:    $CV_{DA} \leftarrow \frac{std(C_{DA})}{mean(C_{DA})}$
4:    **for** $i \leftarrow 0$ to NIP **do**
5:        $ZSC_{DA} \leftarrow Zscore(C_{DA})$
6:        $Protocol \leftarrow Value(C_{PR})$
7:        **if** $|ZSC_{DA}| \geq CV_{DA} \&\& |Protocol| = TCP \&\& |CV_{DA}| \geq 1$ **then**
8:            TCP subnet scan detected on DA subnet
9:        **end if**
10:        **if** $|ZSC_{DA}| \geq CV_{DA} \&\& |Protocol| = UDP \&\& C_D A > mean(C_{DA}) \&\& CV_{DA} \geq 1$ **then**
11:            UDP subnet scan detected on DA subnet
12:        **end if**
13:    **end for**
14: **end procedure**

Algorithm 2. Single host port scan detection algorithm

    Input: Aggregated Flow AF
    Output: R
1: **procedure** $R = \mathsf{Detection}(AF)$
2:    $NIP \leftarrow Number of Rows(AF)$
3:    $CV_{DP} \leftarrow \frac{std(C_{DP})}{mean(C_{DP})}$
4:    $CV_{SP} \leftarrow \frac{std(C_{SP})}{mean(C_{SP})}$
5:    **for** $i \leftarrow 0$ to NIP **do**
6:        $ZSC_{DP} \leftarrow Zscore(C_{DP})$
7:        $ZSC_{SP} \leftarrow Zscore(C_{SP})$
8:        $Protocol \leftarrow Value(C_{PR})$
9:        **if** $|ZSC_{DP}| \geq CV_{DP} \&\& |ZSC_{SP}| \geq CV_{SP}$ **then**
10:            Single host port scan detected on DA
11:        **end if**
12:    **end for**
13: **end procedure**

ESXi 7.0 as a NetFlow Collector. The NetFlow capture daemon (nfcapd), a part of the nfdump tool, was installed on the NetFlow Collector virtual machine to capture all the incoming flows. The NetFlow exporters of two Cisco edge routers (ASR 9K) have been configured to send the traffic to the NetFlow Collector; each router was configured to send the NetFlow statistics to a different port on the traffic Collector. Two instances of the "nfcapd" were launched to listen on two separate ports, each port is dedicated for one router. The "nfcapd" was configured to save the captured flows of each router in a separate file, every one minute.

nfcapd -w -D -l /flow_base_dir/router1 -p 12345
nfcapd -w -D -l /flow_base_dir/router2 -p 12346

The traffic statistics from both routers were collected for one month. Multiple port scans were performed during the mentioned period and a time table was updated after each performed scan to differentiate the normal traffic from the scan traffic. The nfcapd saves the files in raw format. The saved files are converted, by the "nfdump" tool, to the Comma-Separated Values (CSV) format.

4.2 Data Aggregation

A python script was written to customize the aggregation of NetFlow statistics and to visualize the captured flows. The script is based on the concept of grouping the flows by two different methods in order to capture the different scan strategies. The first aggregation method is based on aggregating the flows with the same source address, destination sub-net, and same destination addresses (See Fig. 3a and 3b). The second method is based on aggregating the flows with the same source address, destination address, count of source ports, and count of unique destination ports (See Fig. 4a and 4b).

	sa	subnet	dp	pr	da	ztda	mnda	da_zscore
0	169.54.233.124	212.98.156.0	5060.0	UDP	25	0.52291	1.012163	45.322470
1	169.54.233.118	213.204.124.0	5060.0	UDP	23	0.52291	1.012163	41.543682
238	46.227.2.150	213.204.124.0	53.0	UDP	1	0.52291	1.012163	-0.022980
239	46.226.95.234	212.98.156.0	53.0	UDP	1	0.52291	1.012163	-0.022980
241	46.22.78.51	212.98.156.0	53.0	UDP	1	0.52291	1.012163	-0.022980

(a) UDP based sub-net port scan

	sa	subnet	dp	pr	ibyt	da	ztda	da_zscore
0	108.166.122.103	213.204.124.0	22.0	TCP	1	256	1.949094	2.232790
1	108.166.122.103	213.204.110.0	22.0	TCP	1	256	1.949094	2.232790
2	45.55.21.195	213.204.110.0	179.0	TCP	1	17	1.949094	-0.330717
3	45.55.21.195	213.204.124.0	179.0	TCP	1	17	1.949094	-0.330717
4	85.112.64.9	54.192.46.0	80.0	TCP	1	7	1.949094	-0.437977

(b) TCP based sub-net port scan

Fig. 3. An example of grouped and aggregated NetFlow of UDP and TCP based sub-net port scan

	sa	da	pr	sp	dp	ztsp	ztdp	sp_zscore	dp_zscore
62	169.60.233.124	213.204.150.183	UDP	20	20	0.397941	0.306727	47.131400	61.619802
95	85.112.85.118	224.0.0.252	UDP	16	1	0.397941	0.306727	37.202533	-0.016229
710	8.8.8.8	212.98.156.104	ICMP	5	1	0.397941	0.306727	9.898149	-0.016229
981	218.189.26.10	213.204.100.18	ICMP	4	1	0.397941	0.306727	7.415933	-0.016229
2487	124.238.232.59	213.204.124.18	ICMP	2	1	0.397941	0.306727	2.451499	-0.016229

(a) UDP based Host Port Scan

	sa	da	sp	dp	ztsp	ztdp	sp_zscore	dp_zscore
0	204.93.180.13	213.204.110.170	200	100	2.697029	1.686112	2.999934	2.776694
32	203.12.200.183	213.204.110.169	3	12	2.697029	1.686112	-0.320218	-0.188707
44	87.98.143.182	213.204.124.137	3	5	2.697029	1.686112	-0.320218	-0.424592
58	184.106.52.120	213.204.110.20	2	3	2.697029	1.686112	-0.337071	-0.491987
85	148.251.35.246	213.204.110.225	2	41	2.697029	1.686112	-0.337071	0.788527

(b) TCP based Host Port Scan

Fig. 4. An example of grouped and aggregated NetFlow of UDP and TCP based host port scan

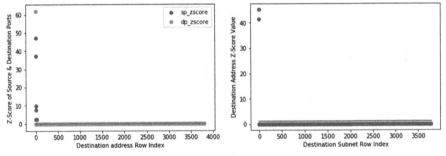

(a) UDP based host port scan Z-score results   (b) UDP based subnet port scan Z-score results

Fig. 5. An example of grouped and aggregated NetFlow of UDP and TCP based host port scan Z-score

4.3   Port Scan Detection

The approach was tested on the collected data-set, the Z-score of each feature was calculated and compared to the threshold, which is in our case the CV for each feature. The results indicate that records with positive Z-score are suspicious and could indicate that port scan is being conducted on the targets. But with the comparison of CV to each feature's Z-score value, we can validate the approach.

The results shown in Fig. 3b for TCP based sub-net scan and in Fig. 3a for UDP based sub-net scan, clearly show that using the coefficient of variation as a dynamic threshold is efficient for correctly detecting sub-net port scan. The results shown in Fig. 6 indicate that the sub-nets 213.204.124.0/24 & 213.204.110.0/24 have received connections from a single source address 108.166.122.103 on 250 different destination addresses in each sub-net.

Table 2. Tested data-setsTested data-sets

Data-set name	Scan type	Protocol	Target	Ports
Normal1	None	-	-	-
Normal2	None	-	-	-
Normal3	None	-	-	-
Normal4	None	-	-	-
TCP1	Full connect	TCP	212.98.156.0/24	21,22,80,8080
TCP2	Full connect	TCP	213.204.124.0/24 and 213.204.110.0/24	22
TCP3	Syn scan	TCP	212.98.156.0/24	22
TCP4	Syn scan	TCP	213.204.110.170	Well Known Range
UDP1	UDP scan	UDP	212.98.156.0/24 and 213.204.124.0/24	5060
UDP2	UDP scan	UDP	213.204.124.0/24	17185
UDP3	UDP scan	UDP	213.204.150.183	Multiple ports

Figure 7 shows that the score value became higher and above the threshold of CV, which is also higher than 1, when sub-net scan is detected. By reviewing Fig. 3b, we can conclude that the sub-net port scan was on port number 22. The CV threshold was 1.94 while the Z-score for the two sub-nets is 2.23 taking into consideration that the next group of communication in Fig. 3b (third row) between the source IP 45.55.21.196 and the sub-net 213.204.110.0/24 has a Z-score value of -0.33. This clearly indicates the abnormality on the first two sub-nets, 213.204.124.0/24 & 213.204.110.0/24 from the attacker source IP 108.166.122.103.

Another sub-net port scan test was performed on UDP ports. Figure 3a shows that the sub-net 212.98.156.0/24 received 23 requests on port 5060 from the source IP 169.54.223.124 and the subnet 212.98.124.0/24 received 25 requests on port 5060 from the source IP 169.54.223.118, while the next group in row 212.98.124.0/24 received only one request from 46.227.2.150. The Z-score values of the scanned sub-nets are above 40, while the rest are below zero and the mean value of destination address count is more than 1. Reviewing Fig. 5b shows that threshold was 1 and all the normal traffic has Z-score values below 0, while the two scanned sub-nets 212.98.156.0/24 & 212.98.124.0/24 have a Z-score value higher than 40 for destination address count.

For TCP based host port scan, the results shown in Fig. 8 indicate that a single host received connections form a single source address on 100 unique destination ports. By reviewing Fig. 9, it is clear that when host port scan is detected, the Z-score values of source ports and destination ports counts were relatively higher and above the threshold line. The CV of source port is 2.69 while the Z-score of source port is 2.99 and the CV of destination port is 1.68

while the Z-score of the destination port is 2.77, and the next group in row has negative Z-score values in both source and destination ports.

The same concept was applied to UDP based host port scan as shown in Fig. 4a. The scanned host received 20 connections on 20 different ports. In the UDP host scan, there are two thresholds, the source port count and destination port count, and in order to consider that a port scan was performed, the Z-score of both values should be above the threshold (see line 9 of Algorithm 2). Reviewing Fig. 5a, we see that there are multiple points crossing the threshold regarding the source port, but only one point has the value of 61 crossing the threshold of destination port, while the next in row is negative.

The same procedure was applied on all data-sets listed in Table 2, and it showed 100% true positive and 0% false negative alerts. Some of the tested data-sets did not contain any port scan (Normal1, 2, 3, and 4) while the others contained multiple types of port scan targeting a single host and sub-nets.

Table 3. Execution time

Data-set name	Size in MB	Number of rows	Loading time	Detection time
TCP1	8	28621	0.453	0.125
TCP2	10.3	29011	0.582	0.234
TCP3	10.2	28740	0.469	0.187
TCP4	9.8	31711	0.4056	0.187
UDP1	11.6	32670	0.5309	0.11
UDP2	9.6	31050	0.406	0.156
UDP3	9.5	30781	0.468	0.078

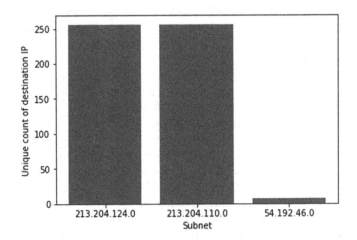

Fig. 6. Sub-net port scan results

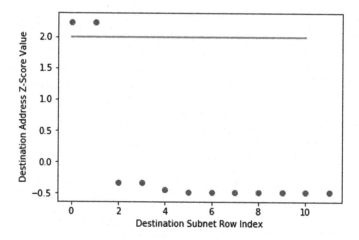

Fig. 7. Sub-net port scan Z-score results

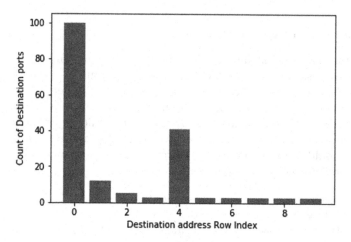

Fig. 8. Host port scan results

Execution Time. In this part, the required execution loading and detection time of each data-set are computed. The loading time represents the time taken for each data-set to be loaded in the memory, and the detection time represents the computing time needed for flow aggregation, filtering, and detection of port scan presence. Table 3 shows these results. It indicated that the loading and detection time varies according to the collected flow size for 60 s. The average time for loading data-set is 0.47 s, the average time taken for detection is 0.15 s. Consequently, this indicates clearly that the proposed solution requires low latency to detect any listed port scan attack variant and especially in the context of huge volume traffic (ISP).

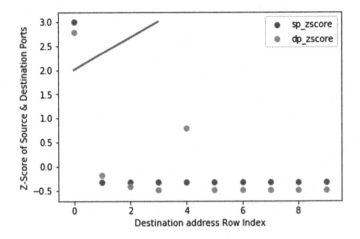

Fig. 9. Host port scan Z-score results

4.4 Proposed Mitigation Process

Based on the statistical results obtained from the previous phase, the ISP may update the Access Control List (ACL), on the edge routers, to block the communication between the attacker and the destination sub-nets or addresses to avoid any further communication between them for a specific period of time. To perform this action, a Secure Shell (SSH) user should be added to the edge router with privileges to create and remove ACL. When port scan is detected, the sensor should connect to the edge router via SSH and append the access list based on the detected scan as follows:

- HOST based: access-list 101 dynamic testlist timeout 10 deny ip host #AttackerIP# host #ScannedIP#
- Subnet Based: access-list 101 dynamic testlist timeout 10 deny ip host #AttackerIP# #Scanned Subnet# 0.0.0.255

The above commands will add a dynamic access list to the edge router in order to block the attacker for 10 min, whenever a scan is detected. The sensor will send the appropriate access-list based on the scan type.

5 Conclusion

Port scanning techniques are real threats to network security. They should be detected and avoided in current and future networks. In this paper, detective, preventive and corrective measures against various possible techniques of port scanning are proposed. The solution is designed to be applied at the ISP level, and it is based on a statistical lightweight scheme. Technically, this method aggregates and filters NetFlow statistics, and then statistical analysis is performed to detect port scan traffic by using the Z-score and co-variation metrics.

To guarantee the detection of a port scan, the proposed method requires 60 s. The experimental results showed that high detection rate (up to 100%) can be achieved using simple measures with a low false positive rate (0%).

Acknowlegments. This paper was partially supported by funds from the Maroun Semaan Faculty of Engineering and Architecture at the American University of Beirut and by the EIPHI Graduate School (contract "ANR-17-EURE-0002").

References

1. Sivanathan, A., Gharakheili, H.H., Sivaraman, V.: Can we classify an IoT device using TCP port scan? In: 2018 IEEE International Conference on Information and Automation for Sustainability (ICIAfS), pp. 1–4. IEEE (2018)
2. Cotton, M., Eggert, L., Touch, J., Westerlund, M., Cheshire, S.: Internet assigned numbers authority (IANA) procedures for the management of the service name and transport protocol port number registry. RFC **6335**, 1–33 (2011)
3. Christopher, R.: Port scanning techniques and the defense against them. SANS Institute (2001)
4. Lyon, G.F.: Nmap network scanning: the official Nmap project guide to network discovery and security scanning. Insecure (2009)
5. Ananin, E.V., Nikishova, A.V., Kozhevnikova, I.S.: Port scanning detection based on anomalies. In: 2017 Dynamics of Systems, Mechanisms and Machines (Dynamics), pp. 1–5 (2017)
6. Balram, S., Wiscy, M.: Detection of TCP SYN scanning using packet counts and neural network. In: 2008 IEEE International Conference on Signal Image Technology and Internet Based Systems, pp. 646–649 (2008)
7. Baig, H.U., Kamran, F., Sheikh, M.A.: An adaptive fuzzy based scan detection technique using time independent feature set. In: 2009 IEEE International Conference on Intelligent Computing and Intelligent Systems, vol. 3, pp. 123–127 (2009)
8. El-Hajj, W., Aloul, F., Trabelsi, Z., Zaki, N.: On detecting port scanning using fuzzy based intrusion detection system. In: 2008 International Wireless Communications and Mobile Computing Conference, pp. 105–110. IEEE (2008)
9. Almseidin, M., Al-Kasassbeh, M., Kovacs, S.: Detecting slow port scan using fuzzy rule interpolation. In: 2019 2nd International Conference on new Trends in Computing Sciences (ICTCS), pp. 1–6. IEEE (2019)
10. Zhang, Y., Fang, B.: A novel approach to scan detection on the backbone. In: 2009 Sixth International Conference on Information Technology: New Generations, pp. 16–21 (2009)
11. Hajdú-Szücs, K., Laki, S., Kiss, A.: A profile-based fast port scan detection method. In: Nguyen, N.T., Papadopoulos, G.A., Jkedrzejowicz, P., Trawiński, B., Vossen, G. (eds.) ICCCI 2017. LNCS (LNAI), vol. 10448, pp. 401–410. Springer, Cham (2017). https://doi.org/10.1007/978-3-319-67074-4_39
12. Aksu, D., Ali Aydin, M.: Detecting port scan attempts with comparative analysis of deep learning and support vector machine algorithms. In: 2018 International Congress on Big Data, Deep Learning and Fighting Cyber Terrorism (IBIGDELFT), pp. 77–80 (2018)
13. Hartpence, B., Kwasinski, A.: Combating TCP port scan attacks using sequential neural networks. In: 2020 International Conference on Computing, Networking and Communications (ICNC), pp. 256–260. IEEE (2020)

14. Wang, Y., Zhang, J.: DeepPort: detect low speed port scan using convolutional neural network. In: Qiao, J., et al. (eds.) BIC-TA 2018. CCIS, vol. 951, pp. 368–379. Springer, Singapore (2018). https://doi.org/10.1007/978-981-13-2826-8_32

15. Soman, K.P., Alazab, M., et al.: A comprehensive tutorial and survey of applications of deep learning for cyber security (2020)

16. Viet, H.N., Van, Q.N., Trang, L.L.T., Nathan, S.: Using deep learning model for network scanning detection. In: Proceedings of the 4th International Conference on Frontiers of Educational Technologies, pp. 117–121 (2018)

17. Chockwanich, N., Visoottiviseth, V.: Intrusion detection by deep learning with tensorflow. In: 2019 21st International Conference on Advanced Communication Technology (ICACT), pp. 654–659. IEEE (2019)

18. Abdulhammed, R., Faezipour, M., Abuzneid, A., AbuMallouh, A.: Deep and machine learning approaches for anomaly-based intrusion detection of imbalanced network traffic. IEEE Sens. Lett. 3(1), 1–4 (2018)

19. Fernández, G.C., Xu, S.: A case study on using deep learning for network intrusion detection. In: MILCOM 2019-2019 IEEE Military Communications Conference (MILCOM), pp. 1–6. IEEE (2019)

Fast and Flexible Elliptic Curve Cryptography for Dining Cryptographers Networks

Briag Dupont, Christian Franck$^{(\boxtimes)}$, and Johann Großschädl

Department of Computer Science, University of Luxembourg,
6, Avenue de la Fonte, 4364 Esch-sur-Alzette, Luxembourg
briag.dupont.001@student.uni.lu
{christian.franck,johann.groszschaedl}@uni.lu

Abstract. A Dining Cryptographers network (DCnet for short) allows anonymous communication with sender and receiver untraceability even if an adversary has unlimited access to the connection metadata of the network. Originally introduced by David Chaum in the 1980s, DCnets were for a long time considered not practical for real-world applications because of the tremendous communication and computation overhead they introduce. However, technological innovations such as 5G networks and extremely powerful 64-bit processors make a good case to reassess the practicality of DCnets. In addition, recent advances in elliptic-curve based commitment schemes and Zero-Knowledge Proofs (ZKPs) provide a great opportunity to reduce the computational cost of modern DCnets that are able to detect malicious behavior of communicating parties. In this paper we introduce X64ECC, a self-contained library for Elliptic Curve Cryptography (ECC) developed from scratch to support all the public-key operations needed by modern DCnets: key exchange, digital signatures, Pedersen commitments, and ZKPs. X64ECC is written in C and uses compiler intrinsics to speed up performance-critical arithmetic operations. It is highly scalable and works with Montgomery curves and twisted Edwards curves of different cryptographic strength. Despite its high scalability and portability, X64ECC is able to compute a fixed-base scalar multiplication on a twisted Edwards curve over a 255-bit prime field in about 145,000 clock cycles on a modern Intel X64 processor. All cryptosystems can be adapted on-the-fly (i.e. without recompilation) to implement DCnets with arbitrary message sizes, and tradeoffs between the cryptographic strength and throughput of a DCnet are possible.

1 Introduction

The possibility to send a message in a way so that nobody can trace it back to the sender is desirable in many settings since anonymity can protect e.g. voters

This research is part of the DCnets project, which is supported by the NLnet Foundation and the NGI Zero PET Fund, see https://nlnet.nl/project/DCnets.

S. Bouzefrane et al. (Eds.): MSPN 2020, LNCS 12605, pp. 89–109, 2021.
https://doi.org/10.1007/978-3-030-67550-9_7

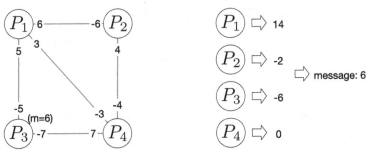

(a) The participants ($P_1...P_4$) pairwise establish mutually inverse secret keys ($k_{ji} = -k_{ij}$), as shown in the graph. P_3 also wants to send the message m here.

(b) Each participant publishes the sum (o_i) of his secret keys (the anonymous sender also adds his message). The sum of all the published values reveals the message.

Fig. 1. An example to illustrate the principle of anonymous communication with a DCnet. In order to anonymously publish a message, the participants (a) first establish secret keys, and then they (b) publish the sum of these public keys (and the message). Since no participant knows all the secret keys of the other participants, nobody can deduce who sent the message, and all participants appear as potential senders.

during (and after) an election, whistleblowers who expose illegal activities, users of online services from tracking/profiling, and so on. A Dining Cryptographers Network (DCnet) [8] is a multi-party protocol that permits one party to send a message in such a way that each participating party appears as the potential sender. How a DCnet works is illustrated in Fig. 1 and explained in more detail in Sect. 2. DCnets are very interesting because they offer the strongest anonymity guarantee, require no trusted third party, and further they permit to communicate with a low latency. They were however considered to be unpractical for many years, because they were too greedy in in terms of bandwidth, and too inefficient at handling participants who do not properly execute the protocol and thereby disrupt the communication. For these reasons, mainly less secure approaches (e.g., relay-based approaches based on onion routing such as [29]) have been used in practice in the past.

With the advent of high speed communication standards like 5G and the upcoming 6G [33], where the peak data rate is expected to be around 1Tbit/s, the prior concerns about the bandwidth usage of DCnets are not as relevant as before. Furthermore, modern DCnet protocols make use of advanced cryptographic techniques and can detect misbehaving participants more efficiently than before. This leads us to think that DCnets will play a more important role in future communications, either for high security applications, for local ad-hoc anonymous networks, or when a very low latency is required.

After the original dining cryptographers protocol was proposed in [8] further improvements were proposed in [6,31,36,37]. These early protocols are unconditionally secure, which means that even an adversary with unlimited time and computational power cannot break the anonymity. However, the main problem of these early DCnets is that a malicious participant could jam the transmission by not properly executing the protocol, and such a participant could remain undetected for a rather long time. A milestone for modern DCnets was [18] with the idea that the values that participants publish should have an algebraic structure, so that one can verify immediately that every participant properly executes the protocol using a corresponding zero-knowledge proof. Unfortunately the algebraic structure could only be achieved by giving up on the unconditional security and by having only computational security instead. The main contribution of [15] was to show that one can replace the algebraic structure by Pedersen commitments, which then allows to have unconditional anonymity and zero-knowledge verification at the same time. Further advantages are that one does not need a reservation, like in [9,13,23,32], but one can use an efficient collision resolution mechanism like in [14,31]. A practical problem is that additionally to digital signatures and key-exchange an efficient implementation of such a DCnet requires a number of cryptographic primitives, such as short-term ECC Pedersen commitments and dedicated zero-knowledge proofs, which are not readily available in other libraries.

We present in this paper an efficient yet flexible ECC library for X64 processors, called X64ECC, that provides all public-key cryptographic operations mentioned above. Even though many open-source implementation of ECC exist, e.g. NaCl, LibSodium, or OpenSSL to mention a few, we found that none of them can fulfill all of the needs and requirements of DCnets. For example, many of the existing ECC libraries (e.g, LibSodium) supports a single curve, providing a single security level, and can not be easily extended. Furthermore, while most libraries provide functions for ECDH key exchange and ECDSA or EdDSA signatures, we are not aware of an open-source library that supports all four public-key functionalities for DCnets. There exist, of course, some specialized libraries for ZKPs, but they do not include key exchange. A a consequence, one would need to combine at least two libraries to cover key exchange, signatures, commitments, and ZKPs, which introduces a lot of overhead and redundancy (since each of them comes with its own low-level functions for field and curve arithmetic). Furthermore, using two or more libraries is also not very programmer-friendly since each library has its own specific API. X64ECC, on the other hand, uses one and the same implementation of the low-level operations (i.e. field and curve arithmetic) for all four kinds of cryptosystems and has a consistent API across all high-level operations. Furthermore, X64ECC is highly scalable and supports three different levels of security, which can be chosen independently for each of the four high-level functionalities. This high level of consistency and self-containedness make X64ECC easy to use for the implementation of DCnets.

2   Elliptic Curve Cryptography for DCnets

The example of a DCnet [8] shown in Fig. 1 can be generalized more formally to a set of participants $P_1, ..., P_n$ who can communicate via a broadcast channel. The DCnet protocol is performed in rounds, each round consisting of

- a key-establishment phase, during which the participants pairwise establish secret keys over a secure channel, for instance P_i and P_j agree on the secret keys k_{ij} and k_{ji}, elements of a finite additive group $\mathcal{G}$, with $k_{ij} = -k_{ji}$; and
- a communication phase, during which every participant computes the sum of all his secret keys, for instance P_i computes $k_i = \sum_j k_{ij}$. Then every participant publishes the value $o_i = k_i$, except if he wants to send an anonymous message m_i, then he publishes the value $o_i = k_i + m_i$.

If one of the participants sends an anonymous message m, then the sum of all the published values o_i reveals this m. Since we have $k_{ij} = -k_{ji}$, all the keys cancel each other out so that $\sum_{i=1}^n k_i = 0$, and therefore $\sum_{i=1}^n o_i = \sum_{i=1}^n k_i + m = m$. Thus, everybody can compute the message m but the sender remains unknown and every participant appears like a potential sender.

Note that a DCnet also provides recipient anonymity, because all participants receive the message, but this property which is due to the broadcast channel is easier to achieve than the sender anonymity and will therefore not be further discussed herein. More details about this can be found in [8,37].

2.1 Key-Establishment

Assuming participants do not collude against each other, the security of the anonymity depends on the quality of the established secret keys. If real random keys are exchanged via a secure channel, then the provided anonymity is unconditionally secure. This means that even an attacker with unlimited time and computational power will not be able to break the anonymity. Such a key exchange could for instance be achieved by two participants physically meeting and exchanging a hard-disc with real random data. A less secure but often more convenient method is to use a cryptographic key exchange, like the Diffie-Hellman key exchange [10]. It can be implemented more easily since participants only have to exchange public keys via a public network to create a shared secret key (which can then be stretched appropriately using a cryptographic pseudo-random number generator). It must be noted however, that the anonymity is then only computationally secure.

2.2 Collisions and Collision Resolution

When multiple participants send a message during the same round, the messages collide and the transmission does not work, e.g., $\sum_{i=1}^n o_i = m_1 + m_2 + m_3$. An efficient way to handle collisions is to make a recursive collision resolution process like in [14,15,31]. The principle is that when multiple messages collide, two new rounds are allocated for the resolution of that collision. The messages that were involved are then resent in either of those two rounds, so the collision is split into two parts. This principle is applied recursively until all collisions are resolved and all messages transmitted. For instance, a collision of 3 messages $(m_1 + m_2 + m_3)$ could be split into $(m_1 + m_3)$ and (m_2), and then $(m_1 + m_3)$ be split again into (m_1) and (m_3). This can be implemented efficiently using inference cancellation, which means that no transmission is necessary for every second round, but every second round can simply be computed instead. For example, when $(m_1 + m_2 + m_3)$ is the initial collision to be split, and then $(m_1 + m_3)$ is received, one can obtain the remaining (m_2) just by making a subtraction.

2.3 Verifiable Collision Resolution

A problem is that a malicious participant can disrupt the communication by creating collisions and interfering with the collision resolution process. The challenge is to detect if somebody is not properly participating to the collision resolution, without compromising the anonymity of the honest participants.

Correct Participation. Proper participation in the collision resolution means that no new messages should be introduced, and a participant P_i who had a message involved in a collision (in $o_i^{(c)}$), can only resend no or exactly the same message (in $o_i^{(r)}$). Thus, a participant P_i can only transmit

1. no message during the retransmission

$$o_i^{(c)} = k_i^{(c)} + m$$
$$o_i^{(r)} = k_i^{(r)}$$

2. or exactly the same message m in both rounds

$$o_i^{(c)} = k_i^{(c)} + m$$
$$o_i^{(r)} = k_i^{(r)} + m$$

Note that no message in both rounds corresponds to $m = 0$. It has been shown in that participants can prove that one of the above holds without revealing if they are transmitting a message or not.

Protocol Extension. The approach proposed in [15] consists of extending the original protocol described in Sect. 2 with Pedersen commitments [30] and zero-knowledge proofs [7]. To sketch this approach by using elliptic curves, assume G and H two publicly known generators of an elliptic curve group $\mathbb{E}$ over which the logarithm problem (ECDLP) problem is hard, and let $\mathcal{G}$ be the additive group modulo $|\mathbb{E}|$. The protocol is then extended so that

– during key-establishment the participants pairwise agree on the secret keys (k_{ij}, r_{ij}) and (k_{ji}, r_{ji}) in $\mathcal{G} \times \mathcal{G}$, with $k_{ij} = -k_{ji}$ and $r_{ij} = -r_{ji}$; and
– in the communication phase every participant P_i computes $k_i = \sum_j k_{ij}$ and $r_i = \sum_j r_{ij}$ and a commitment $C_i = r_i H + k_i G$, and publishes (o_i, C_i), where $o_i = k_i$ (or $o_i = k_i + m_i$). When a collision resolution is in progress, P_i additionally computes a zero-knowledge proof Z_i (as described in more detail below) and publishes (o_i, C_i, Z_i).

After the publication of all the values everybody can verify that nobody cheated.

Verification of Commitments. A first check that has to be made in every round, is done to ensure the integrity of the commitments. Since by construction we have $\sum_{i=1}^{n} k_i = 0$ and $\sum_{i=1}^{n} r_i = 0$ it must hold that $\sum_{i=1}^{n} C_i = \mathbf{0}$. So if this holds for the received commitments, they are considered to be valid. If this is not the case, an investigation can be made during which commitments for individual keys are examined, e.g., like in [15].

Verification of Correct Participation. A second check, which is made in case a round is used for retransmission in the context of collision resolution, consists in verifying the zero-knowledge proofs. To explain the principle on which the zero-knowledge proofs are based, consider for a participant P_i the commitment $C_i^{(c)}$ for the round where there was a collision, and the commitment $C_i^{(r)}$ for the round where there was a retransmission,

$$C_i^{(c)} = r_i^{(c)} H + k_i^{(c)} G$$
$$C_i^{(r)} = r_i^{(r)} H + k_i^{(r)} G$$

Using the techniques presented in [7], a participant can prove in zero-knowledge that he knows a secret witness α, which is either

- $\alpha = r_i^{(r)}$ such that $C_i^{(r)} = \alpha H + o_i^{(r)} G$, or
- $\alpha = r_i^{(r)} - r_i^{(c)}$ such that $C_i^{(r)} - C_i^{(c)} = \alpha H + (o_i^{(r)} - o_i^{(c)}) G$.

without revealing to the verifier which one of both statements is true. The sender is able to prove the first statement if he sent no message during the retransmission because then $o_i^{(r)} = k_i^{(r)}$, or he is able to prove the second statement if he sent exactly the same message M during the retransmission as in the collision because then $o_i^{(r)} - o_i^{(c)} = (k_i^{(r)} + m) - (k_i^{(c)} + m) = k_i^{(r)} - k_i^{(c)}$.

Longer messages can be split into multiple elements $k_1, ... k_l \in \mathcal{G}$, and commitments with multiple bases $C_i = r_i H + k_{i,1} G_1 + ... + k_{i,l} G_l$ can then be used.

2.4   Cryptographic Requirements

In order to implement a DCnet as described above, we need

- Pedersen commitments with a variable number of bases,
- dedicated ZK-proofs to detect malicious activity,
- (optionally) a key-exchange scheme to establish shared secret keys, and
- a digital signatures to sign the values that are published.

To keep the cryptographic elements as compact and as computationally efficient as possible, we use elliptic curve cryptography (ECC). Whereas keys and signatures have a long lifespan and often have to remain secure for several decades, the commitments and the zero-knowledge proofs only need to be secure during the communication. This means that while we have to use strong standard curves for keys and signatures, we can actually gain in efficiency by choosing weaker elliptic curves for Pedersen commitments and zero-knowledge proofs.

3   Implementation Details of X64ECC

Cryptographic software, including libraries for ECC, can be optimized for a wide range of requirements to satisfy the needs of different applications. At one end of the spectrum is high performance, which usually means that an implementer aims to minimize the latency of scalar multiplication and other performance-critical operations. There exists a vast number of papers describing performance-optimized implementations of ECC, e.g. [5], most of which come with hand-crafted assembler code for the field arithmetic. At the opposite end of the spectrum of requirements are flexibility, scalability, maintainability and extensibility. ECC libraries supporting these requirements are usually written in a high-level language like C, C++ or Java, which means they are usually slower than their aggressively speed-optimized counterparts. We call ECC software flexible if it can be built on many different platforms using different compilers and tool chains. Aiming for high flexibility makes sense for our ECC library since protocols and applications using DCnets may run not only on commodity PCs and laptops, but also on mobiles devices like smart phones and tablets. Scalability refers to the ability to support different curves that can provide different levels of security. As mentioned Sect. 1, different target applications can have highly divergent requirements with respect to the period of time during which the cryptographic primitives need to remain secure.

3.1   Requirements and Aims

It should be noted that many of the optimization goals for ECC software are mutually exclusive, which means they can not be achieved with one and the same implementation. For example, ECC libraries that are aggressively performance-tuned often support only a single elliptic curve and a single finite field (e.g. [5]), whereby the low-level arithmetic operations are usually written in Assembly language with fully unrolled loops to reduce the execution time to a minimum. However, such ECC libraries usually lack flexibility since assembler code is architecture-specific and not portable. Furthermore, they are, in general, not scalable since fully unrolled assembler code only works for operands of a specific length. Consequently, if such a library has to support fields of different bit-length, a separate (unrolled) implementation is required for each field. On the other hand, ECC libraries that aim for flexibility and scalability are usually written in a high-level language and parameterized with respect to the length of the operands (i.e. the number of limbs or words they consists of), which means the operand length is passed as parameter to the arithmetic functions along with other parameters like pointers to the arrays in which the operands are stored. In this way, the arithmetic functions can, in principle, process operands of arbitrary length (in steps of w bits, where w denotes the bitlength of a single word or limb). It is clear that scalable arithmetic functions can never reach the performance of speed-optimized functions that support only a single operand length and have fully unrolled loops.

A second, more significant, reason why a flexible and scalable ECC implementation is usually much slower than s speed-optimized one is the performance gap between compiled C code and hand-written Assembler code. What makes things even worse is that high-level languages like C or Java do not allow access to the carry flag, which slows down the execution time of long-integer addition. Furthermore, C and Java do not provide a standards-compliant way of multiplying two 64-bit integers and getting a 128-bit result. Some C compilers like gcc or Clang come with proprietary extensions to support 128-bit data types like int128_t or uint128_t, but these types are not part of the official ISO C standard. Therefore, it can not be taken for granted that such types are generally available (for example, Microsoft's Visual C does not have a 128-bit type). When strict ISO C compliance is desired, developers usually resort to use word or limbs of a length of 32 bits or less, so that a product of two such words or limbs fits into a 64-bit integer. Of course, performing multiple-precision integer multiplication with (32×32)-bit multiply instructions on a 64-bit processor results in poor performance. A well-known example of a "pure" ISO C software for scalar multiplication on Curve25519 is the so-called ref10 implementation that is contained in e.g. LibSodium and SuperCOP.

X64ECC aims for a compromise between flexibility and scalability on the one hand, and good performance on the other hand. To achieve this, we decided to write the library in C and make all arithmetic functions parameterized (so that X64ECC can support curves of many different security levels), but we do not insist on strict compliance with the ISO C standard. This concretely means we use a small set of compiler intrinsics for common operations like addition-with-carry of 64-bit integers or multiplication of 64-bit integers with a 128-bit result. These intrinsics were defined by Intel and are not part of the ISO C standard, but are nonetheless supported by the four major C compiler families, namely gcc, Clang, the Intel compiler, and Microsoft Visual C. Such intrinsics also exist for non-X64 platforms like the 64-bit ARM architecture, though they have slightly different names. These intrinsics allow X64ECC to reach a high flexibility since the source code can be easily ported to other 64-bit architectures, while, at the same time, they allow one to achieve reasonably high speed since the arithmetic can be performed with 64-bit words (or limbs slightly shorter than 64 bits).

3.2 Field Arithmetic

X64ECC provides parameterized functions for arithmetic operation in prime fields whose length is a multiple of 64 minus 1, e.g. 127 bits, 191 bits, or 255 bits. An element of a field (i.e. an integer in the range of $[0, p-1]$) is represented by an array of 64-bit words (i.e. an array of type uint64_t); in the case of a 255-bit prime field the array consists of four words. As mentioned before, the arithmetic functions are parameterized and get, besides pointers to the arrays in which the operands are stored, also a length parameter called *len*. The word with index 0 and index $len-1$ is the least and most significant one, respectively. X64ECC does not insist that field elements, when used as operands, are always fully reduced (i.e. less than p); instead, all arithmetic functions accept incompletely reduced inputs as long as they fit into *len* words. In the worst case, an operand can be slightly bigger than $2p$. Also, the results of the arithmetic functions of our library may not be fully reduced, but this is not a problem since they can still be used as operands for a subsequent arithmetic operation. Only at the very end of the scalar multiplication, the operands get fully reduced (which requires up to two subtractions of p) to have a final result in the range of $[0, p-1]$.

Addition and Subtraction. The straightforward way to perform a modular addition $r = a + b \bmod p$ is to first calculate the sum $s = a + b$ and then subtract a multiple of p from it to obtain a final result that fits into n words. Since each of the operands can be incompletely reduced, the subtrahend is either 0, p, $2p$, or $3p$. However, instead of subtracting a multiple of p, it is, in general, more efficient to add a multiple of c, which is possible since for pseudo-Mersenne primes since $2^n \equiv c \bmod p$. However, the main drawback of such an "add-then-subtract" technique is that it consists of two loops when implemented in a parameterized fashion, each introducing overhead if they are not unrolled. To minimize the loop overhead, we employ a modular addition technique that requires only a single loop, like the one described by Düll et al in [11, Sect. 4.4]. Our implementation is based on their approach and performs an addition in $\mathbb{F}_p$ as follows. First, we add the Most Significant Words (MSWs) of a and b, i.e. we compute the sum $s = a_{len-1} + b_{len-1}$, which can be up to 65 bits long when the operands are incompletely reduced. This sum is then split up into a lower part s_L consisting of the 63 least significant bits, and an upper part s_H with the remaining two bits. We temporarily store s_L in a register and multiply s_H by c. Thereafter, the $len-1$ remaining words of the two operands are added (with carry propagation), starting with the Least Significant Words (LSWs) a_0 and b_0. The main difference to a "conventional" multi-precision addition is that the product of s_H and c is added to the two LSWs and, therefore, the carry to be propagated to the next-higher word can be 0, 1, or 2. Finally, the carry from the last addition (i.e. the addition of the words a_{len-2} and b_{len-2}) is propagated into s_L, which is then at most 16 bits long. The final result fits into *len* words, but may be not fully reduced.

A similar strategy as described above for modular addition is also applicable to modular subtraction $r = a - b \bmod p$. A straightforward implementation performs the subtraction first and then adds a multiple of p to get a non-negative result, which would require two loops. In order to minimize the loop overhead, we compute $r = 4p + a - b \bmod p$ instead, and combine these computations into a single loop similar as above for addition. Adding $4p$ to the difference ensures that the final result will always be non-negative, but it might not be fully reduced.

Multiplication and Squaring. The most basic technique to multiply two elements $a, b \in \mathbb{F}_p$ consists of a normal integer multiplication $t = ab$, followed by a reduction of the product t modulo the prime p. From an algorithmic point of view, there exist two major approaches to implement a long-integer multiplication in software, namely the *Operand-Scanning (OS)* method and the

Product-Scanning (PS) method [19]. These two methods differ in their loop structure and the operation they execute in the inner loops. The OS method performs and operation of the form $S = a \times b + c + d$ in the inner loop, which means two 64-bit words are multiplied, yielding a 128-bit result, and then two further 64-bit words are added to the 128-bit product. On the other hand, the inner loop of the PS method consists of a classical Multiply-ACcumulate (MAC) operation of the form $S = S + a \times b$, i.e. two 64-bit words are multiplied and the 128-bit product is added to a cumulative sum S. When adding up several such 128-products, the length of S will exceed 128 bits and, therefore, S has to be stored in three 64-bit words. X64ECC supports both the OS and PS method; which one is faster depends on the characteristics of the target micro-architecture and the capabilities of the compiler to produce efficient machine code. For example, on Intel processors with ADX (Multi-Precision Add-Carry Instruction Extensions), which was introduced with the Broadwell micro-architecture, the OS method should be faster since the additions in the inner loop can be performed with two independent carry chains. The ADX extensions add two new instructions for add-with-carry, namely `adcx` and `adox`, which perform both an add-with-carry operation like the conventional X64 instruction `adc`. However, while `adc` may set both the carry and overflow flag, the two new instructions affect only one flag, which is the carry flag for `adcx` and the overflow flag for `adox`. Since these two instructions set different flags, it is possible to calculate two chains of addition in parallel, which can be exploited to speed up the OS method as explained in [28].

The $2len$-word product $t = ab$ has to be reduced modulo p to get a result r that consists of len words. Our implementation of the reduction operation takes advantage of the special form of pseudo-Mersenne primes; in particular, we exploit that $2^k \equiv c \bmod p$ and $2^{k+1} \equiv 2^{64len} \equiv 2c \bmod p$. The first step of the reduction is to multiply the len upper words of t by $2c$ and add the product to the len lower words, which yields an intermediate result t' of a length of $len + 1$ words since c is relatively small for the primes we use. Then, t' is split into a lower part t'_L comprising the k least significant bits of the intermediate result and a higher part t'_H that is up to 64 bits long. The final step is the multiplication of t'_H by c and the addition of $t'_H c$ to the lower part t'_L, which is similar to the operation performed in the inner loop of the OS method.

Our implementation of the squaring takes into account that the square $t = a^2$ of an len-word integer a can be computed using only $(len^2 + l)/2$ multiplications of 64-bit words, which is significantly less than the len^2 multiplications required to multiply two distinct len-word integers. A detailed description of how to optimize the squaring operation on Intel processors can be found in [27].

3.3   Curve Arithmetic

X64ECC supports two families of elliptic curves, namely Montgomery curves and twisted Edwards curves. The former are beneficial for variable-base scalar multiplication, such as needed for ECDH key exchange to derive a shared secret, while the latter are better suited for elliptic curve operations that mainly rely on fast fixed-base scalar multiplication, e.g. generation of key pairs for ECDH, generation and verification of signatures, Pedersen commitments, and ZKPs.

A Montgomery curve [26] over a non-binary field $\mathbb{F}_q$ is an elliptic curve governed by an equation of the form

$$E_M : By^2 = x^3 + Ax^2 + x \tag{1}$$

where $A, B \in \mathbb{F}_q$ and $(A^2 - 4)B \neq 0$. These curves are very well suited for the implementation of ECDH key exchange as demonstrated through Curve25519 [1]. The main attraction of Montgomery-form curves is a special algorithm for a variable-base scalar multiplication $Q = kP$, the Montgomery ladder [4], which is not only fast but also provides intrinsic resistance against timing attacks due to its highly regular execution profile. Montgomery curves feature a unique addition law that allows one to efficiently compute the sum $P_1 + P_2$ of two points P_1, P_2 whose difference $P_1 - P_2$ is known at the cost of only three multiplications (3M) and two squarings (2S) in $\mathbb{F}_q$ when using projective coordinates. This so-called "differential" addition involves only the projective X and Z coordinates, i.e. the Y coordinate is not used at all [26]. The doubling of a point in projective X, Z coordinates is even cheaper and costs only $2M$ and $2S$. In summary, the Montgomery ladder has to carry out $5n$ multiplications and $4n$ squarings in $\mathbb{F}_q$ to compute $Q = kP$ when the scalar k is n bits long, i.e. $5M$ and $4S$ per bit.

Twisted Edwards curves (henceforth denoted as TEd curves) were introduced by Bernstein et al in [2] as a generalization of ordinary (untwisted) Edwards curves. A TE curve defined over a prime field $\mathbb{F}_p$ is governed by the equation

$$E_T : ax^2 + y^2 = 1 + dx^2y^2 \tag{2}$$

where a and d are two distinct, non-0 elements of $\mathbb{F}_p$. Like Montgomery curves, TE curves have a co-factor of (at least) 4; therefore, not every elliptic curve can be represented in TE form. Bernstein et al [2] were the first to describe an interesting connection between TE curves and Montgomery curves, namely their birational equivalence over $\mathbb{F}_p$: any TEd curve given by Eq. (2) is birationally-equivalent to a Montgomery curve and vice versa. The TEd model features a unique addition formula that is *unified*, which means it can also be used to double a point. Furthermore, the addition formula is *complete* when a is a square in $\mathbb{F}_p$ and d is a non-square in $\mathbb{F}_p$. Completeness refers to the fact that the obtained sum is correct for any pair $P_1, P_2 \in E_T(\mathbb{F}_p)$, including corner cases like $P_1 = \mathcal{O}$, $P_2 = \mathcal{O}$, or $P_1 = -P_2$. Hişil et al [20] introduced the so-called extended coordinates for TE curves, which enable extremely efficient point addition when $a = -1$. Using such extended coordinates, a "mixed" addition (i.e. an addition of a point in extended projective coordinates with a point given in extended affine coordinates) based on the unified formulae from [20, Section 3.1] costs only seven multiplication (7M) and six additions or subtractions (6A) in $\mathbb{F}_p$. Doubling a point given in extended projective coordinates costs 3M, 4S, and 6A.

3.4   High-Level Cryptosystems

In this section, we review the high-level cryptosystems that are considered herein.

ECDH Key Exchange. The Elliptic Curve Diffie-Hellman (ECDH) protocol was first introduced by Miller [25] and uses scalar multiplication of a point on an elliptic curve as the one-way function for the key-pair generation. The security of the ECDH is based on the assumption that the elliptic curve discrete logarithm problem (ECDLP) is hard. This means that if G is a generator of the elliptic curve and a is a scalar, then it is not practically possible to determine a given aG. Our implementation is based on Montgomery curves as in [24]. The protocol for two parties (Alice and Bob) to establish a shared private key over an insecure channel is as follows:

1. Alice chooses a random number a, and sends $K_A = aG$ to Bob.
2. Bob chooses a random number b, and sends $K_B = bG$ to Alice.
3. Alice and Bob can compute the shared key $K = aK_B = bK_A$.

Because of the assumption that the ECDLP problem is hard, an observer who only knows K_A and K_B but neither a nor b cannot compute K.

Pedersen Commitments. The security of the Pedersen commitment scheme, introduced in 1991 [30], is based on the complexity of the Discrete Logarithm Problem (DLP). Pedersen commitments are computationally binding and unconditionally hiding. The original description of Pedersen commitments uses a prime-order subgroup of $\mathbb{Z}_p^*$ as basic algebraic structure, but it is also possible to embed them into the additive group of points on an elliptic curve over a finite field. In this case, the main computation of a Pedersen commitment is a fixed-based scalar multiplication. X64ECC implements Pedersen commitments using twisted Edwards curves and speeds up the computation with a pre-computed table of multiples of the generator of the group. In essence, our implementation of Pedersen commitments is very similar to [16], expect that we use the low-level field arithmetic functions described earlier in this section.

Edwards Curve Digital Signature Algorithm. The Edwards-curve Digital Signature Algorithm (EdDSA) is a state-of-the-art signature scheme using elliptic curves in (twisted) Edwards form that was developed with the intention of achieving both high performance (especially in software) and high security [3]. A variant of EdDSA as specified in RFC 8032 [22] is one of the digital signature systems supported in the most-recent version of the TLS protocol, i.e. TLS 1.3. EdDSA is a "Schnorr-like" signature scheme that combines the strong security and simplicity of classical Schnorr signatures [34] with the efficiency (and further positive implementation aspects) of twisted Edwards curves [2]. However, unlike the original Schnorr scheme, EdDSA uses a double-size hash function (to help alleviate concerns regarding hash-function security) and generates the per-message secret nonces in a deterministic fashion by hashing each message together with a long-term secret. Thus, EdDSA does not consume fresh randomness for each message to be signed, which makes the scheme less dependent of reliable sources of entropy. In essence, the costly part of the generation of a signature is a fixed-base scalar multiplication $R = kG$, which can be efficiently performed when a table containing multiples of the generator G have been precomputed. To verify an EdDSA signature, one has to check whether an equation of the form $R = kG - lQ$ holds or not. This can be accomplished in different ways; X64ECC splits this computation up into a fixed-base scalar multiplication kG (similar to the signature generation) and a variable-base scalar multiplication lQ, which we perform using the Montgomery ladder on the birationally-equivalent Montgomery curve.

Zero Knowledge Proofs. A Zero-Knowledge Proof (ZKP) [38] convinces a verifier $\mathcal{V}$ that a prover $\mathcal{P}$ knows a secret witness α that verifies a given statement, without revealing α nor anything else. For a DCnet as described in Sect. 2.3, $\mathcal{P}$ has to prove that he knows a scalar α such that

$$(A = \alpha H) \vee (B = \alpha H) = \texttt{true},$$

where H is a generator of an elliptic curve $\mathbb{E}$ on which discrete log problem is assumed to be hard, and A and B are points on that curve $\mathbb{E}$. This proof can be implemented as follows:

- If the prover $\mathcal{P}$ knows the scalar α such that $A = \alpha H$:
  1. $\mathcal{P}$ randomly chooses three integers a, r_2 and c_2 in the range $[0, |\mathbb{E}| - 1]$.
  2. $\mathcal{P}$ computes $t_1 = aH$ and $t_2 = r_2 H - c_2 B$.
  3. $\mathcal{P}$ computes $c = \text{hash}(t_1 | t_2)$
  4. $\mathcal{P}$ computes $c_1 = c - c_2$, $r_1 = a + c_1 k$ and sends (c_1, c_2, r_1, r_2) to $\mathcal{V}$.
- If the prover $\mathcal{P}$ knows α such that $B = \alpha H$:
  1. $\mathcal{P}$ randomly chooses three integers a, r_1 and c_1 in the range $[0, |\mathbb{E}| - 1]$.
  2. $\mathcal{P}$ computes $t_1 = r_1 H - c_1 A$ and $t_2 = aH$.
  3. $\mathcal{P}$ computes $c = \text{hash}(t_1 | t_2)$.
  4. $\mathcal{P}$ computes $c_2 = c - c_1$, $r_2 = a + c_2 k$ and sends (c_1, c_2, r_1, r_2) to $\mathcal{V}$.

The verifier $\mathcal{V}$ computes $t_1' = r_1 H - c_1 A$, $t_2' = r_2 H - c_2 B$ and accepts if $\text{hash}(t_1' | t_2') = c_1 + c_2$. Note that $\mathcal{V}$ cannot distinguish if $\mathcal{P}$ knows α such that $A = \alpha H$ or such that $B = \alpha H$. More details on how to prove statements about discrete logarithms can be found in [7], and the above proof was rendered non-interactive using the Fiat-Shamir heuristic [12] which consists in replacing the challenge c that would come from the verifier $\mathcal{V}$ by a hash function.

4   Benchmarking Results

In this section, measurements of the execution time, in CPU cycles, of the most important operations are presented in order to show the scalability of the operations. First the methodology followed when taking measurements is described in

Table 1. Computation time in CPU cycles of field operations

Prime p	$2^{127} - 19$	$2^{191} - 507$	$2^{255} - 19$
Multiplication	59	84	111
Squaring	56	79	101
Inversion	8764	19775	42098

detail. Then the results obtained for the different operations are presented and analyzed, starting from low-level field operations, then curve operations and finally the high-level operations required for a DCnet.

4.1 Methodology

Obtaining accurate and reproducible measurements of the number of CPU cycles taken for a particular operation can be difficult. The reason for this is that modern CPU technologies allow for changes in the clock frequency and voltages in order to improve both performance and energy consumption. As outlined in [3], reports of measurements can lack details in the set-up used as well as availability of the software tested which makes it difficult to put results into perspective. Therefore, this section provides a detailed description of the experimental set-up and the data analysis process.

All measurements were made on an Intel Core i7-9750H CPU running at 2.60 GHz. This CPU has three main technologies that can affect the measurement of the number of cycles of an operation, namely Turbo Boost, Speed Shift and Hyper-Threading [21]. In order to avoid a change in the processor's frequency while the measurements were taken the cores were set to remain at the maximum frequency (2.6 GHz) and Hyperthreading was turned off. In order to reduce the number of unnecessary background processes running while measurements were taken the OS GUI was turned off producing more consistent results.

Two other problems arise when trying to measure the number of cycles of an operation. The first one is that making the measurement itself takes a number of cycles. The second problem is that if the same operation is conducted in a loop, say a modular multiplication between two constant operands, it is possible that the compiler realizes that the same operation is conducted repeatedly and therefore optimizes the code at compilation time in a way that makes the results unrealistically low. To avoid this issue the operands where modified at each step of the loop and the offset created by those operations and the cycle measurements were evaluated independently and then subtracted from the final measurements.

4.2 Field Arithmetic

As mentioned in Sect. 3, the software is written in ANSI C99 taking advantage of the 64-bit addition and multiplication intrinsics. The software supports field operation for pseudo-Mersenne primes of length 127, 191 and 255 bits. Table 1

Table 2. Computation time in CPU cycles of Montgomery and TEd curve operations

Prime p	$2^{127} - 19$	$2^{191} - 507$	$2^{255} - 19$
Mon. ladder step	701	995	1404
Mon. scalar mul.	102027	214848	404312
TEd point addition	597	923	1233
TEd point doubling	436	754	1093
TEd scalar mul.	40053	81886	145279

shows the cycle counts obtained for 3 low level field operations: modular multiplication, modular squaring and field element inversion.

It can be noted that for the modular multiplication and squaring the computation time seems to increase linearly as the number of bits in the prime increases, meaning that a multiplication with $p = 2^{255} - 19$ takes about twice as many cycles as with $p = 2^{127} - 19$. This is however not the case for modular inversion as an increase of 50% percent in the bit length of the prime yield to an increase of in computation time by about a factor of 2.

In order to put those results into perspective, the modular multiplication implemented in LibSodium was benchmarked in a similar fashion as the described previously. It was found that a modular multiplication with $p = 2^{255} - 19$ took about 88 cycles which is about 20% faster than our implementation, however the LibSodium implementation is optimised for and only supports $p = 2^{255} - 19$ whereas our implementation has the flexibility to support any pseudo-Mersenne prime of length 127, 191 and 255 bits.

4.3 Curve Arithmetic

Table 2 shows the results for Montgomery and Twisted Edwards (TEd) curve operations. The TEd curve parameters used are the same as the ones that can be found in [16] and in [17]. For the Montgomery curves the A parameter is 2678310 for $p = 2^{191} - 507$ and 486662 for $2^{255} - 19$ corresponding to Curve25519.

The scalar multiplication is the main operation of the key exchange cryptosystem. The Montgomery curve representation allows for fast scalar point multiplication for variable base point using the Montgomery ladder step [4]. This allows for a fast computation of a shared key given a public and a private key. The ladder step consists of 5 multiplications, 4 squaring, 1 multiplication by a 64-bit word, 4 additions and 4 subtractions, all of those operations are performed modulo p. The ladder step is implemented to run in constant time to prevent side-channel attacks.

As expected the measurements for the ladder step computation time increases by roughly the same factor as the one obtained for the basic field operations as the bit length of the prime increases. However the scalar multiplication computation time increases by about a factor of 2 when field elements increase from a 191-bit length to a 255-bit length. This is most likely due to the field element inversion and the bitwise operations required in the conditional swapping.

Table 3. Computation time (in CPU cycles) of the high-level cryptosystems

Prime p	$2^{127} - 19$	$2^{191} - 507$	$2^{255} - 19$
ECDH key exchange			
ECDH key pair generation	54699	103904	174571
ECDH shared secret computation	102027	214848	404312
EdDSA signatures			
EdDSA signature generation	59498	109117	180197
EdDSA signature verification	166234	323875	585208
Zero-knowledge proofs			
ZKP computation	558761	1171808	2152412
ZKP verification	486203	1061098	1980074
Simple commitment with 2 base points			
Precomputation	5415148	17549746	48279847
Computation	68926	139511	240251
Multiple commitment with 16 base points			
Precomputation	43325954	140359091	386308058
Computation	479393	981254	1632780
Multiple commitment with 32 base points			
Precomputation	86630512	280727349	772462400
Computation	947432	1938759	3218402
Multiple commitment with 64 base points			
Precomputation	173248206	561929977	1545141239
Computation	1887215	3849720	6391423

Similarly to the Montgomery ladder step, the TEd point addition and doubling consists of basic field operations. The point addition consists of 9 multiplications, 4 subtractions and 5 additions whereas the point doubling consists of 3 multiplications, 4 squaring, 2 subtractions and 4 additions. As expected the computation time for the point addition and doubling scales linearly as the bit length of the prime increases.

The TEd scalar multiplication measurements reported in Table 2 are for a fixed base scalar multiplication. That is to say that the point in the multiplication is known in advance and the scalar multiplication can be done using a precomputed table as described in [16].

4.4 High-Level Cryptosystems

Table 3 shows the results for the four types of high level cryptosystems, namely ECDH key exchange, EdDSA signatures, Zero Knowledge proofs and Pedersen commitments.

As explained in Sect. 3, the ECDH key-pair generation essentially consists of a random-number generation and a fixed-base scalar multiplication, which we perform using the twisted Edwards representation, followed by a conversion of the resulting point to Montgomery representation. The shared key can be derived through a variable-base scalar multiplication on a Montgomery curve. The execution time of the key-pair generation includes the time needed for the generation of a random number (which depends on the operating system) and the fixed-base scalar multiplication. On the other hand, the EdDSA signature scheme uses for both operations (i.e. signature generation and verification) the twisted Edwards form.

The ZKP computation involves three random number generations. Modular reduction of the random number to the order of the generator point of the curve needs to be applied as the ZKP operations described in Sect. 3 are done modulo the order of the generator point. As the order of the base point is not a Mersenne prime, a Montgomery reduction is applied which involves a computational cost. A hash function is also required. We used the BLAKE2b implementation from Monocypher [35] as Monocypher is a lightweight library and BALKE2b is a fast cryptographically secure hash based on the ideas of ChaCha20 which was originally designed by Daniel Bernstein. It is interesting to note that the difference in computation time between the computation and the verification of the ZKP is relatively small, about 10% longer for the computation. Also as expected, the computation time is about 4 times longer when the bit length of the prime is doubled which seems to be consistent with the previous results.

Payload data	Commiment	(ZK-proof)	Signature

(a) Packet structure.

Payload data	1024 bytes		512 bytes	
Prime (commitment & zk-proof)	127 bit	255 bit	127 bit	255 bit
Packet size (bytes)				
Crypto overhead	144	224	144	224
Processing (packets/s)				
Generation	1284.7	653.4	1865.1	881.2
Verification	1315.3	672.3	1930.4	916.0
Bandwidth DCnet (kbit/s)				
10 participants	1052.2	537.8	772.1	366.4
100 participants	105.2	53.7	77.2	36.6

(b) Packet size, estimated cycles needed for the generation and verification of packets, and the estimated throughput of DCnets using 127 and 255 bit curves, and assuming a 4 GHz CPU.

Fig. 2. Estimated performance of DCnets based on our library.

Finally the benchmarks for Pedersen commitments using precomputed points can also be found in Table 3. The advantage of using precomputated tables is that it is possible to trade off RAM memory space for computational speed. For example the computation of simple commitments with 2 base points using the precomputated tables cost about half the number of cycles as a Twisted Edward curve scalar multiplication. This indicates that if the same base points are used repeatedly the overhead cost of the precomputation will be balanced with the later gain when computing commitments. The precomputation and commitment computation time scale linearly with the number of bases used. The commitment computation time appears to also scale in a similar way as the previous operations, that is to say doubling the bit length of the prime result in an increase by a factor of 4 of the computation time.

5   Conclusions

We discussed the cryptographic primitives required to construct verifiable DCnets based on Pedersen commitments and zero-knowledge proofs, we proposed a library specifically designed to efficiently implement those primitives, and we benchmarked the results on a 64bit Intel CPU. Even though X64ECC provides a high level of flexibility and scalability, it still achieves very fast execution times. For example, a variable-base scalar multiplication using a 255-bit Montgomery curve requires only about 400,000 clock cycles on a modern Intel X64 processor. A fixed-base scalar multiplication on a 255-bit twisted Edwards curve is almost three times faster and has an execution time of less than 145,000 cycles.

To conclude we estimate the performance of a DCnet implemented with our library, looking especially at the gain obtained by choosing our 127bit curve rather than a more commonly found 255bit curve. In Fig. 2a, we see the structure of a packet published by a participant. In Fig. 2b, we see that the cryptographic overhead, which is composed of the commitment, the zero-knowledge proof and the digital signature, shrinks from 224 to 144 bytes when we use the 127bit curve for the commitment and the zero-knowledge proof. We further see that also the generation and the verification of a packet is then approximately twice as fast, which is also the case for the throughput of a resulting DCnet. Note that for the computation of the throughput we assume a single Intel CPU running at 4 Ghz and we consider the time it takes for a recipient to verify all the received packets. Further, we assume a collision resolution process with a throughput of 100%, and we assume that every packet contains a zero-knowledge proof, though this is only the case during a collision resolution. In the absolute, we see that a DCnet with 10 participants sending packets of 1kB, can then provide an anonymous channel with a bandwidth of around 1Mbit/s, or a DCnet with 100 participants sending packets of 1kB, can then provide an anonymous channel with a bandwidth of around 100kbit/s.

References

1. Bernstein, D.J.: Curve25519: new Diffie-Hellman speed records. In: Yung, M., Dodis, Y., Kiayias, A., Malkin, T. (eds.) PKC 2006. LNCS, vol. 3958, pp. 207–228. Springer, Heidelberg (2006). https://doi.org/10.1007/11745853_14
2. Bernstein, D.J., Birkner, P., Joye, M., Lange, T., Peters, C.: Twisted Edwards curves. In: Vaudenay, S. (ed.) AFRICACRYPT 2008. LNCS, vol. 5023, pp. 389–405. Springer, Heidelberg (2008). https://doi.org/10.1007/978-3-540-68164-9_26
3. Bernstein, D.J., Duif, N., Lange, T., Schwabe, P., Yang, B.Y.: High-speed high-security signatures. J. Cryptogr. Eng. $2(2)$, 77–89 (2012)
4. Bernstein, D.J., Lange, T.: Montgomery curves and the montgomery ladder. Cryptology ePrint Archive, Report 2017/293 (2017). https://eprint.iacr.org/2017/293
5. Bernstein, D.J., Lange, T., Schwabe, P.: The security impact of a new cryptographic library. In: Hevia, A., Neven, G. (eds.) LATINCRYPT 2012. LNCS, vol. 7533, pp. 159–176. Springer, Heidelberg (2012). https://doi.org/10.1007/978-3-642-33481-8_9
6. Bos, J., den Boer, B.: Detection of disrupters in the DC protocol. In: Quisquater, J.-J., Vandewalle, J. (eds.) EUROCRYPT 1989. LNCS, vol. 434, pp. 320–327. Springer, Heidelberg (1990). https://doi.org/10.1007/3-540-46885-4_33
7. Camenisch, J., Stadler, M.: Proof systems for general statements about discrete logarithms. Technical report/ETH Zurich, Department of Computer Science 260 (1997)
8. Chaum, D.: The dining cryptographers problem: unconditional sender and recipient untraceability. J. Cryptol. $1(1)$, 65–75 (1988)
9. Corrigan-Gibbs, H., Ford, B.: Dissent: accountable anonymous group messaging. In: Proceedings of the 17th ACM Conference on Computer and Communications Security, pp. 340–350 (2010)
10. Diffie, W., Hellman, M.: New directions in cryptography. IEEE Trans. Inf. Theory $22(6)$, 644–654 (1976)
11. Düll, M., Haase, B., Hinterwälder, G., Hutter, M., Paar, C., Sánchez, A.H., Schwabe, P.: High-speed Curve25519 on 8-bit, 16-bit and 32-bit microcontrollers. Des. Codes Crypt. $77(2$–$3)$, 493–514 (2015)
12. Fiat, A., Shamir, A.: How to prove yourself: practical solutions to identification and signature problems. In: Odlyzko, A.M. (ed.) CRYPTO 1986. LNCS, vol. 263, pp. 186–194. Springer, Heidelberg (1987). https://doi.org/10.1007/3-540-47721-7_12
13. Franck, C.: New directions for dining cryptographers. Master's thesis, University of Luxembourg, 2008 (2008)
14. Franck, C.: Dining cryptographers with 0.924 verifiable collision resolution. Ann. UMCS Informatica $14(1)$, 49–59 (2014). https://doi.org/10.2478/umcsinfo-2014-0007
15. Franck, C., van de Graaf, J.: Dining cryptographers are practical (2014)
16. Franck, C., Großschädl, J.: Efficient implementation of Pedersen commitments using twisted Edwards curves. In: Bouzefrane, S., Banerjee, S., Sailhan, F., Boumerdassi, S., Renault, E. (eds.) MSPN 2017. LNCS, vol. 10566, pp. 1–17. Springer, Cham (2017). https://doi.org/10.1007/978-3-319-67807-8_1
17. Ghatpande, S., Großschädl, J., Liu, Z.: A family of lightweight twisted Edwards curves for the internet of things. In: Blazy, O., Yeun, C.Y. (eds.) WISTP 2018. LNCS, vol. 11469, pp. 193–206. Springer, Cham (2019). https://doi.org/10.1007/978-3-030-20074-9_14

18. Golle, P., Juels, A.: Dining cryptographers revisited. In: Cachin, C., Camenisch, J.L. (eds.) EUROCRYPT 2004. LNCS, vol. 3027, pp. 456–473. Springer, Heidelberg (2004). https://doi.org/10.1007/978-3-540-24676-3_27

19. Hankerson, D.R., Menezes, A.J., Vanstone, S.A.: Guide to Elliptic Curve Cryptography. Springer, New York (2004). https://doi.org/10.1007/b97644

20. Hisil, H., Wong, K.K.-H., Carter, G., Dawson, E.: Twisted Edwards curves revisited. In: Pieprzyk, J. (ed.) ASIACRYPT 2008. LNCS, vol. 5350, pp. 326–343. Springer, Heidelberg (2008). https://doi.org/10.1007/978-3-540-89255-7_20

21. Intel Corporation: Intel Core i7–9750H Processor (12M Cache, up to 4.50 GHz) Product Specifications. https://ark.intel.com/content/www/us/en/ark/products/191045/intel-core-i7-9750h-processor-12m-cache-up-to-4-50-ghz.html

22. Josefsson, S., Liusvaara, I.: Edwards-Curve Digital Signature Algorithm (EdDSA). Internet Research Task Force, Crypto Forum Research Group, RFC 8032, January 2017

23. Krasnova, A., Neikes, M., Schwabe, P.: Footprint scheduling for dining-cryptographer networks. In: Grossklags, J., Preneel, B. (eds.) FC 2016. LNCS, vol. 9603, pp. 385–402. Springer, Heidelberg (2017). https://doi.org/10.1007/978-3-662-54970-4_23

24. Langley, A., Hamburg, M., Turner, S.: Elliptic Curves for Security. RFC 7748, January 2016. https://doi.org/10.17487/RFC7748. https://rfc-editor.org/rfc/rfc7748.txt

25. Miller, V.S.: Use of elliptic curves in cryptography. In: Williams, H.C. (ed.) CRYPTO 1985. LNCS, vol. 218, pp. 417–426. Springer, Heidelberg (1986). https://doi.org/10.1007/3-540-39799-X_31

26. Montgomery, P.L.: Speeding the Pollard and elliptic curve methods of factorization. Math. Comput. **48**(177), 243–264 (1987)

27. Öztürk, E., Guilford, J., Gopal, V.: Large integer squaring on intel architecture processors (2013). Intel white paper, available for download at http://www.intel.com/content/dam/www/public/us/en/documents/white-papers/large-integer-squaring-ia-paper.pdf

28. Öztürk, E., Guilford, J., Gopal, V., Feghali, W.: New instructions supporting large integer arithmetic on intel architecture processors (2012). Intel white paper, available for download at http://www.intel.com/content/dam/www/public/us/en/documents/white-papers/ia-large-integer-arithmetic-paper.pdf

29. De la Cadena, W., Kaiser, D., Mitseva, A., Panchenko, A., Engel, T.: Analysis of multi-path onion routing-based anonymization networks. In: Foley, S.N. (ed.) DBSec 2019. LNCS, vol. 11559, pp. 240–258. Springer, Cham (2019). https://doi.org/10.1007/978-3-030-22479-0_13

30. Pedersen, T.P.: Non-interactive and information-theoretic secure verifiable secret sharing. In: Feigenbaum, J. (ed.) CRYPTO 1991. LNCS, vol. 576, pp. 129–140. Springer, Heidelberg (1992). https://doi.org/10.1007/3-540-46766-1_9

31. Pfitzmann, A.: Diensteintegrierende Kommunikationsnetze mit teilnehmerüberprüfbarem Datenschutz. Springer, Heidelberg (1990)

32. Ruffing, T., Moreno-Sanchez, P., Kate, A.: CoinShuffle: practical decentralized coin mixing for bitcoin. In: Kutyłowski, M., Vaidya, J. (eds.) ESORICS 2014. LNCS, vol. 8713, pp. 345–364. Springer, Cham (2014). https://doi.org/10.1007/978-3-319-11212-1_20

33. Samsung: 6G - the next hyper-connected experience for all. Technical report, Samsung Research (2020)

34. Schnorr, C.P.: Efficient identification and signatures for smart cards. In: Brassard, G. (ed.) CRYPTO 1989. LNCS, vol. 435, pp. 239–252. Springer, New York (1990). https://doi.org/10.1007/0-387-34805-0_22
35. Vaillant, L.: Monocypher (2020). https://monocypher.org/manual/hash
36. Waidner, M.: Unconditional sender and recipient untraceability in spite of active attacks. In: Quisquater, J.-J., Vandewalle, J. (eds.) EUROCRYPT 1989. LNCS, vol. 434, pp. 302–319. Springer, Heidelberg (1990). https://doi.org/10.1007/3-540-46885-4_32
37. Waidner, M., Pfitzmann, B.: The dining cryptographers in the disco: unconditional sender and recipient untraceability with computationally secure serviceability. In: Quisquater, J.-J., Vandewalle, J. (eds.) EUROCRYPT 1989. LNCS, vol. 434, p. 690. Springer, Heidelberg (1990). https://doi.org/10.1007/3-540-46885-4_69
38. Wu, H., Wang, F.: A survey of noninteractive zero knowledge proof system and its applications. Sci. World J. **2014** (2014)

Efficient and Lightweight Polynomial-Based Key Management Scheme for Dynamic Networks

Mohammed Nafi[1,2](✉), Samia Bouzefrane[2], and Mawloud Omar[3]

[1] Laboratoire d'Informatique Médicale (LIMED), Faculté des Sciences Exactes,
Université de Bejaia, 06000 Bejaia, Algérie
mohammed.nafi@cnam.fr
[2] CEDRIC Lab, Conservatoire National des Arts et Métiers - CNAM, Paris, France
samia.bouzefrane@cnam.fr
[3] LIGM, ESIEE Paris, Université Gustave-Eiffel, Noisy-le-Grand, France
mawloud.omar@univ-eiffel.fr

Abstract. Wireless sensor networks and Internet of Things (IoT) are part of dynamic networks as new nodes can join while existing members can leave the system at any time. These networks mainly suffer from severe resource constraints like energy, storage and computation, which makes securing communications between nodes a real challenge. Several key establishment protocols have been proposed in the literature. Some of them are based on symmetric polynomials. However, the latter solutions have some limitations, such as the resilience to node capture attacks as well as the storage and computation overheads that are high for constrained nodes. In this paper, we propose a lightweight polynomial-based key management scheme for dynamic networks. The proposed scheme allows nodes to be able to establish secure communications between them, and ensures dynamism by supporting node addition and deletion after the setup phase. It also resists to node capture attack. The performance evaluation shows that our scheme reduces both the storage and computation overheads when compared to other related polynomial-based protocols.

Keywords: Polynomial · Key management · Lightweight

1 Introduction

A dynamic network can be defined as a distributed system whose topology changes continuously over time, where new nodes join the network while existing members leave it at any time. Ad hoc networks, wireless sensor networks and the Internet of Things (IoT) are some examples of dynamic systems since they allow

---

Supported by General Directorate for Scientific Research and Technological Development, Ministry of Higher Education and Scientific Research (DGRSDT), Algeria.

S. Bouzefrane et al. (Eds.): MSPN 2020, LNCS 12605, pp. 110–122, 2021.
https://doi.org/10.1007/978-3-030-67550-9_8

addition and removal of nodes after the deployment phase. These networks are widely used in many application domains such as military, patient and environmental monitoring, agriculture, smart cities and smart homes, etc. The nodes mainly share a wireless communication channel through which they exchange messages. However, this medium is vulnerable to various types of attacks if it is not secured. Securing such a channel should involve the use of cryptographic keys. However, managing these keys is a complex process, due to essentially high resource constraints of some nodes.

Several key predistribution approaches have been proposed in the literature for dynamic networks, especially for wireless sensor networks. Some of them rely on the use of polynomials [1–5], which allows two nodes to establish a pairwise key between them. In these schemes, nodes generally share a common symmetric t-degree polynomial so that any pair of nodes is able to compute the same pairwise key by evaluating the polynomial using as input the identifier of the other node. For instance, Blundo et al. [1] introduced a multi-variate t-degree polynomial-based group key predistribution scheme.

The main drawback of these polynomial-based schemes is that when an adversary physically captures a node, he or she may be able to access its memory and therefore get the shared polynomial. As a result, the adversary could calculate the pairwise key between any pair of nodes by evaluating the polynomial at the identifiers of those nodes. In other words, compromising one node could also affect other communication links between non-captured nodes.

In this paper, we propose a lightweight polynomial-based key management scheme for dynamic constrained networks. Our scheme mainly aims to address the aforementioned limitations of existing polynomial-based schemes. In fact, instead of using the identical polynomial to compute all the secret keys, nodes do not share the same polynomial in our scheme. Accordingly, compromising a node affects the links it shares with its neighbors, but has a little influence on those between non-compromised nodes. In addition, the proposed scheme significantly reduces the storage and computation overheads on the constrained node side. The main features of the proposed scheme are highlighted below:

- Our solution is more resistant to node capture attacks since nodes do not share the same polynomial. In fact, compromising a node has a little influence on the links between two non-captured nodes;
- It reduces the memory overhead. In fact, each node has to store $(d + 1)$ coefficients of a bivariate polynomial instead of $(t + 1)$ shares, where d is the number of neighbors;
- It reduces the computation cost. Indeed, to be able to establish a pairwise key, one node must evaluate only two adequate terms of its polynomial, rather than all the terms of a t-degree polynomial as in the other schemes;
- It enables dynamism following the addition and deletion of nodes. In other words, nodes can join or leave the network at any time. These operations have only impact on the nodes that are in the neighborhood.

The rest of this paper is organized as follows. Section 2 discusses some existing polynomial-based key establishment solutions. Our proposed polynomial-based key management scheme is described in detail in Sect. 3. Its performance evaluation is presented in Sect. 4. Section 5 concludes this paper and gives some future research directions.

2   Related Work

Various mathematical key predistribution schemes have been proposed in the literature for wireless sensor networks. Some schemes make use of matrices [10–12] while others rely on polynomials [1–5]. In this section, we discuss some schemes belonging to the latter category.

Blundo et al. [1] proposed a non-interactive multi-variate t-degree polynomial-based group key predistribution scheme. This scheme uses symmetric polynomial of m variables, where m is the group size. When the group has only two members ($m = 2$), this scheme degenerates into a symmetric bivariate polynomial-based scheme. To obtain the same pairwise key, a pair of nodes evaluates the polynomial at the identifier of the other. This scheme is t-secure and no communication is required between nodes during the key establishment process. However, each node must store $(t + 1)^{(m-1)}$ coefficients, and evaluate all the polynomial's terms when computing a secret key. In addition, compromising more than t nodes leads to the compromise of the entire network.

To improve the resilience to node capture attacks, D. Liu et al. [2] proposed a key predistribution framework based on a pool of polynomials. In this scheme, a set of random bivariate polynomials is used instead of a single polynomial. A subset of polynomials' shares is assigned to each sensor. A pair of nodes establishes a direct key if they have a common polynomial shares. Otherwise, they compute a path key by relying on intermediate nodes. This scheme is more resilient to compromising attacks. However, the storage overhead is increased when compared to the previous scheme.

A. Fanian, et al. [3] introduced a key establishment protocol, called SKEP, based on symmetric t-degree $(k+1)$-variate polynomials, where k is a credential. In their scheme, the network is first divided into separate virtual hexagonal cells. Then, each cell receives a group of sensors, which share the same symmetric t-degree bivariate polynomial. Two members of the same cell establish a direct key, while a pair of sensors from different groups computes an indirect key. In SKEP, each sensor stores the polynomial shares of two distinct t-degree polynomials. This scheme is scalable and resilient to node capture attack. However, the storage overhead remains high when compared to some other related protocols.

J. Zhang et al. [4] proposed a key predistribution scheme for wireless sensor networks that combines both random and polynomial-based key predistribution schemes. Each sensor is assigned with g t-degree polynomials picked from a pool of m elements along with their identifiers. The nodes are also given s keys with their identifiers. Two neighbors can compute a pairwise key if they share the same polynomial or key, or at least a key of one node is derived from the polynomial shares of the other node. This scheme has better resilience to node capture attacks. However, it introduces some additional storage and computation overheads.

A polynomial-based session key establishment scheme in dynamic groups, called NISKC, is presented by V. Kumar et al. in [5]. This scheme uses a multivariate t-degree polynomial, where the number of variables is equal to the group size m. So, each node can compute the session key by putting its private value in the polynomial. This scheme is efficient in terms of communication overhead, and allows node addition and deletion after the deployment phase. However, the storage and the computation costs are still high.

Authors in [6] were the first to introduce a non-interactive group key distribution scheme with revocation that has the self-healing property. The key idea is that only active members have the ability to recover the missed session keys by combining the key shares received before and after the lost. These key shares are complementary to each other. The scheme allows users to be able to establish a group key in an unreliable environment. In addition, it enables users to join or leave the group as well. However, this scheme requires high storage and communication overheads. Moreover, Blundo et al. in [7] presented an attack against the first construction of this scheme.

Another efficient session key distribution scheme for unreliable wireless sensor networks was proposed in [8]. The scheme has also the self-healing and revocation features as the previous one. Each user stores a t-degree polynomial with the initial or current session identifier. From a broadcast message, each non-revoked user is able to compute the current session key, which is in turn used to recover the self-healing keys. The scheme reduces both the storage and the communication overheads. Moreover, authors mentioned that their scheme also ensures forward and backward secrecy since users that join the network at a subsequent session ignore the initial session identifier. However, authors in [9] showed that this scheme does not really resist against forward and backward attacks.

Note that in most existing polynomial-based key establishment protocols, nodes generally share the same t-degree polynomial. Consequently, if more than t nodes are captured, the whole network will be compromised. Moreover, the storage and computation overheads are considerable for constrained nodes. In this paper, we propose a polynomial-based scheme where nodes do not necessarily share the same polynomial, which makes it more resilient to node capture attacks and efficient in terms of storage and computation overheads.

3   ELiPKMS: The Proposed Scheme

In this section, we present our proposed scheme, called ELiPKMS (Efficient and Lightweight Polynomial-based Key Management Scheme), which allows nodes to establish secure links in their neighborhood. ELiPKMS consists of six phases, namely the setup, neighbor discovery, key generation, node addition, node deletion and key refresh phases, which are described in detail in the following. The notation used in this paper is summarized in Table 1.

3.1 Setup

The trusted server generates a bivariate symmetric $2n$-degree polynomial over the finite field $F(q)$, where n represents the number of nodes in the network during the deployment phase. The form of the obtained polynomial, let's say $f(x,y) = \sum_{i=1}^{n} a_i x^i y^i$, and the initial network key K_n are then preloaded into the memory of each node before its deployment.

Table 1. Notation

Notation	Description
x, y	Variables of the polynomial
i, j	Identifiers of nodes i and j
a_i	Secret value of node i (coefficient of the polynomial)
$F(q)$	Finite or Galois field of q elements
K_n	Network key
K_{ij}	Pairwise key shared between nodes i and j
t_i	Neighbor table of the node i
d_i	Degree of the polynomial of the node i
d	Degree of the node (number of neighbors)

3.2 Neighbor Discovery

Once the deployment is done, each node proceeds to discover other nodes that are within its communication range. To do that, each node i generates a random secret value, denoted a_i, and then broadcasts a *Hello* message encrypted with the initial network key K_n. This message contains the sender's identifier and its generated secret value. Each node i holds a neighbor table t_i wherein it stores its identifier along with its secret value as well as those received from its adjacent nodes (j, a_j), with $j \in t_i$. At the end of this discovery phase, each node i orders its neighbor table in ascending order of the identifiers. Afterwards, it uses the polynomial's form to generate its own bivariate d_i-degree polynomial according to its direct neighbors, where $d_i = 2 * Max(j)$, with $j \in t_i$, as described in the equation Eq. 1.

$$f_i(x,y) = \sum a_j x^j y^j, \quad with \quad j \in t_i. \tag{1}$$

where a_j is the secret value of the node j.

3.3 Key Establishment

Two kinds of keys are used: direct and indirect keys that are established as in the following.

Direct Key. When a pair of neighbors i and j want to securely communicate with each other, they first compute a common pairwise key K_{ij} by evaluating only the two appropriate terms of their respective polynomials as follows: $f_i(i,j) = a_i i^i j^i + a_j i^j j^j$ and $f_j(j,i) = a_j j^j i^j + a_i j^i i^i$, where a_i and a_j are the secret values of the nodes i and j respectively. As a result, both nodes obtain the same symmetric secret key as shown in Eq. 2.

$$K_{ij} = f_i(i,j) = f_j(j,i) = K_{ji} \tag{2}$$

Path (Indirect) Key. A node i that needs to communicate in a secure way with a non-neighbor node j, tries to establish a key path via intermediate nodes. To do so, the node i requests assistance from its direct neighbors by sending them a request encrypted with the appropriate direct keys. This request contains the identifier of the sender i as well as its secret value a_i and the identifier of the other node j. A neighbor k that receives such a request, decrypts it with the adequate direct key K_{ki}, and then checks its neighbor table to determine whether or not the node j belongs to its neighbors. If the verification is not successful, the message will simply be ignored. Otherwise, the intermediate node checks the freshness of that message by comparing the received secret value a_i with the one already stored in its neighbor table. If the verification fails, the node discards the message. Otherwise, the intermediate node computes a path key K_{ij} for both nodes i and j in the same way as it is performed between two neighbors by evaluating the corresponding terms of its polynomial. After that, this key is sent back to each of the two nodes within a response message encrypted with the appropriate pairwise keys. Upon receiving the previous message from the intermediate node, both nodes i and j decrypt it and store the path key K_{ij}. The latter nodes are then able to use this indirect key in order to establish secure communication between them.

Example. Let's consider a network initially deployed with three nodes, as shown in Fig. 1.

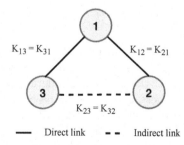

Fig. 1. Network with three nodes

After deployment, the nodes 1, 2 and 3 generate, for instance, the secret values $a_1 = 11$, $a_2 = 22$ and $a_3 = 33$ respectively. At the end of the discovery phase, each node generates its own polynomial as follows:

As the node 1 has two neighbors, hence its polynomial contains three terms:
$f_1(x,y) = a_1 x^1 y^1 + a_2 x^2 y^2 + a_3 x^3 y^3$.
As the degree of the node 2 is equal to one, hence its polynomial has two terms:
$f_2(x,y) = a_1 x^1 y^1 + a_2 x^2 y^2$.
The degree of the node 3 is also equal to one, hence its polynomial has two terms too:
$f_3(x,y) = a_1 x^1 y^1 + a_3 x^3 y^3$.

The nodes 1 and 2 compute the direct pairwise key by evaluating the appropriate two terms of their polynomials as follows:

Node 1 computes the key $K_{12} = f_1(1,2) = a_1 x^1 y^1 + a_2 x^2 y^2 = 11 * 1^1 * 2^1 + 22 * 1^2 * 2^2 = 110$.
Node 2 computes the key $K_{21} = f_2(2,1) = a_2 x^2 y^2 + a_1 x^1 y^1 = 22 * 2^2 * 1^2 + 11 * 2^1 * 1^1 = 110$.

In the same way, both nodes 1 and 3 compute their common direct key.

Node 1 computes the key $K_{13} = f_1(1,3) = a_1 x^1 y^1 + a_3 x^3 y^3 = 11 * 1^1 * 3^1 + 33 * 1^3 * 3^3 = 924$.
Node 3 computes the key $K_{31} = f_3(3,1) = a_3 x^3 y^3 + a_1 x^1 y^1 = 33 * 3^3 * 1^3 + 11 * 3^1 * 1^1 = 924$.

Finally, each pair of neighbors obtains the same direct pairwise key. As a result, they establish a secure channel and can communicate securely. Furthermore, when the node 2 needs to communicate securely with the node 3 that is not inside of its radio range, it solicits the help of the intermediate node 1. The latter computes for them a path key as follows:
$K_{23} = f_1(2,3) = a_2 x^2 y^2 + a_3 x^3 y^3 = 22 * 2^2 * 3^2 + 33 * 2^3 * 3^3 = 7920$.

3.4   Node Addition

Before deployment, a new node has to request the trusted server to obtain the present network key K_n as well as the current polynomial's form used by the network members. After that, the new node generates a secret value, let's say a_n, and broadcasts a *Join* message that contains especially its identifier with that secret value. The *Join* message is encrypted using the network key K_n. A neighbor that receives this message uses the network key to decrypt it and updates its neighbor table by inserting the identifier and the secret value of the new node. Afterwards, it adds to its polynomial a term that corresponds to that new node, and responds back with an acknowledgment *Ack* message, which contains its identifier along with its secret value, let's say a_i. When receiving the *Ack* messages, the new node updates its neighbor table in turn, and constructs its polynomial. Finally, both the current member and the new node are able to compute a common key by evaluating the adequate two terms of their polynomials as follows: $k_{in} = f_i(i, n) = f_n(n, i) = a_i x^i y^i + a_n x^n y^n = a_n x^n y^n + a_i x^i y^i$.

It is important to note that at each node addition, the polynomials of all neighbors of the new node are increased by one term.

Example. Let's assume that the new node 4 joins the network as depicted in Fig. 2. During the setup phase, the node 4 is preloaded with the network key K_n and the form of the current polynomial before its deployment in the area of interest. Just after deploying it, that node generates a secret, let's say $a_4 = 44$, then broadcasts in its neighborhood a *Join* message encrypted with the network key. The nodes 1 and 2 are neighbors of the node 4, so they receive that message. These nodes will then decrypt it and update their neighbor table by adding the ID and secret value of the new node 4. After that, they respond back with an *Ack* message containing their IDs along with their generated secret values. Upon receiving the *Ack* messages, the node 4 decrypts them and adds the IDs as well as these secrets a_1 and a_2 to its neighbor table.

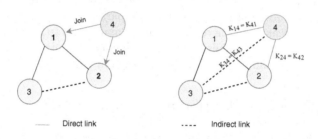

Fig. 2. Node addition

The nodes 1 and 4 respectively and separately compute their direct pairwise key as follows:

$K_{14} = f_1(1, 4) = a_1 1^1 4^1 + a_4 1^4 4^4 = 11 * 1 * 4 + 44 * 1 * 256 = 11308.$
$K_{41} = f_4(4, 1) = a_4 4^4 1^4 + a_1 4^1 1^1 = 44 * 256 * 1 + 11 * 4 * 1 = 11308.$

Note that nodes 1 and 4 obtain the same pairwise key: $K_{14} = K_{41}$.
The nodes 2 and 4 respectively and separately compute their direct pairwise key as follows:

$K_{24} = f_2(2, 4) = a_2 2^2 4^2 + a_4 2^4 4^4 = 22 * 4 * 16 + 44 * 16 * 256 = 181632.$
$K_{42} = f_4(4, 2) = a_4 4^4 2^4 + a_2 4^2 2^2 = 44 * 256 * 16 + 22 * 16 * 4 = 181632.$

Note that nodes 2 and 4 also get the same direct pairwise key: $K_{24} = K_{42}$.
Moreover, the nodes 3 and 4 are also able to secure their communications by using the path key K_{34}, which can be computed by the intermediate node 1.

3.5 Node Deletion

When a node is compromised or leaves the network with its willingness, all its neighboring nodes carry out the following operations:

- Update their neighbor tables by removing the entry corresponding to the leaving node;
- Delete the polynomial's term of that node;
- Erase the pairwise key they share with that node.

It is important to notice that at each node deletion, the polynomials of all nodes adjacent to the outgoing node, are decreased by one term.

3.6 Key Refresh

To counter some kinds of security attacks, the network key and the established pairwise keys must be periodically refreshed. To do so, the server node regularly generates a new network key K'_n, and chooses a completely different symmetric polynomial's form. The latter are then transmitted to the network members in a secure way. Upon receiving these new security parameters, all members replace the old network key and use the received polynomial's form to generate their new symmetric bivariate polynomials. After that, they use the obtained polynomials to compute the new pairwise keys and erase the old keys afterwards.

4 Performance Evaluation and Comparison

To evaluate the performance of the proposed scheme, we focus primarily on efficiency metrics such as the storage and computation overheads. We compare ELiPKMS with the polynomial-based protocols [3,4], and [5] described in Sect. 2. The simulations are developed using MATLAB environment [14]. The nodes are randomly deployed in a square area of 100 m^2. The network size ranges from 10 to 100 nodes. Each node is equipped with a communication radio with a range equal to 10 m. We assume that the number of polynomials picked from the polynomial pool is equal to one ($g = 1$) in [4], while the t-degree polynomial used in [5] is bivariate. Note that these two last parameters are set to their minimum values. The simulation parameters are summarized in Table 2.

4.1 Storage Overhead

In the simulations, we are interested in the storage space occupied by both polynomials shares and their identifiers (IDs). We assume that these coefficients and IDs are chosen from two pools of 100 elements each. Moreover, the polynomial degree is set to 10 in the other schemes. Figure 3 shows the storage overhead in function of the network size. We can clearly see that the memory space required to store polynomials' shares and IDs increases with increasing the number of

Table 2. Simulation parameters

Parameter	Value
Network area	100 m × 100 m
Radio range	10 m
Network size	varies from 10 to 100 nodes
$F(q)$, $F(q')$	Finite fields of 100 elements each
Polynomials' degree	$t = 10$
Number of selected polynomials	$g = 1$
Number of polynomials' variables	$m = 2$

nodes in the network. However, ELiPKMS requires less storage cost when compared to the other schemes. This is because in ELiPKMS, each node needs to store $(d + 1)$ polynomial's coefficients, whereas in the other schemes, each node must save at least $(t + 1)$ polynomial's shares. Accordingly, the total storage space is considerably reduced in our scheme.

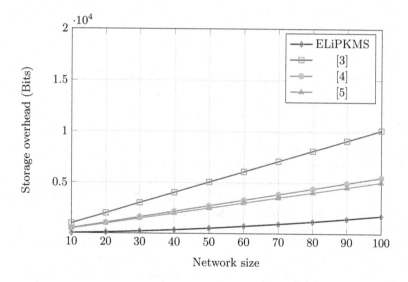

Fig. 3. Storage overhead vs. network size (t = 10, g = 1)

4.2   Computation Overhead

In the experiments, we focused on the computation cost in terms of the number of polynomials' terms evaluated when each node establishes one pairwise key. Figure 4 illustrates the computation overhead depending on the network size. From the figure, we note that ELiPKMS largely outperforms the other schemes.

This is due to the fact that unlike the most existing polynomial-based schemes where a node evaluates all the terms of the same t-degree polynomial in order to compute one pairwise key, in our scheme, each node needs to evaluate only two adequate terms of its polynomial. In this way, ELiPKMS significantly reduces the computation cost at the constrained node side.

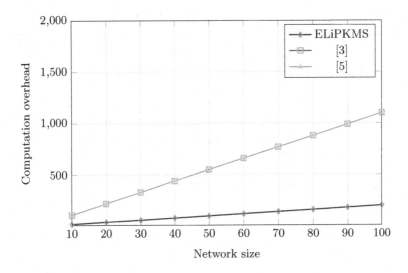

Fig. 4. Computation overhead vs. network size ($t = 10$, $m = 2$)

4.3 Comparison

A fair comparison between our scheme and the related works discussed in Sect. 2 is shown in Table 3. This comparison is made according to the storage and computation overheads. As mentioned before, the storage cost is estimated based on the memory space occupied by polynomials' coefficients and identifications, while the computation overhead is related to the number of polynomials' terms evaluated during the pairwise key establishment. According to [13], each node has to store $(t + 1)^{(m-1)}$ coefficients for a t-degree polynomial of m variables. We have assumed that the polynomial shares are chosen from the same finite field $F(q)$, and the identifications are selected from $F(q')$, with q and q' are two large numbers. The value s represents the number of communication sessions considered in [6].

Table 3. Comparison

Scheme	Storage	Computation
[1]	$(t+1)^{(m-1)} * log\ q$	$(t+1)^{(m-1)}$
[2]	$s'(t+1) * log\ q + s' * log\ q'$	$(t+1)$
[3]	$2(t+1) * log\ q$	$(t+1)$
[4]	$g(t+1) * log\ q + g * log\ q'$	$\leq (t+1)$
[5]	$(t+1)^{(m-1)} * log\ q$	$(t+1)^{(m-1)}$
[6]	$s * (t+1) * log\ q$	$(t+1)$
[8]	$(t+1) * log\ q$	$\geq (t+1)$
ELiPKMS	$(d+1) * log\ q$	2

5   Conclusion

In this paper, we have proposed an efficient and lightweight polynomial-based key management scheme in dynamic networks with high resource constraints. Compared to existing polynomial-based protocols, our proposed scheme ELiPKMS significantly reduces the amount of key material stored in the memory of each node as well as the computation overhead since the number of multiplications and additions operations required to generate a pairwise key is reduced.

As future work, we first intend to assess the energy consumption of the proposed scheme during communication and computation operations, and then expand the security analysis by including a formal verification using AVISPA tool [15], in order to check whether this scheme resists well to some known attacks and satisfies the secrecy, integrity and authentication properties.

References

1. Blundo, C., De Santis, A., Herzberg, A., Kutten, S., Vaccaro, U., Yung, M.: Perfectly-secure key distribution for dynamic conferences. In: Brickell, E.F. (ed.) CRYPTO 1992. LNCS, vol. 740, pp. 471–486. Springer, Heidelberg (1993). https://doi.org/10.1007/3-540-48071-4_33
2. Liu, D.: Establishing pairwise keys in distributed sensor networks. ACM Trans. Inf. Syst. Secur. (TISSEC) **8**, 41–77 (2005)
3. Fanian, A.: An efficient symmetric polynomial-based key establishment protocol for wireless sensor networks. ISeCure-ISC Int. J. Inf. Secur. **2**, 89–105 (2010)
4. Zhang, J.: Key establishment scheme for wireless sensor networks based on polynomial and random key predistribution scheme. Ad Hoc Netw. **71**, 68–77 (2018)
5. Kumar, V., Kumar, R., Pandey, S.K.: Polynomial based non-interactive session key computation protocol for secure communication in dynamic groups. Int. J. Inf. Technol. **12**(1), 283–288 (2018). https://doi.org/10.1007/s41870-018-0140-1
6. Staddon, J.: Self-healing key distribution with revocation. In: Proceedings 2002 IEEE Symposium on Security and Privacy, pp. 241–257. IEEE (2002)
7. Blundo, C.: Design of self-healing key distribution schemes. Des. Codes Crypt. **1**(32), 15–44 (2004)

8. Mukhopadhyay, S. : Improved self-healing key distribution with revocation in wireless sensor network. In: 2007 IEEE Wireless Communications and Networking Conference (2007)

9. Daza, V.: Flaws in some self-healing key distribution schemes with revocation. Inf. Process. Lett. **109**, 523–526 (2009)

10. Nafi, M.: Matrix-based key management scheme for IoT networks. Ad Hoc Netw. **97**, 102003 (2020)

11. Blom, R.: An optimal class of symmetric key generation systems. In: Beth, T., Cot, N., Ingemarsson, I. (eds.) EUROCRYPT 1984. LNCS, vol. 209, pp. 335–338. Springer, Heidelberg (1985). https://doi.org/10.1007/3-540-39757-4_22

12. Du, W.: A key management scheme for wireless sensor networks using deployment knowledge. In: IEEE INFOCOM 2004, vol. 1. IEEE (2004)

13. Harn, L.: Predistribution scheme for establishing group keys in wireless sensor networks. IEEE Sens. J. **15**(9), 5103–5108 (2015)

14. MathWorks. https://www.mathworks.com/. Accessed 20 Aug 2020

15. Armando, A., et al.: The AVISPA tool for the automated validation of internet security protocols and applications. In: Etessami, K., Rajamani, S.K. (eds.) CAV 2005. LNCS, vol. 3576, pp. 281–285. Springer, Heidelberg (2005). https://doi.org/10.1007/11513988_27

Parallel Applications Mapping onto Heterogeneous MPSoCs Interconnected Using Network on Chip

Dihia Belkacemi[1(✉)], Mehammed Daoui[1], and Samia Bouzefrane[2]

[1] Laboratoire de Recherche en Informatique, Université de Tizi-Ouzou,
Tizi Ouzou, Algeria
dihia.belkacemi@yahoo.fr
[2] CEDRIC Lab, CNAM, Paris, France
samia.bouzefrane@cnam.fr

Abstract. To meet the growing requirements of today's applications, multiprocessor architectures (MPSoCs) interconnected with a network on chip (NoC) are considered as a major solution for future powerful embedded systems. Mapping phase is one of the most critical challenge in designing these systems. It consists of assigning application' tasks on the target platform which can have a considerable influence on the performance of the final system. Due to the large solutions' research space generated by both the application complexity and the platforms, this mapping phase can no longer be done manually and hence it requires powerful exploration tools called DSE (Design Space Exploration Environment). This paper proposes a new tool for static mapping applications on NoC based on heterogeneous MPSoCs. This tool integrates several multiobjective optimization algorithms that can be specified in order to explore different solutions' spaces, mainly: exact method, metaheuristics (population-based metaheuristics and single solution-based ones) as well as hybrid ones; it offers different cost functions (defined using analytical or simulation models). The user can specify them or define others easily and it provides an easy way to evaluate the performance of the Pareto front returned by different algorithms using multiple quality indicators. We also present a series of experiments by considering several scenarios and give guidelines to designers on choosing the appropriate algorithm based on the characteristics of the mapping problem considered.

Keywords: Static mapping · Multiobjective optimization · Network on Chip (NoC) · Multi-processor System on Chip (MPSoCs)

1 Introduction

In order to meet today's applications requirements (e.g. multimedia, digital signal processing, image processing, etc.), MPSoCs are becoming increasingly popular solutions for future embedded systems [1]. These MPSoCs are classified

© Springer Nature Switzerland AG 2021
S. Bouzefrane et al. (Eds.): MSPN 2020, LNCS 12605, pp. 123–143, 2021.
https://doi.org/10.1007/978-3-030-67550-9_9

as homogeneous or heterogeneous. Several studies have shown that heterogeneous MPSoCs outperform their homogeneous counterparts [2,3]. Heterogeneous
MPSoCs are composed of PEs of different types such as General Purpose Processor (GPP), Application Specific Integrated Circuit (ASIC), Digital Signal Processor (DSP), hardware accelerators or IP blocks (e.g. video encoder), etc. The
distinct features of different processing elements (PEs) provide high performance
with less energy consumption. Typical examples of heterogeneous MPSoCs are
ST Nomadik for cellular phones [4], NVIDIA's Tegra designed for multimedia in
mobile phones [5], Samsung Exynos 5422 SoC [6], etc. P The growing complexity of heterogeneous MPSoCs requires efficient communication infrastructure.
Network on Chip (NoC) [7] is used as the communication infrastructure which
provides modularity and scalability unlike buses and point to point communication. A NoC consists of a set of processing elements (PEs), routers, links, and
network interfaces (NIs) as shown in Fig. 1. Each PE is connected to a router
and accesses to the network through NI. Routers are interconnected using a
set of links to form a given topology (e.g. 2D Mesh, 2D Torus, etc.). The processing elements (PEs) interconnected to the NoC exchange data in the form
of packets (set of flits). Routing and switching policies are used respectively to
determine the path and how the data is communicated between PEs (source and
destination). NoCs are also characterized by arbitration as well as flow control
techniques. Arbitration is used to solve contentions and flow control technique
defines how NoC resources are allocated to data.

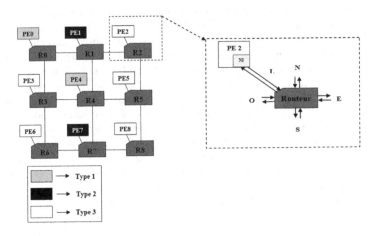

Fig. 1. Example of Heterogeneous MPSoC with three types of processors interconnected using 2D Mesh NoC Topology

One critical problem of heterogeneous MPSoCs interconnected using Network
on Chip is how to map an application on this platform which is a NP-hard [8]
problem. In addition, when solving the mapping problem, the designer is often
called to specify several objectives to be optimized simultaneously. These objectives are often conflicting (e.g. communication vs load, energy consumption vs

total execution time, etc.), so the goal is to find reliable trade-off mapping solutions which simultaneously optimize the different contradictory metrics (objectives) commonly called Pareto Optimal Solutions Set (i.e. Mapping problem is an instance of a multiobjective optimization problem MOP). To tackle all these challenges, designing tools that can automate this step is required. This paper presents a new tool for mapping applications on NoC based on heterogeneous MPSoCs. The work reported in this article extends our prior work [9] with the following contributions:

- In addition to the analytical models used to define the cost (or objective) functions, we propose a simulation model to take into account the dynamic aspect (like contentions) of the system during the mapping process.
- In order to enrich our mapping tool, we have added other metaheuristics like single-solution based metaheuristics (Archived Multiobjective Simulated Annealing (AMOSA) [10] and Parallel Multiobjective Tabu Search (PMOTS) [11]) and hybrid ones.
- We have implemented multiobjective exact method called Multiobjective Branch and Bound (MBB) [12] to check the efficiency of the metaheuristics presented in the tool in solving small mapping problem instances.

The remainder of this paper is organized as follows. Section 2 describes the multiobjective optimization principles. The related works are discussed in Sect. 3. In Sect. 4, the proposed exploration tool is presented. Experimental results are presented and discussed in Sect. 5. Sect. 6 concludes this paper.

2   Multiobjective Optimization

A multiobjective optimization problem (MOP) can be mathematically formulated as given by [22]:

$$
MOP = \begin{cases} \text{``}min\text{''}\, F(x) = (f_1(x), \ldots, f_n(x)) \\ x \in S \end{cases}
$$

where n $(n \geq 2)$ is the number of objectives, $x = (x_1, \ldots, x_k)$ is the vector representing the decision variables, and S represents the set of feasible solutions associated with equality and inequality constraints and explicit bounds. $F(x) = (f_1(x), \ldots, f_n(x))$ is the vector of objectives to be optimized. The objectives in MOP are often conflicting. Before defining a Pareto optimality, a partial order relation could be defined, known as dominance relation.

Definition 1. Pareto dominance *[22]. An objective vector $u = (u_1, \ldots, u_n)$ is said to dominate another vector $v = (v_1, \ldots, v_n)$, denoted as $u \prec v$, if and only if no component of v is smaller than the corresponding component of u and at least one component of u is strictly smaller, that is,*
$\forall i \in \{1, \ldots, n\}, u_i \leq v_i \text{ and } \exists i \in \{1, \ldots, n\} : u_i < v_i.$

Definition 2. *Pareto optimality* [22]. *A solution $x^* \in S$ is Pareto optimal if for every $x \in S$, $F(x)$ does not dominate $F(x^*)$, that is, $F(x) \not\prec F(x^*)$.*

Definition 3. *Pareto optimal set* [22]. *For a given $MOP(F, S)$, the Pareto optimal set is defined as $P^* = \{x \in S / \nexists x^* \in S, F(x^*) \prec F(x)\}$.*

Definition 4. *Pareto front* [22]. *For a given $MOP(F, S)$ and its Pareto optimal set P^*, the Pareto front is defined as $PF^* = \{F(x), x \in P^*\}$.*

3   Related Work

Several authors proposed to use multiobjective optimization algorithms to solve the mapping problem [13–21]. Ascia et al. [13] present an approach based on SPEA2 metaheuristic for exploring the mapping design space. Their aim is to obtain the Pareto mappings that maximize performance and minimize the amount of power consumption. Erbas et al. [14] give a comparative study between two metaheuristics NSGAII and SPEA2. Their aim is to optimize processing time, power consumption, and architecture cost. Zhou et al. [15] address the problem of topological mapping of Intellectual Properties (IPs) on the tile of a mesh-based NoC using NSGA metaheuristic while treating two conflicting objectives: minimizing the average hop and achieving the thermal balance. A multiobjective genetic algorithms MOGA to determine the Pareto-optimal configuration which optimizes average delay and routing robustness is presented in [16]. In [17], authors propose the use of multiobjective evolutionary algorithms (NSGAII and MicroGA) to minimize hardware area, execution time and the total power consumption. Wu et al. [18] propose a new mapping algorithm based on the Genetic Algorithm (GA) and the MAX-MIN Ant System Algorithm (MMAS) called GA-MMAS to optimize power consumption and NoC latency. He and Guo [19] use ACO to solve the mapping problem while optimizing communication power consumption and delay. Chatterjee et al. [20] propose a constructive heuristic method to solve the problem of mapping applications on a NoC (with a mesh topology). Their goal is to optimize the cost of network communications as well as the reliability of the system. Bruch et al. [21] present an optimization flow for mapping applications on a NoC in order to meet the time requirements and minimize the costs of using virtual channels. The approach used is based on the NSGAII algorithm. Authors in [18–20] used the aggregation approach (using a unified cost function) in order to take several objectives into account during the mapping. The disadvantage of their approach comes from the difficulty to adjust the weights which requires knowledge of the problem. Other works like [15,17] did not take into account the dynamic effects (i.e. contentions) of the NoC during mapping. An important limitation of these approaches is that only a few metaheuristics like NSGA [15], NSGAII [14,17,21], SPEA2 [13,14], MOGA [16], etc. are mainly explored. Most of the works take into account the two-dimensional optimization space (i.e. optimize only two cost functions), e.g. performance and energy consumption in [13], minimize the average number of hops and achieves a thermal balance [15], etc.

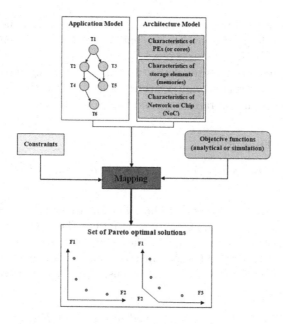

Fig. 2. Inputs and Outputs of the proposed mapping tool

4 Description of the Proposed Tool

Figure 2 gives an overview of the proposed mapping tool. This tool has as inputs (1) the application model represented as an annotated task graph, (2) the high level architecture model, (3) the objective functions defined using analytical or simulation models and (4) the architecture and application constraints. A set of multiobjective optimization algorithms is used to explore the mapping space and to find a set of Pareto optimal solutions.

4.1 Application Model

The application model is represented in the form of a Directed Acyclic Graph (DAG), denoted $G(V, E)$. The set of nodes $V = \{T_0, T_1, \ldots, T_n\}$ represents the application's tasks and E is a set of edges e_i. Each edge e_i in E designates the precedence relation between two tasks connected by e_i labeled with $volume(e_i)$ representing the amount of data exchanged between these tasks. Each task T_i is annotated with $Load(T_i)$ which is the number of instructions of task T_i. Two vectors Ei and Ci contain respectively the energy consumption and execution time of task T_i on each type of processing element. A task T_i may have a deadline $d(T_i)$.

4.2 Architecture Model

The architecture model includes the high level description of the target platform that will run the application. The informations considered in our case are:

- The characteristics of the processors (e.g. number, type, frequency, etc.)
- The characteristics of the storage elements (e.g. maximum memory capacity, etc.) and
- NoC features including: router characteristics (e.g. routing algorithm, switching modes, flow control techniques, arbitration, etc.); the characteristics of the links (e.g. direction, link rate, etc.) and the NoC's topology.

4.3   Objective Functions

We have defined objective functions using two models: analytical and simulation.

Analytical Model. It consists in finding mathematical equations used to evaluate a solution of a given mapping. This model has the advantage of being less expensive in terms of execution time at the expense of the level of precision. In this section, cost functions which measures the quality of a given mapping using analytical model is presented. In the rest of this paper, we use a decision variable $x_{i,j}$ which is defined as follows:

$$x_{ij} = \begin{cases} 1 \text{ if } T_i \text{ is assigned to processor } PE_j \\ 0 \text{ otherwise} \end{cases}$$

Load Balancing. This cost function gives the load balancing between the different PEs for a given mapping, such that all the processing elements in the system are equally loaded (avoiding task concentration in just some processors). This cost function is defined as follows:

$$\sum_{j=0}^{P-1} abs \left(\frac{load(PE_j)}{f(PE_j)} - M \right) \tag{1}$$

where $load(PE_j)$ represents the workload of the processor PE_j expressed as the sum of instructions of tasks that run on it.

$$load(PE_j) = \sum_{T_i \in V} x_{ij} \times load(T_i) \tag{2}$$

M represents the average load.

$$M = \frac{\sum_{j=0}^{P-1} load(PE_j)}{\sum_{j=0}^{P-1} f(PE_j)} \tag{3}$$

$f(PE_j)$ represents the frequency of the processor PE_j and P represents the number of PEs.

Communication. This cost function gives the total amount of communication between all the PEs.

$$Commcost = \sum_{e_i \in E} volume(e_i) \times Distance[PE(Src(e_i)), PE(Snk(e_i))] \quad (4)$$

where E is the set of edges in the application task graph, $volume(e_i)$ is the amount of data exchanged by the tasks connected by the edge e_i. $Src(e_i)$ and Snk (e_i) represent respectively the source and the sink tasks of the edge e_i. $PE(T_i)$ gives the PE on which the task T_i is mapped. $Distance(PE_1, PE_2)$ gives the distance (the hop count number) between PE_1 and PE_2.

Energy Consumption. This cost function estimates the total energy consumption of the system under consideration as follows:

$$E_{total} = E_p + E_{comm} \quad (5)$$

where E_p is the processing energy and E_{comm} is the communication energy. Let E_{ij} be the energy needed to execute the task T_i on a processor PE_j. The processing energy can be computed as follows:

$$Ep = \sum_{i=0}^{NBT-1} \sum_{j=0}^{P-1} x_{ij} \times E_{ij} \quad (6)$$

where P represents the number of processors (PEs) and NBT represents number of tasks. The communication energy is estimated with the same model as the one given in [23]:

$$E_{bit} = E_{S_{bit}} + E_{L_{bit}} \quad (7)$$

where $E_{S_{bit}}$ and $E_{L_{bit}}$ represent respectively the energy consumed on the switch and on the output link of the router. By using the preceding equation, the average energy consumption for sending one bit of data from PE_i to PE_j can be computed as follows:

$$E_{bit}^{i,j} = (nhops + 1) \times E_{S_{bit}} + nhops \times E_{L_{bit}} + 2 \times E_{local} \quad (8)$$

where $nhops$ is the hop count number between routers and E_{local} represents the energy consumed by the link between the router and PEs. We can determine the total communication energy as follows:

$$E_{comm} = \sum_{e_i \in E} volume(e_i) \times E_{bit}^{PE(src(e_i)), PE(snk(e_i))} \quad (9)$$

where $src(e_i)$ and $snk(e_i)$ represent respectively the source and sink tasks of the edge e_i and $PE(T_i)$ gives the PE on which the task T_i is mapped. $volume(e_i)$ is the amount of data exchanged by the tasks connected by the edge e_i. Note that this model does not consider the energy consumed by buffers in presence of contentions. For this purpose, the designer can specify the simulation model presented below (Sect. 4.3).

Overall Completion Time (Schedule Length). To define the total execution time of an application, we have defined two attributes $ST(T_i, PE_j)$ and $FT(T_i, PE_j)$ which represent respectively the Start Time and the Finish Time of the task T_i on the processor PE_j. The values of ST and FT are calculated as follows:

$$ST(T_i, PE_j) = \begin{cases} max(0, FT(T_j, PE_j)), \text{ if } pred(T_i) = 0 \\ \\ max(FT(T_j, PE_j), max_{T_k \in pred(T_i)}(FT(T_k, PE_k) + Tcomm_{ki})), \text{else} \end{cases}$$

$$FT(T_i, PE_j) = ST(T_i, PE_j) + C_{ij} \tag{10}$$

where $pred(T_i)$ is the set of the predecessors of T_i, $FT(T_j, PE_j)$ represents the end time of the last task executed on the same processor PE_j where T_i is mapped. $FT(T_k, PE_k)$ is the end time of the task T_k, where $T_k \in pred(T_i)$. $Tcomm_{ki}$ is the communication time between two tasks T_k and T_i. Eq. (10) gives the end time of the execution of the task T_i. C_{ij} represents the execution time of the task T_i on the processor PE_j. Once all tasks are mapped, the total execution time of the application T_{total} is given by Eq. (11) as follows:

$$T_{total} = \max_{T_i \in V} FT(T_i) \tag{11}$$

As for energy model, this model does not take contentions into account.

Simulation Model. In addition to the analytical model, to compute cost functions, a discrete event-based simulation model has been developed. The advantage of this model over analytical one is that it takes into account the waiting time caused by simultaneous accesses to shared resources (e.g. router output ports). As previously described in [24], the proposed model is composed of an event list ($List_{event}$) to store the system events in a chronological order. The simulation consists of extracting and processing the events one by one until the event list becomes empty (i.e. application's tasks are completed) (see Algorithm 2). Each event occurs at a particular instant of time and generates other events that will be inserted into the event list using Schedule() method. Note that the simulation clock ($current_{Time}$) is advanced to the time of the next event. The *peek*() method retrieves the first item in the list, the retrieved item is not deleted and the *getWhen*() method gives the time when the event occurred. In this work, according to the assumed architecture model, the following events have been considered:

– Event 1. Execute_Task (T_i, PE_j): the simulation starts by executing this first event where the ready tasks of each processor ($R_{list}(PE_j)$) can start their execution if the processor to which they are assigned is free as given by Algorithm 1. $FT(T_k, PE_j)$ is the finish time of the last task running on the same processor PE_j where T_i is mapped and *delta* is the waiting time required to release the processor PE_j so that the task T_i can start its execution on it.

Algorithm 1. $Execute\_Task(T_i, PE_j)$

---

if $(PE_j.state = free)$ then
   $ST(T_i, PE_j) = currentTime$
   $T_i.state = ASSIGNED$
   $PE_j.state = busy$
   $FT(T_i, PE_j) = ST(T_i, PE_j) + C_{ij}$
   $Schedule(Generate\_Packets, FT(T_i, PE_j))$
   $R_{list}(PE_j).remove(T_i)$
else
   delta= $FT(T_k, PE_j) - currentTime$
   $Schedule(Execute\_Task(T_i, PE_j), currentTime+$delta$)$
end if

- Event 2. Generate_Packets: once a given task with successors completes its execution, this second event occurs. It consists of generating packets for each communication. These packets are stored at the network interface's buffer. Each packet contains a set of flits mainly: the header, the payload and the tail.
- Event 3. Transfer_Flits (PE To Router): packet's flits will be sent flit by flit from the processor to the router according to the flow control technique assumed.
- Event 4. Flit_ArrivesAtInputBuffer (Router): after crossing the link between the source processor and router, the flit arrives at input buffer of this router.
- Event 5. Apply_Routing: as soon as a header flit arrives at the router's input buffer, the next hop is calculated according to the assumed routing protocol.
- Event 6. Apply_Arbitration: this event occurs when several packets request the same output port. In this case, the arbitration policy is applied to select the winner packet.
- Event 7. Traverse_Router: the winner packet sends its flits one by one through the router (crossbar) if there is enough space in its output buffer.
- Event 8. Flit_ArrivesAtOutputBuffer (Router): after crossing the router's crossbar, flit arrives at the router's output buffer. If the entire packet has arrived (i.e. flit is queue), a new arbitration for this output buffer can start.
- Event 9. Traverse_Link (Router-Router): according to the flow control technique considered, flits are transmitted between two neighboring routers.
- Event 10. Transfer Flits (Router-Processor): this event occurs if the packet's final destination corresponds to the router's local port.
- Event 11. Flit_ArrivesAtInputBuffer (NI): at the end, the flit arrives at the network interface of the destination processor, where a phase of packet arrival control (flits) and initial message formation will take place.

Overall Completion Time Using Simulation Model: the total execution time of a given application corresponds to the time elapsed between the execution of the first event and the execution of the last event given by T_{total} (see the Algorithm 2).

Algorithm 2. proposed simulation model

$List_{event}$: is the list of events considered
NB_{TT}: is the number of completed tasks initialized to 0
NB_{TTotal}: is the total number of tasks in a given application
$current_{Time}$: is the current time initialized to 0

 Determine the $R_{list}(PE_j)$ (See Algorithm 3)
 for each processor PE_j **do**
  if $R_{list}(PE_j)$ is not empty **then**
   $T_i = R_{list}(PE_j).peek()$
   $Schedule(Execute\_Task(T_i, PE_j), currentTime)$
  end if
 end for
 while $(NB_{TT} < NB_{TTotal})$ **do**
  while $(List_{event}$ is not empty) **do**
   $event = List_{event}.peek()$
   if $(event.getWhen() > currentTime)$ **then**
    $next_{time} = event.getWhen()$
    $break$
   end if
   $event.run()$
   $List_{event}.remove(event)$
  end while
  $currentTime = next_{time}$
 end while
 $T_{total} = currentTime$

Algorithm 3. Determine the $R_{list}(PE_j)$

T_{list} : is a list containing the application's tasks ordered with a given scheduling policy

 for each task $T_i \in T_{list}$ **do**
  $T_i.state = INIT$
  if $(nb(T_i.pred()) = 0$ and $x_{i,j} = 1)$ **then**
   $R_{list}(PE_j).add(T_i)$
   $T_i.state = READY$
  end if
 end for

Energy Consumption Using Simulation Model: unlike the analytical model given above, this model takes into account routing, arbitration and buffer's energies when computing communication energy E_{comm}. It should be noted that this value increases proportionally with the waiting time generated during contentions.

4.4   Application and Architecture Constraints

The proposed tool offers a very efficient mechanism to associate a set of constraints with each solution. The following constraints can be specified by the designer:

Task Assignment. Each task is assigned to exactly one processor, i.e:

$$\sum_{j=0}^{P-1} x_{ij} = 1, \forall i \in [0, NBT - 1] \tag{12}$$

where P is the number of processors (PEs) and NBT is the number of tasks.

Deadline Constraint. We can set a deadline for each task or application. In these two cases their finish time should be less than their deadline.

Pre-assignment. In some cases, one can predefine a tasks assignment on specific processors (like dedicated accelerators) for better performance purposes.

4.5   Mapping Problem

As mentioned above, the mapping problem involves optimization of several objectives (often conflicting) simultaneously. So our goal is to find the Pareto optimal mapping solutions set. For this purpose, in addition to multiobjective optimization algorithms included in jMetal framework [25] which we have adapted to solve mapping problem in our previous work [9], we have added the following multiobjective algorithms:

– AMOSA [10]: is a multiobjective version of Simulated Annealing (SA). Its principal features are: (1) It integrates an archive to store non-dominated solutions found during the search. (2) The archived solutions are also used to determine the probability of acceptance of a new solution (active elitism). The size of the archive is kept limited. (3) AMOSA uses the concept of amount of domination in the calculation of the probability of acceptance of a degrading solution.
– PMOTS [11]: is a multiobjective version of Tabu Search TS, called PMOTS, which means "Parallel-MultiObjective Tabu Search". The algorithm exploits K parallel search trajectories. A tabu list is assigned to each search path. This list is used to prevent cycles and to force the acceptance of degrading solutions (dominated solutions), in order to direct the search to new regions not yet visited. The non-dominated solutions found during the search will be saved in a list. This list will contain the final non-dominated solutions (the optimal Pareto front).

- MBB [12]: is a multiobjective version of Branch & Bound based on Pareto's dominance. The search space is explored by dynamically building a tree whose root node represents the problem being solved and its whole associated search space. The leaf nodes are the potential solutions and the internal nodes are subproblems of the total solution space. The size of the subproblems is increasingly reduced as one approaches the leaves. The construction of such a tree and its exploration are performed using two main operators: branching and pruning [22].
- Hybrid metaheuristics: we have also combined metaheuristics which gives new ones called hybrid metaheuristics. For example, instead of initializing the AMOSA's archive or PMOTS's parallel search randomly, we have used the solutions returned by population-based metaheuristics offered by our tool.

Solving Mapping Problem Using AMOSA [10] **and PMOTS** [11]. To apply these algorithms to the mapping problem, a solution representation and a corresponding neighborhood move operator are to be specified.

- Solution Representation: the potential solution (point) in AMOSA and PMOTS algorithm is like the chromosome representation given in [9].
- Neighborhood Move Operator: all mutations' type provided by jMetal framework [25] can be specified as neighborhood move operator for AMOSA and PMOTS algorithms. These operators have been adapted to solve the mapping problem in [9].

Solving Mapping Problem Using MBB [12]. In this paper, we have used an exact method to check the efficiency of the metaheuristics presented in the tool in solving small and medium mapping problem instances. For this, we have defined these two main operators:

- The branching strategy: it determines the order in which the branches are explored [22]. In our case, at each search level, the non-dominated solutions are explored first (i.e. the best-first strategy), and if more than one non-dominated solutions are found, the depth-first strategy is applied.
- The pruning strategy: it eliminates the partial solutions that do not lead to optimal solutions by computing the lower bound associated with a partial solution [22]. In our work, at each level, the lower bound corresponds to the best solution's evaluation which can be found starting from the partial solution of this level. If the lower bound of a node (partial solution) is dominated by a given solution in the upper bound, the exploration of the node never leads to optimal solution, so the node is ignored. Note that, upper bound set corresponds to a set of non-dominated solutions generated randomly. Figure 3 presents an illustration of the MBB [12] method on the mapping of three tasks (T_0, T_1, T_2) and each task has two permissible processors $(PT_0 = \{0, 1\}$, $PT_1 = \{2, 3\}$ and $PT_2 = \{6, 7\})$.

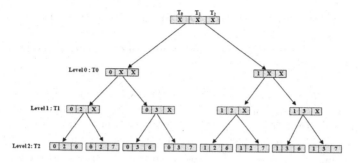

Fig. 3. Illustration of the MBB [12] method on the mapping problem

5   Experimental Results

In this section, we present a set of experiments illustrating the use of our proposed mapping tool to solve several mapping problems' instances (small, medium
and large). These instances differ from each other regarding the task graphs
and platform size used. TGFF [26] is used to generate a set of task graphs
randomly. The architecture model (Platform) consists of k types of processors
interconnected using NoC topology. Table 1 gives the NoC parameters used in
the following experiments. To evaluate and compare multiobjective optimization
algorithms performances, two properties are usually required: convergence and a
uniform diversity. Several quality indicators for measuring these two criteria are
included in jMetal framework [25]. In this paper, we have considered the following evaluation metrics: Inverted Generational Distance (IGD)(convergence and
diversity measure) ([27] and Epsilon (convergence measure) [25]. The smaller
the IGD and Epsilon values are, the better the quality of the obtained solutions.
Since some of the applied metrics require an optimal Pareto set to be computed,
we have constructed it by collecting the results of all the runs of the different algorithms. In all our experiments, we have performed 30 independent runs and the
obtained tables represent the mean and standard deviation values of the quality
indicator applied. The best and the second best metaheuristics are marked with
different levels of gray as background color. Table 2 gives algorithm's parameter
setting used in the following experiments. A PC Intel (R) Core (TM) i7 CPU,
2.7 GHz, with 8 GB of RAM is used to perform all the calculations.

Table 1. NoC's parameters

NoC topologies	2D-Mesh, 2D-Torus and Spidergon
Switching technique	Wormhole switching
Routing technique	XY routing algorithm (2D-Mesh and 2D-Torus)
Arbitration technique	Round Robin (RR)
Flow control	Credit-based

Comparative Study of the Different Algorithms

To make a comparison between the algorithms offered by our mapping tool, we have considered several cases:

- Case1 -*Variation of task graphs and platforms used*- Figure 4 gives comparaison between several multiobjective optimization algorithms offered by our mapping tool (NSGAII, FastPGA, SPEA2, PESAII, IBEA, SMPSO, PAES, FastPGA, OMOPSO, AbYSS, MOCell, AMOSA, PMOTS and MBB) for solving small (P1), medium (P2) and large (P5) mapping instances (see Fig. 4 (a, b and c) respectively). We have fixed some tasks' processors assignement (i.e. pre-assignement constraint). Two conflicting cost functions are optimized: the energy consumption and the overall completion time defined using analytical model and Epsilon and IGD are the quality indicators used to assess the performance of the fronts returned by the different algorithms. These experiments show that the performance order of multiobjective algorithms changes according to the mapping problem considered (task graph and platforms used). For example, for small and medium mapping problems, the two best algorithms are respectively MBB and PMOTS, while for large mapping instance, the best results are given by SMPSO and OMOPSO respectively. This confirms that a mapping tool must provide several metaheuristics in order to explore different solution spaces. We can also see that the algorithms' execution time increases with the size of the problem (task graph and platform used). An example of some algorithms' runtime for solving small, medium and large mapping problems is given in Table 4.
- Case2 -*Variation in the number of objectives to be optimized (NObj)*- The experiments presented in this second case give a comparison between a set of algorithms offered by our mapping tool (NSGAII, SPEA2, MOCell, AbYSS, SMPSO, OMOPSO, AMOSA and PMOTS) by specifying two objectives (load balancing, communication cost), three objectives (load balancing, communication cost and energy consumption) and four objectives (load balancing, communication cost, energy consumption and overall execution time) (see Table 5). These cost functions are defined by analytical models. From Table 5, we see that, firstly, for the same mapping problem (the problem P3 in our case), the performance of metaheuristics changes according to the number of objectives specified. For instance, in these experiments, the results returned by OMOPSO algorithm are poor when considering two objectives, but they are good in the case of three and four objectives. Secondly, these experiments show that metaheuristics' execution time increases with the increase in the number of objectives considered. For example, the execution time of NSGAII for 2, 3 and 4 objectives is respectively $0.560\,s$, $0.950\,s$ and $6.791\,s$.
- Case3 -*Effect of the choice of metaheuristic parameters on the quality of the returned mapping solutions*- In this third case, we present a set of other experiments showing how metaheuristics are sensitive to their parameters. Figure 5 shows several experiments on the effect of some parameters like: the evaluations' number ($MaxEval$), an example of AMOSA's parameter (α), and

Table 2. Algorithms' parameterization

Population-based metaheuristics	(NSGAII, FastPGA, SPEA2, PESAII, IBEA, MOCell, AbYSS, SMPSO and OMOPSO)
NSGAII/FastPGA	
Population size	100
Max iterations	25000/10000 (case 4)
Mutation probability	1.0/L (L: individual length)
Crossover probability	0.8/0.9 (case 4)
SPEA2/PESAII/IBEA	
Population size	100
Archive size	100
Max iterations	25000/10000 (case 4)
Mutation probability	1.0/L (L: individual length)
Crossover probability	0.8/0.9 (case 4)
MOCell	
Population size	100
Archive size	100
Max iterations	25000
Feedback	20
Mutation probability	1.0/L (L: individual length)
Crossover probability	0.8
AbYSS	
Population size	100
Archive size	100
Max iterations	25000
Reference set size	10 + 10
Mutation probability	1.0/L (L: individual length)
Crossover probability	1.0
SMPSO/OMOPSO	
Swarm size	100
Max iterations	500
Archive size	100
Mutation probability	1.0/L (L: individual length)
Single-based metaheuristics	(AMOSA, PMOTS and PAES)
AMOSA	
Initial temperature (T_0)	700/800 (case 4)
Final temperature (T_1)	10^{-3}
Cooling rate (α)	0.8/0.9 (case 4)
Max iterations	1000
Hard limit (HL)	100
Soft limit (SL)	110
Gamma	1.7/1.8 (case 4)
PMOTS	
Max iterations	5000
Max pareto rank (R_{max})	4
Max neighbours	50
Number parallel search paths (K)	10
Size min of tabu list (Tab_{min})	10
Size max of tabu list (Tab_{max})	15
PAES	
Archive size	100
Max iterations	25000
Mutation probability	1.0/L (L: individual length)

Table 3. Mapping problems' instances (MPs)

MP	Task graph	Platforms
P1	7 tasks	3 × 3 2D-mesh with 3 processors' types
P2	10 tasks	4 × 4 2D-mesh with 3 processors' types
P3	100 tasks	8 processors interconnected with Spidergon topology (3 processors' types)
P4	100 tasks	4 × 4 2D-mesh with 3 processors' types
P5	100 tasks	8 × 8 2D-torus with 6 processors' types

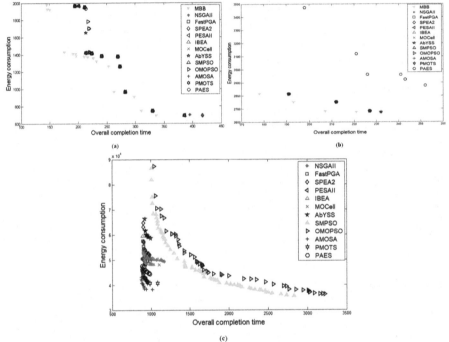

Fig. 4. Algorithms' comparison: (a) Solving small mapping instance, (b) Solving medium mapping instance, (c) Solving large mapping instance.

mutation operator on the performance of some metaheuristics proposed by our mapping tool such as: SMPSO, AMOSA and SPEA2. In all these experiments, we varied one parameter for each algorithm and other parameters were set. The study was done on P3 problem presented in Table 3. Load balancing and communication were specified as objective functions to be optimized in these experiments. Figure 5(a) shows clearly that the more the evaluations are, the better the quality of the mapping solutions found at the expense of the execution time (see Table 1 in Fig. 5). Another example of a parameter affecting the AMOSA algorithm is given in Fig. 5(b). It is the parameter α

Table 4. Algorithms' runtime

MPs	NSGAII	IBEA	MOCell	AbYSS	SMPSO	OMOPSO	AMOSA	PMOTS	PAES	MBB
P1 (small)	0.235s	2.027s	0.177s	0.169s	0.222s	0.216s	0.242s	11.653s	0.122s	3.595m
P2 (medium)	0.272s	2.080s	0.209s	0.208s	0.302s	0.287s	0.384s	11.720s	0.153s	17.95m
P5 (large)	3.560s	5.496s	3.572s	3.499s	6.166s	6.064s	7.577s	5.601m	3.0576s	–

whose value varies between $]0, 1[$. The closer the value of this parameter is to 1, the better is the performance of AMOSA, also at the expense of its execution time (see Table 2 in Fig. 5). Other important parameters affecting the performance of metaheuristics are the reproduction operators: (1) mutation (type and probability) and (2) crossover (type and probability). This is clearly demonstrated in the experiment shown in Fig. 5 (c) which indicates that *Flip mutation* operator gives better results compared to the other types of mutation operators (polynomial and uniform mutations).

– Case4 -*Comparing between hybrid and non hybrid metaheuristics*- As the last experiments, we compared hybrid (HNSGAII, HSPEA2 and HPESAII) and non hybrid metaheuristics (NSGAII, SPEA2 and PESAII) for solving P5 problem (see Table 3). Two conflicting cost functions are optimized: the energy consumption and the overall completion time defined using simulation model. From Fig. 6, we see that the proposed hybrid algorithms give promising results (better fronts) compared to non-hybrid algorithms at the expense of time (see Table 6). This extra time of the hybrid algorithms compared to the non-hybrid algorithms in these experiments is due to the AMOSA runtime used for the improvement of the Pareto fronts resulting by NSGAII, SPEA2 and PESAII metaheuristics. It is important to note that the parameters of the hybrid algorithms are a combination of those given in Table 2 (with the same configuration values).

Table 5. IGD. Mean and standard deviation

NObj			NSGAII	SPEA2	MOCell	AbYSS	SMPSO	OMOPSO	AMOSA	PMOTS
2	IGD	MOY	$8.18e-02$	$8.86e-02$	$8.13e-02$	$8.30e-02$	$2.78e-02$	$1.16e-01$	$7.88e-02$	$8.99e-02$
		ET	$8.5e-03$	$8.5e-03$	$6.8e-03$	$6.9e-03$	$1.4e-03$	$1.5e-02$	$5.9e-03$	$3.2e-03$
		Runtime	0.560s	1.144s	0.568s	0.368 s	1.086s	0.777s	0.349s	2.522s
3	IGD	MOY	$6.59e-02$	$6.91e-02$	$6.56e-02$	$5.33e-02$	$2.72e-03$	$1.82e-02$	$5.72e-02$	$6.50e-02$
		ET	$5.6e-03$	$4.8e-03$	$3.7e-03$	$8.3e-03$	$1.5e-04$	$6.0e-04$	$2.1e-03$	$2.0e-03$
		Runtime	0.950s	1.580s	0.928s	0.727s	1.527s	1.325s	0.930	5.139s
4	IGD	MOY	$2.17e-02$	$2.41e-02$	$2.20e-02$	$1.61e-02$	$6.50e-03$	$1.21e-02$	$2.53e-02$	$2.44e-02$
		ET	$1.5e-03$	$1.1e-03$	$1.1e-03$	$2.7e-03$	$3.9e-04$	$4.4e-04$	$5.0e-04$	$4.6e-04$
		Runtime	6.791s	7.162s	6.687s	8.910s	265.742s	377.501s	8.953s	35.616s

Table 6. Runtime of hybrid and non hybrid algorithms

	NSGAII	HNSGAII	SPEA2	HSPEA2	PESAII	HPESAII
Runtime (in minutes)	3.12 m	6.354 m	2.933 m	6.121 m	2.639 m	5.83 m

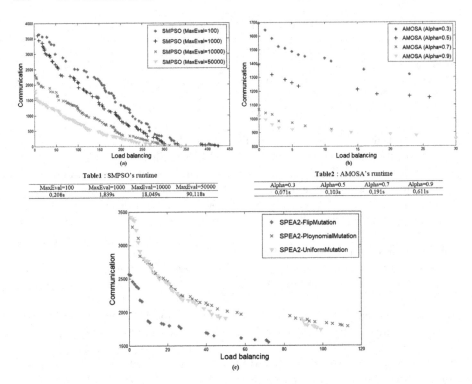

Fig. 5. Algorithms' parameters setting effect: (a) varying of the evaluations' number (MaxEval) of SMPSO algorithm, (b) varying AMOSA's cooling rate (α), (c) varying SPEA2's mutation operators.

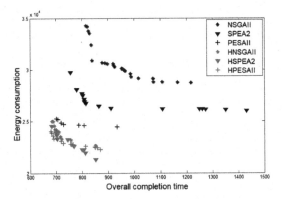

Fig. 6. Comparative study of hybrid and non hybrid algorithms.

5.1 Discussion

The proposed mapping tool offers several multiobjective algorithms that can be specified when solving the mapping problem. The question is: "*What is the most efficient algorithm (quality of solutions and runtime) to solve a given mapping problem?"* In this section, we try to summarize our experimental study, and thus we give a series of guidelines on the use of the proposed tool. According to the experimental results presented above, we concluded that:

– For small (or medium) instances of the mapping problem, the exact method (MBB) as well as metaheuristics with "good parameter" give good compromise solutions (i.e. good Pareto fronts). The exact method (MBB) gives the exact Pareto front. Therefore, the exact method (MBB) is preferable in this case (see case 1).

– For large mapping problems' instances, only metaheuristics can be used. The exact method (MBB) does not give results in polynomial time considering a large search space. Therefore, the exact method (MBB) cannot solve large mapping problems' instances (see Table 4 in case 1).

– Although metaheuristics can deal with all mapping problems' instances (small, medium or large), their main disadvantage is their sensitivity to parameters. Therefore, a sensitivity analysis must be done in order to estimate the right parameters for each algorithm. It should be noted that there is no standard optimal setting for metaheuristics since this is strongly related to the mapping problem under consideration (see case 3).

– No metaheuristic is better than another for any kind of mapping problem. This depends on several factors such as: the task graph and the platform used (see case 1), objectives' number specified (see case 2) and metaheuristics' parameters (see case 3).

– Metaheuristics' execution time (runtime) depends on several factors such as: the problem's size (task graph and platforms used) (see Table 4 in case 1), the number of objectives to be optimized (case 2), the parameters' configuration of the algorithm (see Table 1 and Table 2 in Fig. 5) and the type of objective function specified (analytical (case 1) vs. simulation (case 4)).

– The solution-based metaheuristics, for example AMOSA can effectively improve P-metaheuristics like NSGAII, SPEA2 and PESAII (see Fig. 6). The major disadvantages of these resulting hybrid metaheuristics are their additional runtime compared to non hybrid ones (see case 4) and the difficulty of configuring their parameters, since they consist of a combination of parameters of the metaheuristics which are, also by their nature, very sensitive to their parameters.

6   Conclusion

In this paper, a new tool for mapping applications on NoC based on heterogeneous MPSoCs is proposed, in which several multiobjective optimization algorithms can be specified to explore the mapping space. Our tool offers the designer the flexibility to easily add a new cost function or any application and architecture constraints. It offers also an easy way to assess the performance of the front returned by different algorithms. In our future work, we are planning to consider real time constraints during the mapping and generalize the mapping solution proposed in this paper in simultaneous mapping of several applications (critical and/or non-critical) on the same target platform.

References

1. Tariq, U.U., Wu, H., Ishak, S.A.: Energy and memory-aware software pipelining streaming applications on NoC-based MPSoCs. Future Generation Computer Systems **111**, 1–16 (2020)
2. Pipelined Multiprocessor System-on-Chip for Multimedia. Springer, Cham (2014). https://doi.org/10.1007/978-3-319-01113-4_9
3. Suriano, L., Otero, A., Rodríguez, A., Sánchez-Renedo, M., De La Torre, E.: Exploiting Multi- Level Parallelism for Run-Time Adaptive Inverse Kinematics on Heterogeneous MPSoCs. IEEE Access **8**, 118707–118724 (2020)
4. STMicroelectronics, Nomadik application processor, http://www.st.com
5. NVIDIA Tegra: Next Generation Mobile Development, https://developer.nvidia.com/tegra-development
6. Mobile processor exynos 5 octa (5422), https://www.samsung.com/semiconductor/minisite/exynos/products/mobileprocessor/exynos-5-octa-5422/
7. Benini, L., De Micheli, G.: Networks on Chips: A new SOC paradigm. IEEE Computer **35**(1), 70–78 (2002)
8. Michael R. Garey and David S. Johnson.: Computers and Intractability: A Guide to the Theory of Np-Completeness. W.H.Freeman & Co Ltd, New York (1979)
9. D. Belkacemi, Y. Bouchebaba, M. Daoui, and M. Lalam.: Network on Chip and Parallel Computing in Embedded Systems. In: 2016 IEEE 10th International Symposium on Embedded Multicore/Many-core Systems-on-Chip (MCSOC), pp. 146–152. IEEE, (September 2016)
10. S. Bandyopadhyay, S. Saha, U. Maulik, and K. Deb.: A Simulated Annealing-Based Multiobjective Optimization Algorithm: AMOSA. IEEE Transactions on Evolutionary Computation 12(3), 269–283 (June 2008)
11. Jaffrs-Runser, K., Gorce, J.-M., Comaniciu, C.: A Multiobjective Tabu Framework for the Optimization and Evaluation of Wireless Systems. In: Jaziri, Wassim (ed.) Tabu Search. I-Tech Education and Publishing, Vienna, Austria (2008). ISBN 978-3-902613-34-9
12. J. Carlos Soto-Monterrubio, Alejandro Santiago, H. J. Fraire- Huacuja, Juan Frausto-Solís, and J. David Terán-Villanueva: Branch and Bound Algorithm for the Heterogeneous Computing Scheduling Multi-Objective Problem. International Journal of Combinatorial Optimization Problems and Informatics 7(3), 7–19 (2016)
13. Ascia, G., Catania, V., Palesi, M.: Mapping Cores on Network-on-Chip. International Journal of Computational Intelligence Research **1**(2), 109–126 (2005)
14. Erbas, C., Cerav-Erbas, S., Pimentel, A.D.: Multiobjective optimization and evolutionary algorithms for the application mapping problem in multiprocessor system-on-chip design. IEEE Transactions on Evolutionary Computation **10**(3), 358–374 (2006)
15. Zhou, W., Zhang, Y., Mao, Z.: Pareto based Multi-objective Mapping IP Cores onto NoC Architectures. Circuits and Systems, APCCAS (2006)
16. R. Tornero, V. Sterrantino, M. Palesi, and J. M. Orduna: A multi-objective strategy for concurrent mapping and routing in networks on chip. 2009 IEEE International Symposium on Parallel Distributed Processing, pp. 1–8. IEEE, (May 2009)

17. N. Nedjah, M. Vinícius Carvalho da Silva, and L. de Macedo Mourelle: Customized computer-aided application mapping on NoC infrastructure using multi-objective optimization. Journal of Systems Architecture 57(1), 79–94 (January 2011)
18. N. Wu, Y. Mu, and F. Ge : GA-MMAS: an Energyand Latency-aware Mapping Algorithm for 2D Network-on-Chip. IAENG International Journal of Computer Science 39(1), (2012)
19. He, T., Guo, Y.: Power consumption optimization and delay based on ant colony algorithm in network-on-chip. Engineering Review 33(3), 219–225 (2013)
20. N. Chatterjee, S. Reddy, S. Reddy, and S. Chattopadhyay: A reliability aware application mapping onto mesh based Network-on-Chip. In 2016 3rd International Conference on Recent Advances in Information Technology (RAIT), pp. 537–542. (March 2016)
21. J.V. Bruch, E.A. da Silva, C.A. Zeferino, and L.S. Indrusia: Deadline, Energy and Buffer-Aware Task Mapping Optimization in NoC-Based SoCs Using Genetic Algorithms. In 2017 VII Brazilian Symposium on Computing Systems Engineering (SBESC), pp. 86–93. IEEE, (November 2017)
22. Talbi, El-Ghazali: Metaheuristics: from design to implementation. John Wiley & Sons, Hoboken, N.J., New Jersey and canada (2009)
23. Jingcao Hu and R. Marculescu: Energy-aware mapping for tilebased NoC architectures under performance constraints. In Proceedings of the ASP-DAC Asia and South Pacific Design Automation Conference, pp. 233–239. IEEE, (January 2003)
24. Belkacemi, D., Daoui, M., Bouzefrane, S., Bouchebaba, Y.: Parallel Applications Mapping onto Network on Chip Based on Heterogeneous MPSoCs Using Hybrid Algorithms. International Journal of Distributed Systems and Technologies 10(2), (2019)
25. Durillo, Juan J., Nebro, Antonio J.: jMetal: A Java framework for multi-objective optimization. Advances in Engineering Software 42(10), 760–771 (2011)
26. R.P. Dick, D.L. Rhodes and W. Wolf: TGFF: task graphs for free. Workshop on Hardware/Software Codesign, (1998)
27. Nebro, Antonio J., Luna, Francisco., Alba, Enrique., Dorronsoro, BernabÉ., Durillo, Juan J., Beham, Andreas: AbYSS: Adapting Scatter Search to Multi-objective Optimization. IEEE Transactions on Evolutionary Computation 12(4), 439–457 (2008)

Budget-Aware Performance Optimization of Workflows in Multiple Data Center Clouds

Karima Oukfif[1]([✉]) [iD], Fares Battou[2], and Samia Bouzefrane[3] [iD]

[1] LARI Lab, Mouloud Mammeri University of Tizi-Ouzou, Tizi-Ouzou, Algeria
karima.oukfif@gmail.com
[2] University of Lille, Lille, France
[3] CEDRIC Lab, Conservatoire National des Arts et Metiers, Paris, France

Abstract. Users pay to use resources in cloud systems which makes them more demanding on performance and costs. Optimizing the response time of the applications and meeting user's budget needs are therefore critical requirements when scheduling applications.

The approach presented in this work is a scheduling based-HEFT algorithm, which aims to optimize the makespan of tasks workflow that is constrained by the budget. For this, we propose a new budget distribution strategy named Estimated task budget that we integrate in our budget-aware HEFT algorithm. We use a multiple datacenters cloud as a real platform model, where data transfer costs are considered. The results obtained by our algorithm relative to recent work, show an improvement of makespan in the case of a restricted budget, without exceeding the given budget.

Keywords: Workflow · Multiple data centers cloud · Makespan optimization · Budget distribution · HEFT

1 Introduction

Cloud platforms have become the trend for running applications. The cloud-computing paradigm has revolutionized the way of assessing computing resources by proposing a highly versatile availability of resources through a pay-as-you-go model. These features have enabled users to migrate their applications to cloud platforms. Workflows are examples of scientific applications which involve a higher performance-computing environment to be executed and cloud platforms offer huge opportunities to solve them. A workflow is a popular model for representing scientific computing, including complicated simulation and precise analysis of massive data [10]. Scheduling workflows, considered as NP-hard [4] problem, still remains a fundamental issue in cloud computing although it has been widely studied over the years [11,12].

During workflows scheduling in the cloud, both cloud providers and users are most involved with the makespan and monetary costs criteria. Makespan

© Springer Nature Switzerland AG 2021
S. Bouzefrane et al. (Eds.): MSPN 2020, LNCS 12605, pp. 144–160, 2021.
https://doi.org/10.1007/978-3-030-67550-9_10

refers to the completion time of the entire workflow and the price that users need to pay due to the usage of cloud resources is the monetary cost. In cloud computing, resources of different capabilities at different prices are provided. Normally, faster computing resources are more expensive than slower ones. Thus, different scheduling strategies of a workflow using different resources may result in different makespan and different monetary cost. Therefore, the problem of workflow scheduling in the cloud requires both time and cost constraints to be satisfied [16].

These two criteria have conflicting objectives, and it is important to suggest a trade-off between them. This trade-off influences the different scheduling objectives, which include reducing costs while meeting the deadline, optimizing makespan while meeting the budget, or achieving the deadline and budget as a more flexible objective [10].

In this work, we focus on optimizing makespan while meeting the budget constraint. The intuition behind this strategy is to finish a workflow at a given budget as soon as possible. The objective is to minimize makespan under budget restrictions. Several authors have worked on this issue in single data center clouds, as detailed in the related work section. In this work, we are dealing with the same problem in the context of multiple data centers clouds. Indeed, currently cloud providers have tens of thousands of servers for providing sufficient computing resources for applications. These resources are deployed in multiple data centers.

We propose a budget-aware HEFT algorithm for performance optimization of workflows in IaaS multiple data centers cloud. Our goal is to optimize the makespan and meeting the budget while scheduling workflows. For this, we propose a novel budget distribution approach based on estimating task features.

The rest of this paper is organized as follows. Section 2 gives an overview of the related work, followed by our budget-aware scheduling algorithm formalization in Sect. 3. The proposed scheduling algorithm based on HEFT is outlined and evaluated in Sects. 4 and 5 respectively. Finally, Sect. 6 summarizes the results and concludes the paper.

2   Related Work

It is generally accepted that the problem of workflows scheduling upon distributed systems is NP-hard [4]. In this mind, heuristic and meta-heuristic strategies are used to generate high-quality and approximate solutions with polynomial time complexity. Makespan and cost still remain the most relevant criteria to optimize while scheduling workflows in clouds. Several approaches have been proposed to optimize makespan, cost or both.

Work such as [15] and [8] proposed budget and deadline constrained heuristics based upon Heterogeneous Earliest Finish Time (HEFT) to schedule workflow over cloud resources. The proposed heuristics present a beneficial trade-off between execution time and execution cost under given constraints.

A list multiobjective optimization technique is designed by [9] to minimize monetary costs for deadline constrained workflows in cloud environments.

The authors select the non-dominated solutions by combining the quick non-dominated sorting approach with the crowding distance.

In [2,18], the authors focus on budget and deadline aware workflow scheduling. Their idea presented in [2] is to satisfy both budget and deadline constraints while introducing a tunable cost-time trade off over heterogeneous instances. In [18] a workflow scheduling algorithm to find a feasible solution for a workflow that meets budget and deadline constraints is proposed. Based on the execution cost of the task on the slowest resources and the optimistic spare budget, the algorithm generates the task optimistic available budget. Then, it builds the set of suitable resources according to the task's optimistic available budget to control the range of resources selection, and thus controls the task execution cost.

Many studies have addressed the issue of scheduling workflows effectively given budget constraints. In order to achieve this goal, many works apply budget distribution strategies for workflow scheduling in the cloud. A budget distribution strategy consists of assigning a sub-budget for each task of the workflow.

The algorithm presented by [17] is an extension of the HEFT heuristic except for the selection phase (task-ressource assignment). The algorithm distributes the budget to all tasks in proportion to their average execution time on the available resources. Then, the resource chosen is the one that allows the task to be accomplished early at a cost not greater than its allocated sub-budget.

The authors in [1] propose a workflow partitioning that focuses on the dependency structure inherent to workflow tasks. The partitioning leads to several levels each containing independent tasks. Several methods are introduced to distribute the global budget over these levels. According to the authors, the most effective strategy is the so-called 'All-in' which places the entire budget on the entry-level. Thus any remainders are trickled down to later levels. In our work, we implemented this strategy for comparison purposes.

In [13] authors propose a scheduling algorithm whose objective is to optimize a workflow's execution time under a budget constraint. Their approach focuses on finer-grained pricing schemes that provide users with more flexibility and the ability to reduce the inherent wastage that results from coarser-grained ones. Their approach partitions the DAG into a bag of tasks prior to its execution and then distributes the budget over the tasks. The drawback of their clustering phase is the parallelism limitation because of grouping several dependent tasks of workflow at the same level, which leads to the performance degradation of the workflow.

The authors in [5] extended the two well-known algorithms, MIN-MIN [3] and HEFT [14] to budget-aware scheduling algorithms for scientific workflows with stochastic task weights on heterogeneous. In addition, they improved these versions with refined ones that aim to re-schedule some tasks on faster VMs.

In [6], the authors proposed a normalization-based budget for constraint workflow scheduling algorithm. Their algorithm controls the resource selection phase of each task according to the available budget, thereby increasing the probability of the 'best' resource selection.

All of these studies deal with the workfow scheduling problem in a single data center cloud and eliminate or underestimate data transfer costs, unlike today's cloud providers that rely on multiple data centers. The cost model used in previous studies did not consider the charge of data transfers in the cloud although most cloud providers charge for the actual data storage depending on the amount of data being stored. Moreover, we propose a new way of distributing the budget over the workflow tasks defined based on estimating their characteristics.

In this paper, we assume a multiple data centers cloud platforms that provide for workflow applications heterogeneous resources under budget and we consider a charged peer-to-peer transfer mode instead of resorting external global storage.

3   Problem Formalization

This section begins by detailing the application and the platform models, then we formalize the workflow scheduling problem. The aim of our scheduling heuristic is to find a schedule S for the workflow (w) with a minimum makespan while respecting the budget.

3.1   Application Model

A scientific workflow application (w) is modeled as a DAG (Directed Acyclic Graph): $G = (V, E)$, where V is a set of n vertices representing tasks t_i $(1 \leqslant i \leqslant n)$, and E is a set of directed edges. An edge $e(i, j) \in E$ corresponds to a dependence constraint between task t_i and t_j, in which t_i is an immediate parent task of t_j, and t_j the immediate child task of t_i. A child task cannot be executed until all of its parent tasks are completed. A task with no parent tasks is called an entry task and a task with no children tasks is called an exit task. The data matrix, with $n \times n$ dimensions, represents the data volume exchanged between tasks.

3.2   Cloud Resource Model

We consider platforms defined by an IaaS cloud where computer resources (instances) can be deployed on different data centers. During this section, we use the time model that specifies the data transfer times between data centers that we detailed in our previous work [12]. Then we present a cost model that takes into account the costs of the instances as well as those of the transferred data.

Time Model. In IaaS clouds, computer resources are instantiated as Virtual Machines (VMs) which are deployed on different data centers. Typically, cloud providers offer multiple types of VM; $VM = vm_1, vm_2, ..., vm_q$ is the set of VMs with heterogenous processing capacity.

The estimated execution time of the task t_i in a VM of type vm_p is defined by the computing time $(CT(t_i, vm_p))$.

The transfer time $TT_{(i,j)}$ (see Eq. (1)) taken to transfer data from task t_i (executed on vm_p lodged in data center DC_a) to task t_j (executed on vm_k lodged in data center DC_b) corresponds to an edge $(i,j) \in E$ in the application graph (DAG).

$$TT_{(i,j)} = \frac{data_{ij}}{Transfer_{rate_{(p,k)}}} \tag{1}$$

The transfer time $TT_{(i,j)}$ is proportional to the size of the output data $data_{ij}$ produced by task t_i and transferred to t_j, and is inversely proportional to the heterogeneous transfer rates or the bandwidths $Transfer_{rate_{(p,k)}}$ when the tasks are executed on different data centers.

We note that when two communicated tasks are executed on the same VM, the transfer time is equal to zero and when they are executed on different VMs that are lodged in the same data center also the transfer time is neglected. Thereby, the total computing time $TCT(t_i, vm_p)$ of a task in a VM is computed as shown in Eq. (2).

In this equation, m refers to the number of parent tasks of t_i (predecessors). The boolean s_m is equal to 0 if t_i and t_j run on the same virtual machine ($p = k$) or to 1 otherwise. Besides, the value r_m is equal to 1 to indicate that the VMs can be hosted in different datacenters.

$$TCT(t_i, vm_p) = CT(t_i, vm_p) + \sum_{j=1}^{m} s_m.r_m.TT_{(j,i)} \tag{2}$$

In the formula (2) the product $s_m \times r_m$ indicates the inclusion of data transfer times between the VMs according to the following two cases:

1. Transfer time between VMs in the same datacenter is neglected:

$$r_m = \begin{cases} 1 \text{ if } DC_a \neq DC_b \\ 0, \text{ else} \end{cases}$$

2. Transfer time between VMs in the same datacenter is not neglected:

$$r_m = 1 \text{ , then } s_m \times r_m = s_m$$

In order to calculate the makespan, which refers to the total execution time $TCT(w)$ of all the tasks of the workflow, it is necessary to define for each task these two attributes $EST(t_i, vm_p)$ (*Earliest Start Time*) and $EFT(t_i, vm_p)$ (*Earliest Finish Time*) as following:

The $EST(t_i, vm_p)$ of the task t_i on the machine vm_p, is calculated according to the following recursive procedure: If the task has no parent tasks, then $EST(t_i, vm_p) = 0$, otherwise the task can start executing as soon as its parent tasks are finished and their output data is transferred. However, if the resource is occupied by another task at this point, the execution of the task t_i should be delayed until this virtual machine vm_p is free again.

The procedure (3) calculates the value of $EST(t_i, vm_p)$:

$$EST(t_i, vm_p) = \begin{cases} 0, \text{if } t_i \text{ has no parent tasks} \\ \max\{avail[vm_p], \max_{t_k \in pred(t_i)}\{EFT(t_k, vm_q)\}\}, \text{ else} \end{cases}$$
(3)

Where: $pred(t_i)$ is the set of immediate predecessors of the task t_i (parents of t_i), $avail[vm_p]$ is the next instant time when the resource vm_p will be ready or available for task execution.

To determine $EST(t_i, vm_p)$, the maximum value between $avail[vm_p$ and $\max_{t_k \in pred(t_i)}\{EFT(t_k, vm_q)\}$ is selected, where $avail[vm_p]$ is the maximum completion time of previous tasks of t_i on the same virtual machine vm_p. The value $avail[vm_p]$ guarantees that a virtual machine processes one task at a time, while $\max_{t_k \in pred(t_i)}\{EFT(t_k, vm_q)\}$ guarantees that a child task starts after all of its parents have finished their execution.

The $EFT(t_i, vm_p)$ of the task t_i on the machine vm_p is given by the following equation:

$$EFT(t_i, vm_p) = EST(t_i, vm_p) + TCT(t_i, vm_p)$$
(4)

The makespan or the total computing time $TCT(w)$ of the workflow is defined by the Eq. (5), and which corresponds to the completion time of the last task in the workflow.

$$TCT(w) = \max\{EFT(t_i, vm_p)\}$$
(5)

Cost Model. To deal with the pay-as-you-go cost model of the cloud, we need to incorporate the budget constraint in our approach.

The total cost of the whole workflow execution is the sum of the cost due to the execution of all its tasks in the platform.

The cost due to the execution of a task on a given VM vm_p is defined by the Eq. (6) and the cost of data transfers for this task is given by the Eq. (7).

$$Cost(t_i, vm_p) = CT(t_i, vm_p) \times UC_{vm_p}$$
(6)

$$Trcost(t_i) = \sum_{i=j}^{m} data_{ij} \times r_m \times UC_{data}$$
(7)

Where UC_{vm_p} is the per time unit cost for using the vm_p, UC_{data} is the unit cost for transferring data and m the number of successor tasks of t_i. In the Eq. (7), $data_{ij}$ refers to the data transferred from t_i to t_j. The boolean r_m indicates if the data transfers are achieved in the same datacenter ($r_m = 0$) thereby the data transfers fees are eliminated, or within different ones ($r_m = 1$). The cost for a task is then given by the Eq. (8).

$$Cost(t_i) = Cost(t_i, vm_p) + Trcost(t_i)$$
(8)

Altogether, we give the total cost for the workflow execution as (9):

$$Cost(w) = \sum_{i=1}^{n} Cost(t_i) \tag{9}$$

Objective. Given a budget B, our objective is to find the schedule that minimizes the makespan while the budget is respected, namely: $\min\{TCT(w)\}$ while $Cost(w) \leq B$.

4   Budget-Aware HEFT Based Scheduling Algorithm

In this section, we will first describe the HEFT algorithm, then we propose a new budget distribution approach named Estimated task budget. Afterward, we present the Budget-aware HEFT heuristic for scheduling workflows with budget constraints in multiple datacenter cloud. HEFT heuristic is one of the most popular list-based scheduling algorithms. It determines the scheduling of a DAG in a heterogeneous environment in order to minimize the makespan of the application. HEFT is integrated into important projects like ASKALON project [7] to provide scheduling for a quantum chemistry application.

4.1   HEFT Algorithm

HEFT is a well-established list scheduling algorithm that prioritizes a workflow task with a higher rank. It determines the rank value for each task, based on the average execution time and the average communication time between the resources of two successive tasks.

The HEFT algorithm orders the tasks on the different resources in a given order based on a value of a rank attribute. Ranks in HEFT are calculated based on the estimated average computation and communication times of the tasks. Indeed, the tasks are sorted according to their scheduling priorities, which are based on the increasing rank (upward rank, noted $rank_u$). The value $rank_u$ is the maximum distance of a task from the DAG output task. The rank of a task is defined recursively as follows:

$$rank_u(t_i) = \begin{cases} \overline{CT}(t_{exit}), & \text{if } t_i = t_{exit} \\ \overline{CT}(t_i) + \max_{t_j \in succ(t_i)}\{\overline{TT}_{(i,j)}, rank_u(t_j)\}, & \text{else} \end{cases} \tag{10}$$

Where:

- $succ(t_i)$ is the set of immediate successors of task t_i.
- $\overline{CT}(t_i)$ the average cost of running the task t_i.
- $\overline{TT}_{(i,j)}$ is the average cost of the communications of the edge (i,j).

This rank is calculated for all the tasks of the DAG starting with the exit task. The exit task has as rank only the average of the computation times on the different resources since it has no successor tasks.

The HEFT algorithm works in two phases; (i) The prioritization phase during which the priorities of all tasks are calculated using $rank_u$. Next, a list of tasks is generated by sorting the tasks according to their decreasing rank (priorities). (ii) The resource selection phase during which the tasks are assigned to computing resources which minimize their (*Finish Time*). The time $FT(t_i, vm_p)$ of a task i on a computational resource vm_p corresponds to the time at which the task finishes its execution, that is to say, the time of its start time $ST(t_i, vm_p)$ (*Start Time*) added to the time of its execution.

The HEFT algorithm proceeds according to the Algorithm (1).

Algorithm 1: HEFT algorithm

Data: W: workflow, PF: platform ;
Result: S: a schedule;

1 **begin**
2   Calculate the rank for all the tasks by traversing the DAG upwards from the exit tasks according to the equation (10);
3   Sort the tasks in a list following the rank in descending order ;
4   **while** *there are unscheduled tasks in the list* **do**
5   Select the first task t_i in the task list;
6   **foreach** vm_p *with* $p = 1..VM$ **do**
7   Calculate $FT(t_i, vm_p)$;
8   Assign the task t_i to the machine vm_p such that $FT(t_i, vm_p)$ is minimum ;
9   **end**
10   **end**
11 **end**

Before detailing our algorithm, we explain the new budget distribution strategy that we designed for our budget-aware HEFT scheduling algorithm.

4.2 Budget Distribution

The main of budget distribution is to scatter the provided budget (B) to the workflow tasks. Each task receives a fragment of this budget. Several methods of budget distribution have been proposed. Example of recent strategies we quote [1,5] cited in the related work section. In this work, we propose a novel budget distribution strategy for our budget-aware scheduling algorithm, the Estimated Task Budget. With the Estimated Task Budget (ETB) strategy, we estimate the budget required for each task according to the costs of its processing time and the costs of the data transfers that it needs. This estimation is much closer to the specific needs of each task than any other fair approach. The ETB approach better reflects the needs of the tasks when the workflow is running in multiple data centers clouds. This is possible by also estimating the costs of transfers made between datacenters, which are not always free. Therefore, the initial budget used to cover the total execution of a workflow w can be distributed to the workflow tasks according to the features of each of them. We propose to estimate the proportional budget $B(t_i)$ reserved for a task t_i using the Eq. (11).

$$B(t_i) = \frac{\overline{CT}(t_i)}{\sum_{i=1}^{n} CT(t_i)} \times UC_{vm_p} + \frac{\sum_{j=1}^{m} \overline{data}_{ji}}{\sum_{(x,y) \in E} data_{(xy)}} \times UC_{data} \qquad (11)$$

For each ready task, we calculate the corresponding sub-budget $B(t_i)$ of the initial budget (B) in proportion to the entire workflow. The first summand in the Eq. (11) concerns the unit cost of an instance by the ratio of the average computing time of a given task to the overall computing time of the workflow. The second summand represents the unit transfer cost by the ratio of the required data of a given task t_i to the total data to be transferred in the workflow.

Any unused fraction of the budget consumed when assigning previous tasks is recovered by the algorithm. For this purpose, the algorithm uses the variable B_{remain} which is initialized to zero for entry tasks but reclaims any remaining budget in previous assignments for the other tasks.

4.3 Budget-Aware HEFT Algorithm

In this subsection, we present a budget-aware HEFT algorithm to allow its execution on workflows in multi-datacenter cloud platforms with budget constraints. We call this algorithm $B - HEFT$.

Initially, the HEFT heuristic [14] is presented to schedule a task graph on a set of heterogeneous processors. The adaptation of the HEFT heuristic, for the execution of workflow on platforms such as multi-datacenters clouds with budget constraint, requires rethinking the stage of instance selection to a given task (or the assignment of tasks to VMs phase).

Using the proposed time model described in Sect. 3.2, we adapted the HEFT heuristic to the multi-datacenter cloud model. Moreover, we use the Estimated task budget for distributing the global budget over the workflow tasks.

The $B - HEFT$ is described by the following Algorithm (2).

Our algorithm started by sorting the tasks in a list following the $rank_u$ in descending order (lines 2 and 3). Initially, for each task t_i in the ordered list, our algorithm affects the cheapest VM in the platform PF (lines 7 and 8) as the best VM, which does not necessarily provide the minimum earliest finish time for this task. The $EFT(t_i, vm_p)$ is obtained using the Eq. (4)(line 9). The algorithm calculates the share of the budget for each task using the proposed Estimation task budget (line 10). In addition, the algorithm recovers any part of the remaining budget from previous tasks (line 11). From line 12 to line 19, the algorithm calculates the $EFT(t_i, vm_p)$ according to the Eq. (4) with each VM vm_p. Then, the task cost is generated using Eq. (8). The B-HEFT algorithm verifies the finish time, checks if the budget $B(t_i)$ is not exceeded, and updates the minimal finish time and the best vm if it's necessary. Afterward, the algorithm evaluates the remaining budget by subtracting its real cost from its own reserved budget. Finally, the algorithm returns the best vm for the task (line 19).

5 Evaluation and Results

In this section, we present the experiments carried out to evaluate the performance of the proposed approach.

To assess the performance of our approach, we tested the algorithms with workflows generated based on the characteristics of two well-known real workflow applications, Montage and CyberShake, from two different scientific fields.

The CyberShake workflow is a data-intensive application of seismology used to describe earthquakes by generating synthetic seismograms. The Montage workflow is used in astronomy for generating mosaics personalized from the sky

---

Algorithm 2: B-HEFT algorithm

Data: W:workflow, PF: platform, B: Budget;
Result: S: a schedule;

1 **begin**
2   Calculate the rank for all the tasks according to the equation (10);
3   Sort the tasks in a list following the rank in descending order ;
4   **while** *there are unscheduled tasks in the list* **do**
5   Select the first task t_i in the task list;
6   // initialization: $Best_{VM}$ as the cheapest VM ;
7       $UC_{vm} = \min\{UC_{vm_p}\}$ with $p = 1..VM$;
8       $Best_{VM} = vm$;
9   Calculate $EFT(t_i, Best_{VM})$ according to the equation (4) ;
10   Calculate $B(t_i)$ according to the equation (11) ;
11      $B(t_i) = B(t_i) + B_{remain}$;
12   **foreach** vm_p *with* $p = 1..VM$ **do**
13   Calculate $EFT(t_i, vm_p)$ according to the equation (4) ;
14   Calculate $Cost(t_i)$ according to the equation (8) ;
15   **if** $((EFT(t_i, vm_p) < EFT(t_i, Best_{VM}))$ *and* $(cost(t_i) \le B(t_i)))$ **then**
16             $EFT(t_i, Best_{VM}) = EFT(t_i, vm_p)$;
17             $Best_{VM} = vm_p$;
18             $B_{remain} = B(t_i) - cost(t_i)$
19   **end**
20   Assign t_i to $Best_{VM}$;
21   **end**
22   **end**
23 **end**

using a set of input images. Most of its tasks are I/O intensive. These workflows are generated by WorkflowGenerator[1] tool. The structure of the small workflows are shown by Fig. 1.

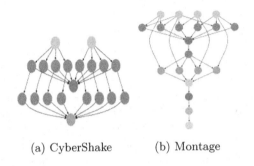

(a) CyberShake   (b) Montage

Fig. 1. Structure of the small scientific workflows

We modeled an IaaS provider platform with a platform of three data centers with 125 MBps as Bandwidth and \$0.055 per GB as data transfer cost. In each data center, three types of VMs can be allocated. Their characteristics (CPU power and cost) are similar to the c4 compute-optimized instance types offered by Amazon EC2. The configurations of the VM type used are shown in Table 1.

Table 1. Type and prices of VMs

VM type	Name	vCPU	Price per Seconde (\$)
1	small	2	0.0045
2	medium	4	0.009
3	large	8	0.018

In the experiments, different budget intervals were employed. We assume that the minimum budget (B_{min}) for running the workflow equals the cost of running all tasks on the single cheapest VM. We establish four different budget intervals based on this minimum budget as indicated in Eq. (12), then we use the rounding to an integer value for B.

$$B = \alpha \star B_{min} \quad where \quad 0 < \alpha < 5 \tag{12}$$

We assessed different workflows to compare performance with respect to workflow size. We used 25, 50 and 100 tasks for Montage workflow and used 30, 50 and 100 tasks for CyberShake workflow.

---

[1] https://confluence.pegasus.isi.edu/display/pegasus/WorkflowGenerator.

To afford a baseline comparison, we implemented a 'uniform' distribution as a basic strategy and an adapted version of the 'All-in' distribution proposed in [1].

The uniform distribution strategy operates blindly, sharing the budget provided over the set of tasks by equal sharing. Except for the number of tasks, no other information concerning the workflow structure or task characteristics is considered. With the 'All-in' distribution strategy, the total budget is assigned to the first level. After serving all tasks at this level, any remaining budget is trickled to the next level. Since our B-HEFT algorithm does not perform level building preprocessing, we implement an 'All-in' version based on the ordered list of tasks instead of levels. In this case, the total budget is given for the first ready task in the workflow. Then after serving this first task, the remaining budget will be devoted to the next ready task in the list, and so on.

5.1 Montage Workflow

Figure 2 shows the makespan achieved for Montage workflow using different budgets. With the different sizes of Montage workflow, our algorithm, plotted as 'Estimated' for Estimated task budget shows identical makespan as 'All-in' approach. Both 'Estimated' and 'All-in' perform better than the 'Uniform' strategy. This is due to the fact that when 'uniform' equitably distributes a restricted budget ($B = 1$, $B = 2$ for Montage-25 for example) between all the tasks, the share of each becomes insufficient. Then the algorithm assigns the tasks to the cheap instances, thus increasing the makespan (since the cheap instances are also slow). We point out the power of our algorithm to improve makespan compared to 'All-in' using a minimal budget.

In fact, our algorithm, using the 'Estimated' approach for sharing the budget, distributes for each task a sufficient sub-budget which is close to its real cost. On the other hand, 'All-in' is more generous with the first tasks of the workflow (starting with the input tasks) by assigning them the maximum budget, therefore being able to run on faster instances. Unfortunately for the last tasks, if the budget is not sufficient, they run on slow instances which lengthens the makespan.

The costs recorded for Montage workflow based on different budgets are shown in Fig. 3. The costs recorded by our strategy are very close to those obtained by the 'All-in' case. The 'Uniform' strategy got reduced costs for the restricted budgets because it assigns the tasks to the cheap instances in this case to the detriment of the makespan. These benefits are visible in particular for significant sizes workflows like Montage with tasks sizes 50 and 100 (Fig. 3 (b) and (c)). In most cases, the three strategies meet the budget.

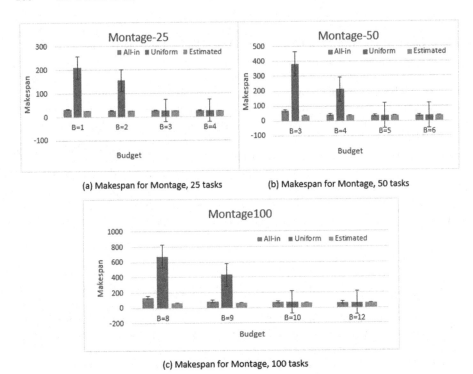

(a) Makespan for Montage, 25 tasks   (b) Makespan for Montage, 50 tasks

(c) Makespan for Montage, 100 tasks

Fig. 2. Makespan for Montage workflows grouped by Budget

5.2 CyberShake Workflow

Figure 4 shows the makespan achieved for CyberShake workflow using different budgets. With CyberShake, our approach also achieves makespan identical to those obtained by 'All-in' with relaxed budgets, but rather better in the case of a restricted budget for all the CyberShake task sizes (Fig. 4 (a), (b) and (c)).

The makespan obtained by 'Uniform' is high compared to 'Estimated' and 'All-in' especially in with restricted budgets. Note that in the case of Cyber-Shake with 100 tasks, 'Uniform' fails to optimize the makespan even with a relaxed budget (Fig. 4) (c)). Our approach achieves performances identical to those obtained by the 'All-in' strategy with relaxed budgets, but rather better in the case of a restricted budget.

As shown in Fig. 5, the results of CyberShake workflow regarding the costs are plotted. The costs realized by our approach are very close to those obtained by 'All-in' except for the workflow of size 100. In this case, 'All-in' behaves better compared to our approach. This is due eventually to the fact that the estimated values of the task's characteristics are not sufficiently accurate when dealing with a large number of tasks.

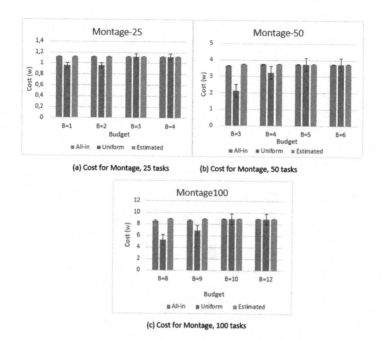

(a) Cost for Montage, 25 tasks   (b) Cost for Montage, 50 tasks

(c) Cost for Montage, 100 tasks

Fig. 3. Cost for Montage workflows grouped by Budget

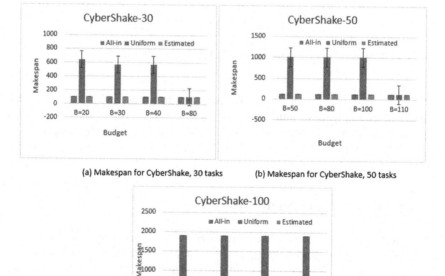

(a) Makespan for CyberShake, 30 tasks   (b) Makespan for CyberShake, 50 tasks

(c) Makespan for CyberShake, 100 tasks

Fig. 4. Makespan for CyberShake workflows grouped by Budget

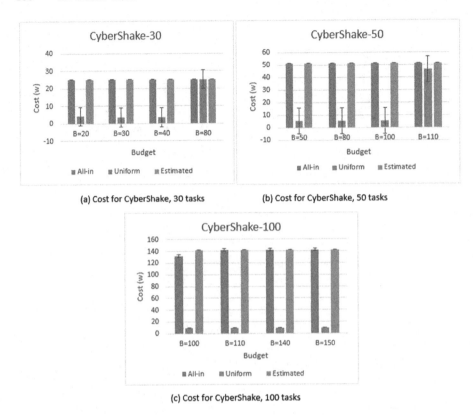

(a) Cost for CyberShake, 30 tasks   (b) Cost for CyberShake, 50 tasks

(c) Cost for CyberShake, 100 tasks

Fig. 5. Cost for CyberShake workflows grouped by Budget

With the 'Uniform' strategy, the tasks costs are reduced. But in reality, the approach is unable to offer sufficient budgets for tasks with restricted budgets. It just runs them on cheap instances without actually meeting the task's needs. When offering a relaxed budget, 'Uniform' recorded costs as high as these of the other two approaches.

6   Conclusion and Future Work

In this paper, we presented a budget-aware HEFT algorithm for optimizing makespan when meeting the budget. The budget-aware algorithm is based on an estimated task budget which calculates the budget share required for each task in the workflow. We target as a platform the multi-datacenter clouds so that the costs of data transfers between data centers are considered.

We evaluated the makespan and costs using two real-world workflows with budget scenarios. Our approach shows identical makespan as 'All-in' distribution strategy but surpasses it in the case of restricted budgets. The 'Uniform' approach is far from being competitive with our algorithm by recording slower makespan. This makes the power of our algorithm to improve makespan with a minimal budget. In most cases, our algorithm behaves as an 'All-in' approach, without exceeding budget constraints.

Future work will focus on extending the experimental tests with large scale workflows. Other more precise performance metrics will be used to better assess the proposed algorithm.

References

1. Arabnejad, V., Bubendorfer, K., Ng, B.: Budget distribution strategies for scientific workflow scheduling in commercial clouds. In: 2016 IEEE 12th International Conference on e-Science (e-Science), pp. 137–146. IEEE (2016)
2. Arabnejad, V., Bubendorfer, K., Ng, B.: Budget and deadline aware e-science workflow scheduling in clouds. IEEE Trans. Parallel Distrib. Syst. **30**(1), 29–44 (2018)
3. Braun, T.D., et al.: A comparison of eleven static heuristics for mapping a class of independent tasks onto heterogeneous distributed computing systems. J. Parallel Distrib. Comput. **61**(6), 810–837 (2001)
4. Brucker, P.: Scheduling Algorithms, vol. 3. Springer, Heidelberg (2007). https://doi.org/10.1007/978-3-540-69516-5
5. Caniou, Y., Caron, E., Chang, A.K.W., Robert, Y.: Budget-aware scheduling algorithms for scientific workflows with stochastic task weights on heterogeneous IAAS cloud platforms. In: 2018 IEEE International Parallel and Distributed Processing Symposium Workshops (IPDPSW), pp. 15–26. IEEE (2018)
6. Kalyan Chakravarthi, K., Shyamala, L., Vaidehi, V.: Budget aware scheduling algorithm for workflow applications in IAAS clouds. Cluster Comput. 1–15 (2020)
7. Fahringer, T., Jugravu, A., Pllana, S., Prodan, R., Seragiotto Jr., C., Truong, H.-L.: Askalon: a tool set for cluster and grid computing. Concurrency and Computation: Practice and Experience **17**(2–4), 143–169 (2005)
8. Ghafouri, R., Movaghar, A., Mohsenzadeh, M.: Time-cost efficient scheduling algorithms for executing workflow in infrastructure as a service clouds. Wireless Pers. Commun. **103**(3), 2035–2070 (2018)
9. Han, P., Du, C., Chen, J., Ling, F., Du, X.: Cost and makespan scheduling of workflows in clouds using list multiobjective optimization technique. J. Syst. Archit. 101837 (2020)
10. Pingping, L., Zhang, G., Zhu, Z., Zhou, X., Sun, J., Zhou, J.: A review of cost and makespan-aware workflow scheduling in clouds. J. Circuits, Syst. Comput. **28**(06), 1930006 (2019)
11. Oukfif, K., Bouali, L., Bouzefrane, S., Oulebsir-Boumghar, F.: Energy-aware DPSO algorithm for workflow scheduling on computational grids. In: 2015 3rd International Conference on Future Internet of Things and Cloud (FiCloud), pp. 651–656. IEEE (2015)
12. Oukfif, K., Oulebsir-Boumghar, F., Bouzefrane, S., Banerjee, S.: Workflow scheduling with data transfer optimisation and enhancement of reliability in cloud data centres. Int. J. Commun. Networks Distrib. Syst. **24**(3), 262–283 (2020)
13. Rodriguez, M.A., Buyya, R.: Budget-driven scheduling of scientific workflows in IAAS clouds with fine-grained billing periods. ACM Trans. Auton. Adapt. Syst. (TAAS) **12**(2), 1–22 (2017)
14. Topcuoglu, H., Hariri, S., Min-you, W.: Performance-effective and low-complexity task scheduling for heterogeneous computing. IEEE Trans. Parallel Distrib. Syst. **13**(3), 260–274 (2002)

15. Verma, A., Kaushal, S.: Cost-time efficient scheduling plan for executing workflows in the cloud. J. Comput. **13**(4), 495–506 (2015)
16. Fuhui, W., Qingbo, W., Tan, Y.: Workflow scheduling in cloud: a survey. J. Supercomput. **71**(9), 3373–3418 (2015)
17. Zheng, W., Sakellariou, R.: Budget-deadline constrained workflow planning for admission control. J. Grid Comput. **11**(4), 633–651 (2013)
18. Zhou, N., Lin, W., Feng, W., Shi, F., Pang, X.: Budget-deadline constrained approach for scientific workflows scheduling in a cloud environment. Cluster Comput. 1–15 (2020)

IoT-Edge-Cloud Computing Framework for QoS-Aware Computation Offloading in Autonomous Mobile Agents: Modeling and Simulation

Leila Ismail[1,2]([⊠]) [iD] and Huned Materwala[1,2] [iD]

[1] Distributed Computing and Systems Research Laboratory, Department of Computer Science and Software Engineering, College of Information Technology, United Arab Emirates University, Al Ain, Abu Dhabi 15551, United Arab Emirates
[2] National Water and Energy Center, United Arab Emirates University, Al Ain, Abu Dhabi 15551, United Arab Emirates
leila@uaeu.ac.ae

Abstract. Edge-cloud computing is an emerging computational model that allows offloading of service requests by the autonomous mobile agents from the edge-server to the cloud-server. This is to reduce the network latency prevalent in the cloud-IoT model. However, Quality-of-Service (QoS)-Aware computation offloading in a heterogeneous and dynamic edge-cloud environment remains an open problem. In this paper, we propose a queuing theory-based edge-cloud computing framework for QoS-aware offloading in mobile autonomous agents. This framework model decides whether to execute an incoming request to the edge-server on the edge itself or to offload to one of the heterogeneous cloud servers such that the request's execution time is the minimum. To model a request's execution time, we consider the processing capabilities and the queues overheads of the edge and cloud servers, and the edge-cloud communications' time. The details of the evaluation results, using dataset generated from real-life scenarios, are presented in the paper.

Keywords: Cloud computing · Computation offloading · Edge computing · Internet of things · Modeling · Quality-of-service · Queuing theory · Simulation

1 Introduction

Internet of Things (IoT) is a network of interconnected physical devices and systems that can wirelessly communicate and transfer data without human intervention to fulfil tasks [1]. There are various applications of IoT in the context of smart cities such as smart transportation, smart healthcare, smart homes, smart education, smart energy and smart industry [2]. However, IoT devices are often limited in terms of data storage and access, scalability, networking and computing capabilities. These limitations are complemented by the cloud computing paradigm [3] to solve the complex analysis required by smart city applications.

© Springer Nature Switzerland AG 2021
S. Bouzefrane et al. (Eds.): MSPN 2020, LNCS 12605, pp. 161–176, 2021.
https://doi.org/10.1007/978-3-030-67550-9_11

Cloud computing is a computing paradigm that provides on-demand scalable shared pool of hardware and software resources to end-users over the internet, with minimal interaction by the cloud service provider. IoT applications tap into the cloud computing resources to increase the quality-of-service (QoS) in terms of execution time. This gives the rise to Cloud-IoT applications [4]. However, the massive amount of end users and data generated by the IoT devices push the network to its limit, making it difficult for the cloud computing to guarantee the QoS for the applications. This delay in execution time is not acceptable particularly for applications that require real-time decision-making. For instance, a delay in execution for applications in healthcare or transportation domain can cause a serious threat to human life. Cloud-IoT suffers from performance issues leading to the introduction of edge computing [5] to optimize the performance of the cloud-IoT systems. This is by providing data storage and processing capabilities at the edge of the network near the IoT devices.

Edge computing shifts the data, applications and the associated services from the distant cloud to the logical extremes of the network. Consequently, the network latency between the IoT devices and the cloud can be significantly reduced, thus enhancing the applications' QoS by reducing the communications' cost. However, compared to the cloud servers, the processing capabilities and the storage capacity of the edge servers are limited, resulting in performance degradation due to these bottlenecks. Consequently, it becomes crucial to offload computations from the edge to the cloud whenever required to enhance the QoS. Consequently, there should be a decision to be taken based on: 1) the network capabilities of the edge-cloud infrastructure, 2) the storage capacities of the edge and cloud, 3) the computing capabilities of the edge and cloud and 4) the requirements of an application in terms of QoS. Several works in the literature propose an edge-cloud model for computation offloading to enhance an application's performance [6–11]. However, these models have not been evaluated in a heterogeneous and dynamic edge-cloud environment. In this paper, we propose a queuing approach-based edge-cloud model for QoS-aware computation offloading in autonomous mobile agents. Autonomous mobile agents are intelligent software or hardware components that works independently without a human intervention for decision-making. The model either executes an agent's request on the receiving edge or offloads the execution to the one of the heterogeneous cloud servers such that the request's execution time is the minimum. The main contributions of this paper are as follows:

1. We explain the background of edge-cloud computing and present an overview of 3-tier IoT-edge-cloud computing framework.
2. A queuing theory-based IoT-edge-cloud computing model is proposed for QoS-aware computation offloading in autonomous mobile agents. For each incoming agent's request to the edge, the model decides whether to execute it on the edge itself or to offload it to one of the heterogeneous cloud servers. This is in a way that the total execution time of the request is minimized.
3. The computation capabilities and the queue overheads of the edge and cloud servers and the data communications' time between the edge and the cloud are considered while modeling a request's execution time.

4. We evaluate the performance of the proposed model in a heterogenous IoT-edge-cloud environment using a dataset generated from real-life scenarios. This is in a dynamic edge-cloud environment.

The remainder of the paper proceeds as follows. Section 2 provides an overview of related work. Section 3 presents the background of cloud and edge computing along with a 3-tier IoT-edge-cloud framework. Our proposed IoT-edge-cloud computing system model for computation offloading is explained in Sect. 4. The experimental setup, experiments and results analysis of our model, in terms of execution time in a heterogeneous IoT-edge-cloud computing environment, are presented in Sect. 5. Section 6 concludes the paper and highlights future research directions.

2 Related Work

Several works in the literature propose computation offloading models for edge-cloud computing [6–22]. However, most of these works focus on 2-tier architecture which consists of the mobile devices as one tier and the cloud a second tier. In these models, the computation offloading is from the mobile device to the cloud, i.e., either executing the partial/full requests locally on the mobile device or the cloud-server [12–22]. Very few works in the literature focus on the problem of scheduling requests on either an edge-server or on a cloud-server in case that IoT devices does not have resources for computing and storage in a 3-tier architecture [6–11].

Ko et al. [6] proposed a spatial and temporal computation offloading decision algorithm based on Markov decision process. The mobile device decides either to process the request on itself or to schedule it to an edge or a cloud-server. An objective function considers the energy consumption, the processing time and the data transmission cost. Zhao et al. [7] proposed a collaborative computation offloading and resource allocation optimization scheme for vehicular networks. This is to decide on either to execute users' requests on the vehicle itself, edge or the cloud-server such that the system utility and the computation time is improved. Hong et al. [8] proposed a multi-hop cooperative computation offloading using a game-theoretic approach for the IoT device to decide on either to execute the request on itself, edge or the cloud. This is in a way that the cost of computation in terms of computation time and the energy consumption is the minimum. Huang et al. [9] formulated a dynamic optimization problem to schedule a user's request on an edge-server or the cloud in a way that the request's response time is the minimum. However, the authors do not consider the communication time between the user and the edge. To reduce the scheduling time by reducing the search space, the authors applied goal softening to the optimization problem. Ma et al. [10] proposed a queuing model approach for scheduling dynamic users' requests either to an edge-server or one of the cloud instances in a way that the computational resource cost is the minimum while satisfying the QoS of the requests in terms of response time. Liu et al. [11] proposed an energy-efficient collaborative request computation offloading algorithm to execute requests on either the IoT device itself, on the edge-server or the cloud-server. This is in a way that the energy consumption of the request execution is minimized while considering the requests-dependency and the completion time requirements.

However, none of the above-discussed work considers the impact of a dynamic heterogeneous edge and cloud servers on the model performance. In this paper, we propose a queuing approach-based IoT-edge-cloud computing model to decide whether to execute an incoming request on the edge itself or to offload it to one of the heterogeneous cloud servers. This is in a way that the total execution time of the request is minimized. In our model, we consider the computation capabilities and the queue overheads of the edge and cloud servers and the data communications' time between the edge and the cloud to optimize the execution time. Therefore, we evaluate the performance of the proposed model with increasing number of edge servers, cloud servers and mobile agents in a heterogenous IoT-edge-cloud environment.

3   Overview of IoT-Edge-Cloud Computing Framework

In this section, we discuss the background knowledge of cloud and edge computing and present an overview of the IoT-edge-cloud computing framework. In addition, we highlight the applications of IoT-edge-cloud computing in the context of a smart city.

3.1   Cloud Computing

The Cloud computing revolutionizes the way computing is performed; not only relying on limited user resources, but also tapping into large-scale resources, whether hardware and/or software, that are available all the time [3]. It enables delivery of services and resources over the internet. This is by allowing convenient and timely network access to a shared pool of scalable and configurable resources and all of this can be provisioned with least management effort or cloud service provider interaction. These resources can be of type computing, storage, or networking and allocated based on a pay-per-use model. Cloud computing is mainly characterized by features such as on-demand service, elasticity, broad network access, resource pooling and measured services.

Cloud computing provides mainly three service models: 1) software as a service which allows multiple users to use web-based software services remotely, 2) platform as a service which makes available the necessary environment and tools that are required to develop web-based applications and 3) infrastructure as a service that offers virtualized processing, storage and networking hardware that are hosted in a cloud center to multi-tenant remote users. With the emergence of smart cities applications, cloud computing helps to increase business opportunities as these applications are developed to be used as software as a service in the cloud, thus participating in the economic ecosystems of a nation. Moreover, with the trend towards the use of sensors and mobile devices as an integral part of smart cities, IoT as a service is evolving to assist end-users with easy deployment and management of smart cities applications.

3.2   Edge Computing

With the emergence of smart cities applications and the increase of IoT devices on the edge, a massive amount of data is generated to be computed at cloud data centers, pushing the network bandwidth to its limit. Despite technological advancements in networking, cloud data centers cannot guarantee an application's execution time. Therefore, it becomes crucial to bring applications' contents and processing close to the mobile devices and sensors; giving birth to the edge computing to deliver networks contents more efficiently [23]. Edge computing can be seen as a cache running services and storing data in the edge rather than the cloud. The cache is capable of exploiting mobile agents' proximity to the edge and nearby smart objects to perform tasks on behalf of the cloud on the edge that is closest to the mobile agents leading to better execution time. This is crucial for applications that need faster decision-making, such as industrial distributed control systems, autonomous vehicles, healthcare, e-commerce, education and robotics.

3.3 IoT-Edge-Cloud Computing Framework

Figure 1 shows an overview of a 3-tier IoT-edge-cloud computing framework. It mainly consists of three layers:

1. IoT layer: This layer consists of ubiquitous devices and sensors generating data/requesting services to/from different smart cities applications such as smart transportation, smart healthcare, smart industry, smart energy and smart home. The IoT devices in this layer are connected to the edge devices/servers in the edge layer based on proximity.
2. Edge layer: This layer consists of the edge devices/servers depending on the smart city application. For instance, the edge layer consists of hospitals or local clinics in the context of smart healthcare, base stations or Wi-Fi access routers for smart homes and colleges/schools for smart education. The main functions of the edge layer are 1) to schedule users' requests either to the edge or the cloud-server and 2) to process the requests being executed on the edge-server in real-time.

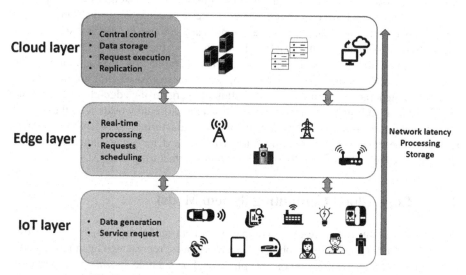

Fig. 1. Overview of IoT-edge-cloud computing framework.

3. Cloud layer: This layer consists of cloud resources such as processing servers, storage, virtual machines and network facilities. The main functions of this layer are: 1) to have central control over the network, 2) to serve as storage for sensor data, 3) to process the agents' requests that are sent from the edge and 4) to aid in fault tolerance by replication of the data over multiple clouds.

The IoT-edge-cloud architecture introduces the edge layer between the IoT and the cloud layers to reduce the network delays between the IoT and cloud. This allows the IoT devices to be in the proximity of the edge and get the services more efficiently. However, in this architecture the processing capabilities and the storage capacities increase while moving upwards through the layers. The cloud resources have more storage and processing capabilities compared to the edge resources, while the IoT devices typically have no to little capabilities.

3.4 Smart City Applications on IoT-Edge-Cloud Computing

A smart city has been closely associated with edge-cloud computing due to the processing and storage requirements of the dynamic data and users' requests [24]. Cloud solutions along with the edge computing can overcome the limitations of these individual computing paradigms and enhance the QoS of the smart cities applications such as smart transportation, smart healthcare, smart home, smart energy and smart industry.

Smart transportation is one of the main applications of smart cities where the daily commute lives of the citizens will be more efficient and sustainable. This is by collecting traffic data in real-time and processing them in the edge-cloud computing framework [25, 26]. The healthcare system has been revolutionized over the past decade with the involvement of medical sensors and devices monitoring individuals 24/7 and generating a huge amount of data. Edge-cloud computing can enhance the quality of patient care with more real-time prognosis/diagnosis while utilizing fewer resources [27, 28].

A smart home is a place of living that uses internet-connected devices and sensors to remotely monitor and manage home appliances and systems in an efficient, real-time and cost-effective manner using an edge-cloud computing platform [29]. Smart energy is the revolution in the business models, technologies and policies of the traditional energy generation and distribution system by using smart meters-based monitoring. This is for efficient generation, storage and distribution of energy using edge-cloud computing [30, 31]. Smart industry is connecting the physical and digital worlds with the help of sensors and digitization to revolutionize the way manufacturing industries and factories function. The edge-cloud computing framework is used for smart industry for safe, efficient, flexible and eco-friendly workflow and manufacturing [32, 33].

4 IoT-Edge-Cloud Computing System Model

Figure 2 shows our IoT-edge-cloud computing system model that consists of M edge servers, N cloud servers and K mobile IoT devices that are represented by mobile agents. A mobile agent is an integral part of an application. For example, in smart transportation a vehicle is a mobile agent, in smart education students carrying smart phones that are represented by mobile agents, and in smart healthcare patients carrying biosensors and smart phones are considered as mobile agents. For each mobile agent $k \in \{1, 2, ...,$ K\}, let $l_i(t)$ denote the geographical location of the agent i at time t. Each mobile agent is connected to the nearest edge-server based on Euclidean distance [34]. The requests from a mobile agent are sent to the edge-server to which the agent is connected. For each edger-server $m \in \{1, 2, ..., M\}$, there exists two queues: 1) decision queue, where the decision is made whether to execute the agent's request on the same edge m or offload the request on a cloud-server $n \in \{1, 2, ..., N\}$ for execution and 2) service queue, where the requests will be executed on the edge.

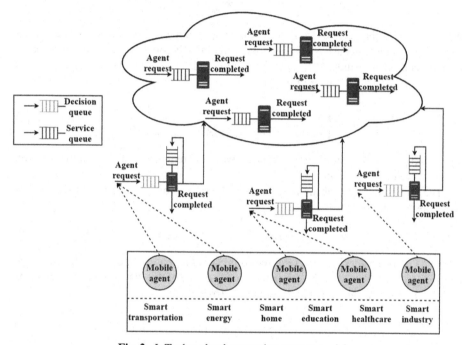

Fig. 2. IoT-edge-cloud computing system model.

Each request by a mobile agent is characterized by its length in Million Instructions (MI). When an agent sends a service request r_i, $r \in \{1, 2, 3, ...\}$, to the connected edge-server m, the request enters the decision queue of that edge. The decision queue computes the request's execution time on the edge itself and all the cloud servers considering the computation capabilities and the queue overheads of the edge and cloud servers and the edge-cloud data communications' time. After computing the execution time of the request r_i on the edge-server m and the all the cloud servers N, the decision queue of server m schedules the request to the server (either to itself or to one of the cloud servers) that gives the minimum execution time as shown in Eq. (1).

$$r_i \in j, \; s.t. \; j = \min(ET_{i,j}), j \in \{m\} \cup N \qquad (1)$$

where $ET_{i,j}$ is the execution time of request r_i on the server j.

4.1 Execution Time for Edge Computing

The execution time $(ET_{i,m})$ for processing the request r_i on the edge-server m is calculated using Eq. (2).

$$ET_{i,m} = PT_{i,md} + PT_{i,ms} \tag{2}$$

where $PT_{i,md}$ and $PT_{i,ms}$ are the processing times of the request (r_i) by the decision and the service queues of the edge-server m, respectively. The processing time of r_i by the decision queue is calculated using Eq. (3).

$$PT_{i,md} = DT_{i,md} + WT_{i,md} = c + WT_{i,md} \tag{3}$$

where $DT_{i,md}$ is the decision computing time required to decide on whether the request should be executed on the edge or the cloud. This value is constant (c) for any considered infrastructure under study. $WT_{i,md}$ is the waiting time of r_i in the decision queue of the edge-server m calculated using Eq. (4).

$$WT_{i,md} = \begin{cases} 0, & i = 1 \\ \max\{0, PT_{i-1,md} - IAT_{\{i,i-1\},md}\}, & i > 1 \end{cases} \tag{4}$$

where $IAT_{\{i,i-1\},m}$ is the inter arrival time between the requests r_i and r_{i-1} at the decision queue of the edge-server m.

The processing time of the request r_i by the service queue of the edge-server m is calculated using Eq. (5).

$$PT_{i,ms} = ST_{i,m} + WT_{i,ms} \tag{5}$$

where $ST_{i,m}$ is the service time required to process the request r_i on the edge-server m and $WT_{i,ms}$ is the waiting time of r_i in the service queue of the edge-server m. The values of $ST_{i,m}$ and $WT_{i,ms}$ are calculated using Eqs. (6) and (7).

$$ST_{i,m} = \frac{L(r_i)}{PS_m} \tag{6}$$

$$WT_{i,ms} = \begin{cases} 0, & i = 1 \\ \max\{0, PT_{i-1,ms} - (PT_{i,md} - PT_{i-1,md})\}, & i > 1 \end{cases} \tag{7}$$

where $L(r_i)$ is the length of the request r_i in MI and PS_m is the processing speed of the edge-server m in Million Instructions per Second (MIPS). The value $(PT_{i,md} - PT_{i-1,md})$ depicts the inter arrival time between the requests r_i and r_{i-1} at the service queue of edge-server m.

4.2 Execution Time for Cloud Computing

The execution time $(ET_{i,n})$ for processing the request r_i on the cloud-server n is calculated using Eq. (8).

$$ET_{i,n} = PT_{i,md} + PT_{i,ns} + CT_{n,m} \tag{8}$$

where $PT_{i,md}$ is the processing time of the request (r_i) by the decision queue of the edge-server m (Eq. (3)), $PT_{i,ns}$ is the processing time by the service queue of the cloud-server n and $CT_{n,m}$ is the communication time to send the request response from the cloud-server n to the edge-server m. A constant value for $CT_{n,m}$ is considered in this paper. The processing time of r_i by the service queue of cloud-server n is calculated using Eq. (9).

$$PT_{i,ns} = ST_{i,n} + WT_{i,ns} \tag{9}$$

where $ST_{i,n}$ is the service time required to process the request r_i on the cloud-server n and $WT_{i,ns}$ is the waiting time of r_i in the service queue of the cloud-server n. The values of $ST_{i,n}$ and $WT_{i,ns}$ are calculated using Eqs. (10) and (11).

$$ST_{i,n} = \frac{L(r_i)}{PS_n} \tag{10}$$

$$WT_{i,ns} = \begin{cases} CT_{m,n}, & i = 1 \\ max\{0, PT_{i-1,ns} - (PT_{i,md} - PT_{i-1,md}) + CT_{m,n}\}, & i > 1 \end{cases} \tag{11}$$

where PS_n is the processing speed of the cloud-server n in MIPS and $CT_{m,n}$ is the communication time to send the agent's request from the edge-server m to the cloud-server n. The value $(PT_{i,md} - PT_{i-1,md})$ depicts the inter arrival time between the requests r_i and r_{i-1} at the service queue of cloud-server n. The value of $CT_{m,n}$ is considered similar to that of $CT_{n,m}$ in this paper.

5 Performance Evaluation

In this section, we explain the experimental environment, experiments, and the experimental results analysis. We evaluate our model in terms of execution time with increasing number of edge servers, cloud servers and mobile agents in a heterogenous IoT-edge-cloud environment.

5.1 Experimental Environment

To evaluate the performance of our IoT-edge-cloud computing model, we create a heterogeneous IoT-edge-cloud environment made of five different types of edge servers and four different types of cloud servers. The edge and the cloud servers are implemented using Matlab R2016a [35]. The processing speed (MIPS) of these servers are shown in Table 1.

Table 1. Edge and cloud-servers' types used in the experiments.

		Type 1	Type 2	Type 3	Type 4	Type 5
MIPS	Edge-server	750	1000	1150	1200	1350
	Cloud-server	2750	2000	3500	3000	–

To acquire the geographical position of the mobile agents for connecting them to the nearest edge-server, we use the Vehicle-Crowd Intraction (VCI) - DUT dataset [36]. The values from the x_est and y_est columns of the dataset, that represent the estimated vehicle position, are used as the positions of mobile agents. Each mobile generates a load of requests in terms of MI that represent an intensive smart application service. This is by generating loads between 1000 and 10,000 MI randomly by each mobile agent. Table 2 shows the experimental parameters.

Table 2. Experimental parameters

# Edge servers	5, 10, 15, 20, 25
# Cloud servers	20, 25, 30, 35, 40
# Mobile agents	100, 200, 300, 400, 500
Minimum (Request's length in MI)	1000
Maximum (Request's length in MI)	10000
Communication time between edge and cloud	2 s
Service time of the decision queue at the edge	2 s
Requests' mean arrival rate	0.5

5.2 Experiments

We first simulate the IoT-edge-cloud computing network with 100 mobile agents, 5 edge servers, 20 cloud servers. For the mobile agents' geographical locations, we take the first 100 locations from the VIC-DUT dataset. For the geographical location of each edge-server, we randomly generate the x and y coordinates between the minimum and maximum values of x and y coordinates values of the mobile agents respectively. Each mobile agent generates randomly a request between 1000 and 10,000 MI. For each request, an exponential arrival time to the decision queue is generated with mean arrival rate of 0.5 s per request. Each mobile agent is then connected to the nearest edge based on Euclidean distance. For each request on edge-server, the server computes the request's execution time when executed on the edge itself or when executed on a cloud-server. This is considering the computation capabilities and the queue overheads of the edge and cloud servers and the IoT-edge-cloud data communications' time. The request is then scheduled by the edge's decision queue to the server that executes the request in the minimum time. The execution time for each agent's request on each-server is computed, and then the average execution time of all the requests is computed. This experiment is repeated for three scenarios: 1) with increasing number of edge servers, while keeping the number of cloud servers and mobile agents constant at 20 and 100 respectively, 2) with increasing number of cloud servers keeping the edge servers and mobile agents constant at 5 and 100 respectively, and 3) with increasing number of mobile agents keeping the number of edge and cloud servers constant at 5 and 20 respectively. The execution time for each request and the average execution time for each experiment are computed.

5.3 Experimental Results Analysis

In this section, we evaluate our IoT-edge-cloud computing model in terms of execution time. We also give insights and conclusions on these evaluations.

Figure 3 shows the execution times of the mobile agents' requests with increasing number of edge servers. It shows that the execution times of the requests decreases with the increasing number of edge servers, which is intuitive. This is because of the distribution of the agents' requests among multiple edge servers. Figure 4 shows the average execution time for all the requests with increasing number of edge servers. It shows that the average execution time decreases with increasing number of edge servers with an average reduction of 0.40886 s.

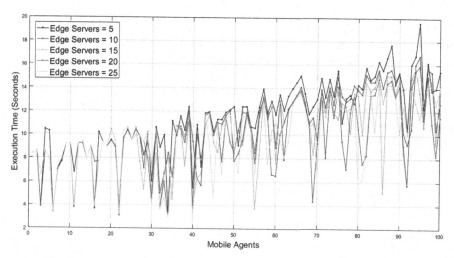

Fig. 3. Requests' execution times when the number of edge servers increases.

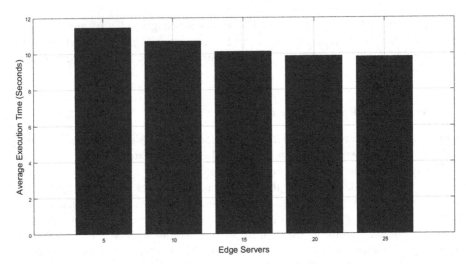

Fig. 4. Average requests' execution time when the number of edge servers increases.

Figure 5 shows the execution times of the mobile agents' requests with increasing number of cloud servers and a constant number of edge servers and mobile agents. It shows that the execution times of the requests decreases with the increasing number of cloud servers. This is because of the distribution of the agents' requests among multiple cloud servers. However, comparing the execution times with increase cloud servers (Fig. 5) to that with increasing edge servers (Fig. 3), there is not much difference even though the processing capability of the cloud servers is higher compared to that of the edge servers. This is because all the requests will first go to an edge-server that will decide whether to execute the request on edge or send it to the cloud. Thus, increasing

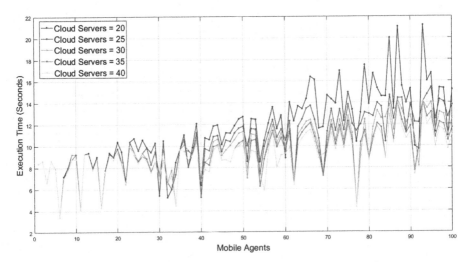

Fig. 5. Requests' execution times when the number of cloud servers increases.

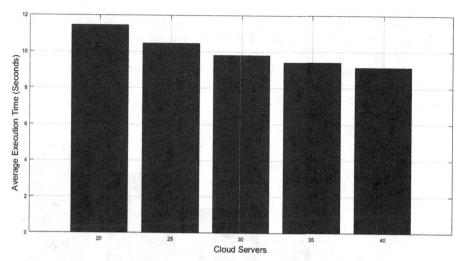

Fig. 6. Average requests' execution time when the number of cloud servers increases.

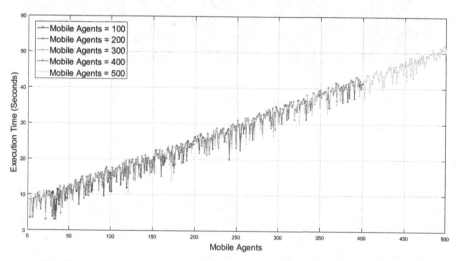

Fig. 7. Requests' execution times when the number of mobile agents increases.

the cloud servers will not have a significant impact as the requests need to wait in the decision queue of the edge-server leading to increase in execution time. Figure 6 shows the average execution time for all the requests with increasing number of cloud servers. It shows that the average execution time decreases with increasing number of cloud servers with an average reduction of 0.57462 s, which is not significantly high compared to that with increasing number of edge servers (Fig. 4).

Figure 7 shows the requests' execution times with increasing number of mobile agents and constant number of edge and cloud servers. It shows the execution times increases linearly with the number of mobile agents. This is because the increasing requests with constant number of servers will create overhead in the service queue of the edge and the cloud servers. Figure 8 shows the average execution time for all the requests with increasing number of mobile agents. It shows that the average execution time increases with increasing number of cloud servers with an average increment of 4.32118 s, which is contradicting to that when the number of edge and cloud servers increases (Figs. 4 and 6 respectively).

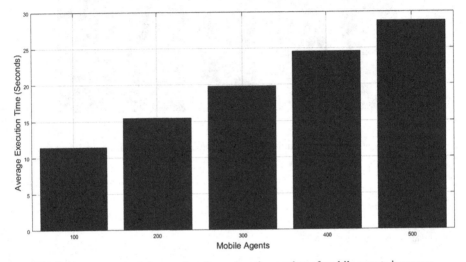

Fig. 8. Average requests' execution time when the number of mobile agents increases.

6 Conclusion

QoS-aware computation offloading is an important problem in a heterogeneous and dynamic IoT-edge-cloud environment with increasing smart cities applications. In this paper, we propose a queuing theory-based IoT-edge-cloud computing framework for QoS-aware offloading in mobile autonomous agents. The proposed model decides whether to execute an agent's request on the edge-server or schedule it to a cloud-server such that the request's execution time is the minimum. Our modeling and simulation for execution time takes into consideration the capabilities and queuing overhead of the edge and cloud servers and the edge-cloud communications' time.

We evaluate our proposed model using a dataset generated from real-life scenarios in a heterogeneous IoT-edge-cloud environment with increasing number of edge servers, cloud servers and mobile agents. Our experimental results reveal that increasing cloud servers with high capabilities while keeping constant number of edge-servers will not lead to significant performance improvement because of the decision-making overhead on the edge servers. Consequently, we learned from this paper that one should scale up the number of edge servers as well. Our future research direction would focus on the modeling of optimal number and locations of the edge servers required for better performance.

Acknowledgements. This work was funded by the National Water and Energy Center under Grant 31R215.

References

1. Buyya, R., Dastjerdi, A.V.: Internet of Things: Principles and Paradigms. Elsevier Science (2016)
2. Mehmood, Y., Ahmad, F., Yaqoob, I., et al.: Internet-of-things-based smart cities: recent advances and challenges. IEEE Commun. Mag. **55**, 16–24 (2017)
3. Mell, P., Grance, T.: The NIST definition of cloud computing recommendations of the national institute of standards and technology. NIST Spec. Publ. **145**, 7 (2011). https://doi.org/10.1136/emj.2010.096966
4. Ismail, L., Materwala, H.: Energy-aware VM placement and task scheduling in cloud-iot computing: classification and performance evaluation. IEEE Internet Things J. **5**, 5166–5176 (2018). https://doi.org/10.1109/JIOT.2018.2865612
5. Shi, W., Cao, J., Zhang, Q., et al.: Edge computing: vision and challenges. IEEE Internet Things J. **3**, 637–646 (2016)
6. Ko, H., Lee, J., Pack, S.: Spatial and temporal computation offloading decision algorithm in edge cloud-enabled heterogeneous networks. IEEE Access **6**, 18920–18932 (2018)
7. Zhao, J., Li, Q., Gong, Y., Zhang, K.: Computation offloading and resource allocation for cloud assisted mobile edge computing in vehicular networks. IEEE Trans. Veh. Technol. **68**, 7944–7956 (2019)
8. Hong, Z., Chen, W., Huang, H., et al.: Multi-hop cooperative computation offloading for industrial IoT–edge–cloud computing environments. IEEE Trans. Parallel Distrib. Syst. **30**, 2759–2774 (2019)
9. Huang, J., Lan, Y., Xu, M.: A simulation-based approach of QoS-aware service selection in mobile edge computing. Wirel. Commun. Mob. Comput. **2018**, 1–10 (2018)
10. Ma, X., Wang, S., Zhang, S., et al.: Cost-efficient resource provisioning for dynamic requests in cloud assisted mobile edge computing. IEEE Trans. Cloud Comput. (2019)
11. Liu, F., Huang, Z., Wang, L.: Energy-efficient collaborative task computation offloading in cloud-assisted edge computing for IoT sensors. Sensors, **19** (2019). Article No. 1105
12. Chen, X., Jiao, L., Li, W., Fu, X.: Efficient multi-user computation offloading for mobile-edge cloud computing. IEEE/ACM Trans. Netw. **24**, 2795–2808 (2015)
13. Li, X., Dang, Y., Aazam, M., et al.: Energy-Efficient Computation Offloading in Vehicular Edge Cloud Computing. IEEE Access **8**, 37632–37644 (2020)
14. Tao, X., Ota, K., Dong, M., et al.: Performance guaranteed computation offloading for mobile-edge cloud computing. IEEE Wirel. Commun. Lett. **6**, 774–777 (2017)
15. Chen, W., Wang, D., Li, K.: Multi-user multi-task computation offloading in green mobile edge cloud computing. IEEE Trans. Serv. Comput. **12**, 726–738 (2018)
16. You, C., Huang, K., Chae, H., Kim, B.-H.: Energy-efficient resource allocation for mobile-edge computation offloading. IEEE Trans. Wirel. Commun. **16**, 1397–1411 (2016)
17. Ren, J., Yu, G., Cai, Y., He, Y.: Latency optimization for resource allocation in mobile-edge computation offloading. IEEE Trans. Wirel. Commun. **17**, 5506–5519 (2018)
18. Liu, L., Chang, Z., Guo, X., Ristaniemi, T.: Multi-objective optimization for computation offloading in mobile-edge computing. In: 2017 IEEE Symposium on Computers and Communications (ISCC), pp 832–837 (2017)
19. Chen, M., Hao, Y., Hu, L., et al.: Edge-CoCaCo: Toward joint optimization of computation, caching, and communication on edge cloud. IEEE Wirel. Commun. **25**, 21–27 (2018)

20. Hao, Y., Chen, M., Hu, L., et al.: Energy efficient task caching and offloading for mobile edge computing. IEEE Access **6**, 11365–11373 (2018)
21. Mao, Y., Zhang, J., Letaief, K.B.: Dynamic computation offloading for mobile-edge computing with energy harvesting devices. IEEE J. Sel. Areas Commun. **34**, 3590–3605 (2016)
22. Zhang, J., Xia, W., Yan, F., Shen, L.: Joint computation offloading and resource allocation optimization in heterogeneous networks with mobile edge computing. IEEE Access **6**, 19324–19337 (2018)
23. Dilley, J., Maggs, B., Parikh, J., et al.: Globally distributed content delivery. IEEE Internet Comput. **6**, 50–58 (2002)
24. Zhao, L., Wang, J., Liu, J., Kato, N.: Optimal edge resource allocation in IoT-based smart cities. IEEE Netw. **33**, 30–35 (2019)
25. Jaisimha, A., Khan, S., Anisha, B., Kumar, P.R.: Smart transportation: an edge-cloud hybrid computing perspective. Inven. Commun. Comput. Technol. **89**, 1263–1271 (2020)
26. Chen, W., Liu, B., Huang, H., et al.: When UAV swarm meets edge-cloud computing: The QoS perspective. IEEE Netw. **33**, 36–43 (2019)
27. Oueida, S., Kotb, Y., Aloqaily, M., et al.: An edge computing based smart healthcare framework for resource management. Sensors, **18** (2018). Article No. 4307
28. Abdellatif, A.A., Emam, A., Chiasserini, C.-F., et al.: Edge-based compression and classification for smart healthcare systems: concept, implementation and evaluation. Expert Syst. Appl. **117**, 1–14 (2019)
29. Albataineh, H., Nijim, M., Bollampall, D.: The design of a novel smart home control system using smart grid based on edge and cloud computing. In: 2020 IEEE 8th International Conference on Smart Energy Grid Engineering (SEGE), pp. 88–91 (2020)
30. Liu, Y., Yang, C., Jiang, L., et al.: Intelligent edge computing for IoT-based energy management in smart cities. IEEE Netw. **33**, 111–117 (2019)
31. Chen, S., Wen, H., Wu, J., et al.: Internet of Things based smart grids supported by intelligent edge computing. IEEE Access **7**, 74089–74102 (2019)
32. Georgakopoulos, D., Jayaraman, P.P., Fazia, M., et al.: Internet of Things and edge cloud computing roadmap for manufacturing. IEEE Cloud Comput. **3**, 66–73 (2016)
33. Afrin, M., Jin, J., Rahman, A., et al.: Multi-objective resource allocation for Edge Cloud based robotic workflow in smart factory. Futur. Gener. Comput. Syst. **97**, 119–130 (2019)
34. Danielsson, P.-E.: Euclidean distance mapping. Comput. Graph Image Process **14**, 227–248 (1980)
35. MATLAB - MathWorks - MATLAB & Simulink. https://www.mathworks.com/products/matlab.html. Accessed 7 Apr 2020
36. Yang, D., Li, L., Redmill, K., Özgüner, Ü.: Top-view trajectories: a pedestrian dataset of vehicle-crowd interaction from controlled experiments and crowded campus. In: 2019 IEEE Intelligent Vehicles Symposium (IV), pp 899–904 (2019)

Toward a Privacy Guard for Cloud-Based Home Assistants and IoT Devices

Radja Boukharrou$^{(\boxtimes)}$, Ahmed-Chawki Chaouche, and Khaoula Mahdjar

MISC Laboratory, University Abdelhamid Mehri - Constantine 2,
Ali Mendjeli Campus, 25000 Constantine, Algeria
{radja.boukharrou,ahmed.chaouche,khaoula.mahdjar}@univ-constantine2.dz

Abstract. The Internet of Things is a technology which is dominating our lives, making it more comfortable, safer and smarter. Using smart speakers as voice assistants for smart homes provides valuable service and an easy control of IoT devices, despite allowing the emergence of privacy threats and disclosing sensitive data about users. In this paper, we propose to associate with any smart personal assistant a privacy guard gateway (PGG for short) in order to mitigate privacy issues related to cloud-based devices, like profiling and linkage. In an original way, the PGG system is based on a noise addition mechanism that injects dummy requests according to some selected strategy, without the user's activities being stored during the operation. A case study of our approach is experimented with a Google Home Assistant, in order to show its effectiveness.

Keywords: Internet of Things · Smart home Personal Assistants · Cloud-based devices · Privacy issues · Privacy guard gateway · Scrambling mechanism

1 Introduction

Internet of things (IoT) is a new generation of Internet, composed of objects capable of both connecting to an IP network and sharing their data. These objects are interconnected using several wired and/or wireless networks in order to provide users with the most appropriate and transparent services. The ubiquity of IoT objects allows the true emergence of the internet towards a smart environment.

With the growth of integrated and intelligent devices like smartphones and smart wearables, the interaction of humans with computers has changed due to the intelligence embedded in these devices that act proactively using the knowledge gathered about the user [6]. Moreover, other devices have emerged, offering voice interaction with the user by means of natural languages, such as Smart Home Personal Assistants (SPA) [2]. In fact, with the SPA system, we can manage and monitor home devices. While such systems changed the user lifestyle making it easier, comfortable, and smarter, however, their control and confidentiality are compromised [10].

© Springer Nature Switzerland AG 2021
S. Bouzefrane et al. (Eds.): MSPN 2020, LNCS 12605, pp. 177–194, 2021.
https://doi.org/10.1007/978-3-030-67550-9_12

Nowadays, security and privacy are considered the topmost challenges of IoT [6,18], especially in home, because user activities are captured all the time, often without asking his permission. Thereby, the data collected on a user can harm his privacy, especially sensitive data. Privacy of users may be exposed as a result of serious breaches of users' sensitive information, which may occur in devices, storage, during communication, and at processing too. According to [2], most of the smart device owners are oblivious to their collected data being stored in device manufacturers clouds. With the larger adoption of the cloud-based home assistants, several threats are accrued; mobile applications and clouds collect both wanted and unwanted data about the users including their locations, names, addresses, purchases, vocation, etc. These hubs can collect user's habits that can be used and learned by some data analytics engines that analyze user routines by means of machine learning techniques [4,9]. They can go much further and analyze the recorded voices by smart speakers to get profiles about the user concluding much data about his health, whether he is suffering from chronic disease, and so on. In addition, their data analysis is able to understand the context of interactions between users. As shown in [9], by using SPA data they could have the capability to profile the intimacy of a couple and infer how healthy their relationship is, through acoustic analysis of communication between them in a given conversation.

In any home assistant, data analytics is an essential concept, allowing the system to conclude fine-grained decisions and to offer appropriate services, although it compromises users' privacy. The huge amount of data gathered by the home assistant can be stored locally or remotely in cloud servers. Untrusted cloud providers can perform privacy attacks against their clients, by exploiting the collected data for profiling or by selling them to third parties to gain profit. Therefore, it is hard to construct software solutions for such devices that look like a black-box and use encrypted data [11].

In this paper, we aim at strengthening the privacy of SPA within IoT device use cases. In fact, we propose a novel system based on a user-centered approach, called Privacy Guard Gateway (PGG). This system is physically associated with any SPA, in order to mitigate privacy concerns which can be violated by it. Our proposed solution consists to collect the user speech the same as the assistants do and to perform thereafter a noise addition based mechanism. The main role of this mechanism is to fix the profiling concerns and thus ensure data scrambling, as said "too much information is equal to no information". Besides, knowing that the majority of SPAs only support over-IP devices, therefore, the PGG system allows them to be interconnected with non-IP devices too.

The present paper is organized as follows: Sect. 2, introduces an overview of IoT devices manipulation within the possible deployments. In Sect. 3, we present our privacy guard system, which strengthens the privacy of IoT devices and SPA users. The proposed scrambling mechanism is well-developed. In Sect. 4, we experiment the functioning of our system with Google Home assistant as a case study. Section 5 discusses our approach with regard to related works. The last section concludes and brings out our next perspectives.

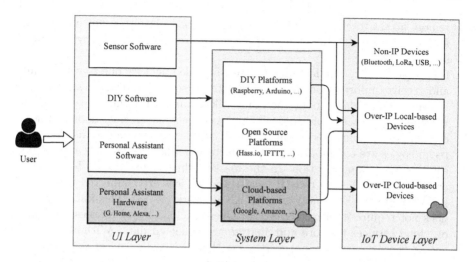

Fig. 1. Overview of IoT systems

2 Internet of Things and Privacy Issues

2.1 Overview of IoT Systems in Smart-Environments

Different IoT architecture has been suggested since its emergence [6]. In fact, there are several ways to control IoT devices in a smart-environment, including user interfaces (UI) and processing platforms. In Fig. 1, we give an overview of IoT architecture that can be applied in smart-environment, like smart-home. We classify the different components of the architecture, in three distinct layers:

UI Layer. Through this layer, the user controls and manages his IoT devices remotely and in a flexible way. The user can use two categories of interfaces: (1) By using installed apps in their mobiles, such as smartphones, tablets, smart TV, laptops, etc. Usually, the user manipulates UI buttons and switches to control the devices (2) Through hardware assistants, like Google Home and Amazon Echo, that interpret user commands using multi-modal interfaces, such as voice, gestures, or eyes (using mixed reality). The main role of this kind of device is to capture, analyze and then execute the user's requests. Both of the aforementioned categories can be built by device manufacturers or by a developer user in a DIY project (Do It Yourself).

System Layer. This layer allows the heterogeneous IoT devices to interact with each other through some software platforms. Beside ensuring the interaction with the UI layer, it often includes filtering, encryption, authentication and authorization policies to provide security and privacy services. The platforms that can be used in this layer are: (1) The DIY platform which is a newly built system by the owner, or by changing the firmware of an existed products, which is not possible for all users; (2) the open source platform which is a ready-made platform that supports many device brands, without the need for remote access to clouds; and (3) the cloud-based platforms which is seen as a black box [11]. It usually supports a hardware assistant, to provide remote services.

IoT Device Layer. The IoT objects are embedded devices, one that transmits and receives information over a network. These devices can be sensors collecting physical data about the home (like temperature, humidity, position, voice, etc.) and actuators controlling objects such as lighting, doors, camera, etc. They are connected using wired or wireless communications. Wireless technologies are commonly used within the household as an easy and flexible solution for communication. In the market, three categories of IoT devices are distinguished: (1) Over-IP local-based devices are connected directly to a LAN network (Ethernet) or a WLAN network (WiFi). This kind of device does not require internet access; (2) Over-IP cloud-based devices are based on cloud services to store and analyze the collected data. Without internet access, these devices can not work correctly; (3) Non-IP devices communicate by using non-IP protocols such as Bluetooth and LoRa (for wireless communications) and RS-232 and USB (for wired communication). To access an IP network, they are generally connected to a gateway [17].

According to the horizontal view of the presented architecture, four main deployments are possible:

Direct Access. Some IoT devices offer a mobile app to control and monitor them. These devices are connected directly to the app over-IP or non-IP network communication. In this kind of deployment, internet access is not required, and collective and intelligent behaviors are not possible due the heterogeneity of devices and/or apps. Privacy is preserved in case of using local-based devices for storage, analyzing and process.

DIY Deployment. is based on scratch development at all levels and the user should be a software developer. In fact, the user should implement a custom system (over a microcontroller, as Arduino or a single-board computer like Raspberry Pi), to control the IoT devices, and develop a mobile app to interact with it. The communication between the mobile app and the platform can be own, however, the one between the platform and IoT devices is conditioned by the protocol used by the IoT devices. Here, the privacy is taken care of by the user, but remains dependent on the types of used IoT devices.

Open Source Platforms. There are ready-made platforms, like Hauss.io and IFTTT (If This Than That [16]), that support many device brands. Powered by a worldwide community of tinkerers and DIY enthusiasts, they provide a free and efficient home automation without the access to clouds or remote servers. Privacy in this stage depends on open source development of platforms, and used IoT devices.

Cloud-Based Assistants. The cloud-based platforms, such as Google Home and Amazon Echo interact with the user through mobile apps, or hardware SPA assistants, knowing that SPAs are considered more simpler and user-friendly [2]. A SPA generally uses voice recognition skills to perform user's requests [9]. Viewed as a black box for final users, cloud-based platforms don't ensure the user privacy because they always depend on the manufacturer cloud which can gain access to the user's data without his knowledge. Indeed, users never have the ability to filter their voice commands, even if the manufacturers promise that they clear all the recorded voices. In addition, some platforms give the possibility to manipulate Non-IP devices, thus they can save the collected data and send it later silently and on with small amounts to their cloud [11].

Currently, the cloud-based assistants are the most widely used type, and the easiest for users, and their privacy is very limited, especially for sensitive data. Therefore, it is necessary to propose a solution to this problem.

2.2 Smart Personal Assistants (SPA)

Smart Personal Assistants (SPA) voice interaction device, allow us to complete tasks quickly and efficiently using natural language [2,9]. Through connected devices, smart hubs provide easy and remote control of the smart home. In fact, they can support different manufacturers IoT devices and connect to their cloud services to trigger pertinent services. Standard protocols are defined to ensure compatibility of SPAs with different IoT devices. Actually, there are two types of smart hubs:

SPA Without Interfaces: allows the user to perform commands by using voice only, usually involves smart speakers, such as Google Home and Amazon Echo, and cloud based voice personal assistant such as Amazon Alexa and Google Assistant. Thus, speech recognition and analysis are based on cloud services. By taking Google Home as an example, this one can respond to all the requests of home users that start their request with the expression "Ok, Google". Google Home allows us to manage emails, ask questions, and control different IoT devices of the home.

SPA with Interfaces: allows users to perform commands from touchable interfaces, like Samsung SmartThing and Hubitat Home Hub. Completely managed using screens, they connect different devices in a smart home for easy automation. Thanks to additional dongles, Hubitat can find and control all the Z-wave and Zigbee devices in the smart home. Some SPAs without interfaces can operate offline, thus not compromising user privacy.

2.3 Privacy Concerns in SPA

In [6], different IoT architectures proposed in the literature are discussed, in terms of security and privacy, and as it is expected privacy was the last interest. Whereas security is concerned about the way that the data appears and transmitted, privacy concerns about the data itself, by answering to many questions: What kind of data is collected? How is it managed? Who is allowed to store thereby use it? And what is the purpose it is used for? In the context of smart

environments, it is also important to know the used IoT devices and their impact
and scope.

In this paper, we focus on Cloud-based SPA which raises many privacy issues
and threats. In fact, SPA Systems pose serious privacy threads as speech is a rich
source of sensitive acoustic and textual information about the users and their
environment. According to [7,9,18], the main privacy threats to which SPA suffer
are:

- **Weak Authentication.** The authentication is done just with wake-up
  words, so the SPA accepts any command preceding the wake-up keyword
  from anyone;
- **Weak Authorization.** The absence of a pertinent method in SPA for permissions and access control which defines to the users their role in smart home,
  allows to any user to control any device, and/or modify the SPA set-up;
- **Identification.** IoT devices in home can be related with private data about
  the owners such as (name, addresses, location, ...);
- **Profiling.** Being attentive to the wake-up keyword, SPA is always on and
  always listening. This would allow to process data about users' activities and
  actions during a long period of time, to classify users according to some features. Usually, the results are sent to cloud and exploited as advertisements;
- **Inventory and Linkage.** Data can be illegitimately gathered about the
  existence and characteristics of IoT devices in specific places, opening the
  opportunity to other types of attacks such as profiling and tracking. In addition, separate data sources can be linked and combined to conclude new facts
  that are not perceived;

To preserve user privacy, any device should be designed to interrogate users
about any sensitive data dissemination and even for software updates and also
allow him to reset and review the permissions, and data policies.

Actually, the data collection process from IoT devices is more passive, pervasive and less intrusive [2]. To better protect the SPA users, collected data should
be untraceable and unlinkable, making it difficult to identify hiding information
about the relationship between any device [5]. Moreover, the anonymity of users
is very important, by hiding information about the user who performed a given
action and by using pseudonyms instead of using real identifiers.

The more important threat faced by the SPA user is profiling. The collected
user data includes his personal information, his location, and his habits that
can be learned by some data analytics engines that analyze user routines. The
analytics engines are generally deployed in the cloud. Thereby, the cloud services
already support a number of speech processing functions like speaker identification, vocal recognition and text analysis such as topic modeling, document
categorization, sentiment and relations analysis and identity detection that can
extract sensitive information. Applying these functions can significantly under-
mine the user's privacy. Most of the time, data are exploited as advertisements,
but this might be a great problem for users with sensitive positions (like govern-
ments, commercial parties, etc.), or could be used for account settlement between

enemies. Moreover, another problem that disturbs smart home owners is related to the home control, which could be used by thieves.

3   PGG: The Privacy Guard Gateway System

In this paper, we propose a privacy approach dedicated to SPA operating in smart environments. This approach, called Privacy Guard Gateway (PGG for short), aims at strengthening the privacy guard of users.

PGG is based on a software platform embedded in a hardware system. It is physically associated with any SPA, in order to mitigate privacy concerns caused by the use of this kind of IoT device. PGG collects the user speech the same as the SPA does and to perform thereafter a noise addition based mechanism. The main role of this mechanism is to fix the profiling concerns and thus ensure data scrambling, where "Too much information is equal to no information".

Besides, knowing that the majority of SPAs only support over-IP devices, therefore, the PGG system allows them to be interconnected with non-IP devices.

3.1   Privacy Guard Architecture

Figure 2 depicts the main physical entities composing the proposed architecture and the interactions between them.

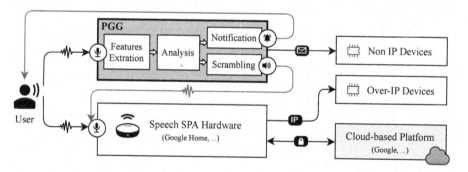

Fig. 2. Privacy guard architecture

SPA and Cloud-Based Platform. The majority of SPAs use voice recognition skills to perform user requests. Viewed as a black box for the final users, SPAs are cloud-based assistants, which always depend on the manufacturer cloud which can gain access to the user's data without his knowledge.

Usually, SPAs are based on over-IP protocols to communicate with IoT devices, therefore, they don't allow to control non-IP devices, requiring an interoperability gateway. Moreover, communication between the SPA and cloud platform is over-IP encrypted, i.e. no request can be interpreted or analyzed. Although this ensures the confidentiality of the communication, Thereby it does not allow any intermediary system of privacy guard to filter the interaction between the SPA and the cloud platform.

PGG System. In order to provide a privacy guard, PGG is physically placed beside the SPA and embeds a microphone and a speaker, as for SPA. Its role is to collect the same speech forwarded to the SPA in order to apply a scrambling mechanism after processing the user requests. First, through the microphone, PGG retrieves the speech and proceeds to the extraction of the request features. Then, an analysis of the request is performed to situate it in a feature tree. Based on the analysis phase and its feature tree, PGG can then start the scrambling mechanism which consists of producing some dummy requests by using the speaker. We have so much information and this way allows us to reinforce the privacy.

Moreover, knowing that the SPA cannot control non-IP devices, therefore, PGG can be used as a gateway between SPA and non-IP devices while applying the privacy guard mechanism.

Hence, in our approach, PGG should satisfy the two main requirements: (1) *Controlling non-IP devices* connected to it and handling the authentication and the authorization of smart-home users, while minimizing private and sensitive data storage gathered by the devices; and (2) *Supervising SPAs*, from the collection of voices and feature analysis to the scrambling mechanism.

3.2   Privacy Guard Process

As stated by Fig. 2, the PGG system operates in four processing phases:

Features Extraction. Firstly, PGG captures the speech of the user request and translates it into text by using any Speech to Text technique, like [1]. Then, it proceeds to the extraction of the so-called *request features*. These features are keywords and synonyms generated from the user request, that are sorted according to several types of context features, like devices or actions.

Definition 1. *(Request feature)*
Let $\mathcal{N}$ be the set of all possible feature names, and $\mathcal{T}$ be the set of possible types of request features, such as: Device, Action, Space and Time. A request feature is a pair $\langle name, type \rangle$, where $name \in \mathcal{N}$ is the name of the feature and $type \in \mathcal{T}$ is the corresponding type. The mapping $\lambda : \mathcal{T} \to 2^{\mathcal{N}}$ yields the set of feature names corresponding to a given type, whereas $\lambda^{-1} : \mathcal{N} \to \mathcal{T}$, gives the type of a feature name.

As shown in Fig. 3, in this paper only four types are considered. For instance, the *Device* type contains many IoT devices, such as $Bulb_1$, $Door_1$, and Fan_1, whereas *Space* one contains room names of a given smart-home, for examples, $\lambda(Space) = \{Living\ room, Bedroom, Kitchen, Garden, ...\}$ and $\lambda^{-1}(Kitchen) = Space$.

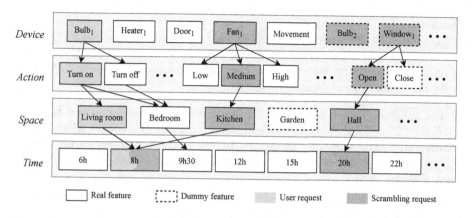

Fig. 3. The IoT feature tree

Let $\mathcal{I}$ be the set of possible interpreted sentences of the user, and $\mathcal{F}$ be the set of all possible request features. The function $extract : \mathcal{I} \rightarrow 2^{\mathcal{F}}$, allows to extract a set of request features from an interpreted sentence given by the speech to text mechanism. In this phase, the words of a sentence that cannot correspond to any type are ignored and don't be considered in the next phases. In addition, some features can be implicitly extracted without appearing in the sentence of the request, such as the temporal context of it (i.e. Time features). For instance, $extract$ ("*Turn on the living room bulb*") = $\{\langle Turn\ on, Action \rangle, \langle Living\ room, Space \rangle, \langle Bulb, Device \rangle\}$.

Feature Analysis. In this phase, the features previously extracted are classified and matched to some predefined *request pattern*. The request patterns represent the possible and expected requests that the user can launch.

Definition 2. *(Request pattern)*
A request pattern P ($P \in 2^{\mathcal{F}}$) is a set of request features, such that $\forall f_1, f_2 \in P, f_1 = \langle name_1, type_1 \rangle$ and $f_2 = \langle name_2, type_2 \rangle$, then $name_1 \neq name_2 \wedge type_1 \neq type_2$.

In Fig. 3, the request features are represented by rectangles, and the arrows connecting them constitute the request patterns. For example, the request pattern "$Bulb_1 \rightarrow Turn\ off \rightarrow Bedroom \rightarrow 9h30$" means that this is a request to turn off the primary bulb in the bedroom at 9h30. Note that the devices with the same type in some space, like $Bulb_1$, $Bulb_2$ and $Bulb_3$ respectively correspond to primary, secondary and tertiary bulbs. The devices having only one instance are simply represented without the indexes, e.g. *Movement*.

The structure illustrated in Fig. 3, is called *Request Feature Graph*, where nodes correspond to request features and paths to request behaviors. The matching of extracted features with some request pattern yields a *user request*. It is based on a matching threshold, allowing to determine if the extracted features are eligible or are to be discarded.

Definition 3. *(User request)*
Let $D \in [0,1]$ be the matching threshold used to determine the eligibility of the extracted features. A user request is a triplet $\langle EF, P, d \rangle$, where $EF \in 2^{\mathcal{F}}$ is the set of the extracted request features, P is the matched request pattern and $d \in [0,1]$ is the matching degree, such that $d \geq D$.

Let $\mathcal{UR}$ be the set of all possible user requests. We define the function $analyze : 2^{\mathcal{F}} \times [0,1] \rightarrow \mathcal{UR}$, to yield a user request from a set of extracted features and some matching threshold. In Fig. 3, the user requests are graphically represented by the path of yellow features, e.g. "$Bulb_1 \rightarrow Turn\ on \rightarrow Living\ Room \rightarrow 8h$".

User Notification. This phase consists in notify the user of the extracted features that are potentially exploited by the SPA. The user is notified using several ways: e-mails, SMS, or mobile notifications.

The notification process depends on the availability and scope of the analyzed requests in PGG, thus two modes of notification are possible: stateful or stateless notifications. In the case of stateless mode, the analyzed requests are not stored and are only reactively sent to the user as informative messages. Otherwise, by using the stateful mode, the analyzed requests are stored in PGG, providing a global and historical view of the user activities. Therefore, the notification process is more sophisticated and more intelligent using data analysis and machine learning techniques. Thereby, the detection of anomalies about user requests becomes possible, for example, the detection of opening a door in a late hour of the day.

Although this mode provides an efficient notification mechanism thanks to stored data, it harms the user's privacy as does the SPA. Thus, the choice of notification mode must be requested from the user, in order to allow him to control the storage or not of data.

Scrambling Mechanism. Now that the user request has been analyzed and approved, PGG can apply the scrambling mechanism. Based on a speaker and on some Text to speech technique, the proposed scrambling mechanism consists of forwarding dummy requests in order to frustrate the profiling and linkage problems of SPAs. This technique enables the interference of the information that the cloud can extract from the orders forwarded to the over-IP devices, adopting an engineering saying "too much information is equal to no information".

Thereby, two types of request features are considered, *real* and *dummy features*. A dummy feature can be introduced at any type by implementing it in PGG and this one can be configured with SPA to respond to it. For instance, dummy features can be dummy devices, actions, spaces or times. These dummy features are added when configuring real features. In Fig. 3, the real features are represented by solid line rectangles, whereas dummy ones are depicted by dotted line rectangles.

Definition 4. *(Scrambling request)*
A scrambling request R $(R \in 2^{\mathcal{F}})$ is a request whose features can be real or dummy. Let $\mathcal{SR}$ be the set of all possible scrambling requests. We define a mapping $scramble^{-1} : \mathcal{SR} \to \mathcal{UR}$, which yields the user request from which a given scrambling request originated.
As the scrambling mechanism is dedicated to IoT device controls, if the device feature of a scrambling request is real, then all other features must be real. Indeed, it is not possible to perform a dummy action in a real device, because this one provides only predefined (real) actions.

Let $\mathcal{S}$ be the set of scrambling strategies. The function $scramble : \mathcal{UR} \times \mathcal{S} \to 2^{\mathcal{SR}}$, is used to give a set of scrambling requests from the pattern of a given user request based on a scrambling strategy. A simple strategy would be to generate $n \in \mathbb{N}^*$ scrambling requests for each user request. The choice of dummy and real (device) features in scrambling requests would be based on some probabilistic law.

In Fig. 3, the scrambling requests are depicted by red features, e.g. "$Window_1 \to Open \to Hall \to 20\,\text{h}$".

The algorithm 1 synthetically highlights the PGG process for reinforcing the privacy guard of SPAs. PGG starts by extracting features (EF) from the interpreted sentences (I_{in}) of the user request. Then, the features are analyzed to determine if the user request (ur) is eligible or not, and a supervision notification is sent to the user. In case the scrambling mechanism is activated, PGG produces a set of scrambling requests (SR). For each scrambling request, a sentence is made (I_{out}) and emitted using the PGG speaker.

4   Google Home Case Study

Many types of SPAs provide an easy remote control of the smart home. They support different manufacturers devices and connect to their cloud services such as Google Home, Amazon Echo and Philips hue. Using such assistants, we avoid installing the controlling apps of all appliances in the smart home. In this paper, we take Google Home as a case study for our proposed approach. Indeed, Google

---

Algorithm 1.   PGG process

```
 1: Require:
 2:   D := 0.5 ∈ [0, 1]  /* Matching threshold */
 3:   isScrambling ∈ {True, False}
 4:   S ∈ S    /* Scrambling strategy */

 5: while speech_in := listen() do
 6:     I_in := speechToText(speech_in)
 7:     EF := extract(I_in)
 8:     ur := analyze(EF, D)
 9:     if ur ≠ Null then
10:         notify(ur)
11:         if isScrambling then
12:             SR := scramble(ur, S)
13:             for sr ∈ SR do
14:                 I_out := sentence(sr)
15:                 speech_out := textToSpeech(I_out)
16:                 emit(speech_out)
17:             end for
18:         end if
19:     end if
20: end while
```

Home is a cloud based platform, which is able to collect IoT device data and send it to the cloud. Although this allows to enhance the quality of service of Google Home, it can cause profiling and linkage problems for the user. In this section, we propose an implementation and a concrete deployment of the PGG system to reinforce privacy of Google Home users. Google Home is a smart speaker developed by Google under the Google Nest brand, enabling users to speak voice commands not only to interact with services like shopping and music, but also to control smart home devices [13], including IFTTT service. It is based on over-IP protocols, often HTTPS, to wirelessly communicate with IoT devices.

Table 1. Common commands for Google Home

Command type	Examples [Ok, Google, ...]	Extracted features
Useful information	– How's the weather today? – What's 35 times 12? – What's the latest with the coronavirus?	Interest, Information, Time
Phone and calls	– Call Mom. – Call the nearest restaurant. – Find my phone.	Contacts, Position, Habit, Time
Broadcasting	– Broadcast 'Dinner is ready!'. – Broadcast 'Time to leave for school'.	Day plan, Habit, Time
Time, timers and alarms	– What's the time in London? – Snooze the alarm. – Cancel the alarm for 7h30.	Morality, Health situation, Time
Smart home control	– Turn on the living room lights. – Lock the front door.	Device, Action, Space, Time

Google Home responds to all speech commands forwarded from the users which start by the wake-up word "Ok, Google" (or "Hey Google"). So, it is always on, always listening to be able to react instantly to the user. Many types of commands can be accepted by Google Home. Table 1 illustrates some common ones and shows how they can be exploited. All the commands extract several features on user requests. For example, call commands can collect the contacts and habits of the user and sometimes even his position.

In our approach, we focus on smart home control commands, which allow the user to control several types of IoT devices, like turn on/off lights or open doors. As mentioned in Sect. 3, the extracted features in smart home control requests concern mainly the requested device and the performed action on it. Note that it is possible to trigger some complex commands, by using customized sentences for IFTTT services, e.g. "Hey Google, activate home security."

The Google Home SPAs (Speaker or display) are set up through an associated mobile app. The user has to follow some steps that require a Google Account and an internet connection over Wi-Fi network to remotely authenticate the user. It is possible to change some settings at any time after the complete setup of Google Home.

We can remotely control smart devices that are declared "Compatible with Google Home". To connect them to Google Home, we should select the manufacturer of a given device from a Google predefined list and we follow the in-app steps to complete setup. Moreover, it is possible to use IFTTT commands with Google Home. For this end, we need to connect the IFTTT account to that of Google, to give it the required access permissions.

4.1 PGG Deployment

Fig. 4. Deployment of the case study

As illustrated in Fig. 4, we experiment our approach by developing a hardware project embedding the proposed PGG system[1]. In this project, we opted for Raspberry Pi 3 Model B (RPi3) as nano-computer, due to its interesting hardware features, such as the performances of CPU, RAM and peripherals. Although RPi3 can be operated by several high-level OS, this one provides an owner OS, called Raspbian (a Debian-based Linux distribution) allowing to exploit efficiently the integrated hardware. In addition, RPi3 not only has the main input/output ports, including microphone and speaker, but also provides general-purpose input/output (GPIO) capabilities allowing to control low level sensors and actuators. For efficiency reasons of the PGG system, the RPi3 with its microphone and speaker should be beside Google Home with a distance between 10 cm and 50 cm. Moreover, the closer PGG is to the Google Home, the greater the noise nuisance caused by the volume of the speaker.

---

[1] The hardware used in this experiment is: Google Home Mini, Raspberry Pi 3 Model B, Logitech USB Mic, Rokit Boost Orbit Speaker, and Horsky WiFi Outlet.

The entire development of PGG is done in Python language (v3.8), because Raspbian promotes Python as its main programming language. Moreover, Python offers many ready-to-use modules that we use in speech synthesis.

4.2 Non-IP Devices Control

The GPIO capabilities of the RPi3 allow it to increase its connectivity in terms of communication. Indeed, thanks to the different dongles that can be plugged into the RPi3, the PGG system is able to control non-IP devices (e.g. Bluetooth, Z-wave or Zigbee).

After its authentication, the user can control the non-IP devices through its voice, in the same way as for IP devices. However, in this case the RPi3 is used as an IP gateway to the various non-IP devices.

4.3 Dummy Device Implementation

Some scrambling requests include dummy device (and action) features, therefore, it is necessary to virtually implement them, like on real device firmware. As for real devices, dummy devices must be accessible from Google Home, and configured with it. Although each one of them can be implemented in a separate connected hardware, they all can be integrated in one same hardware. Moreover, to avoid using an additional hardware, the RPi3 can embed all dummy devices, in addition to containing the PGG system. The communication between Google Home and RPi3 is done over-IP, like for real devices.

The PGG process is triggered when the user requests are listened to by the microphone of PGG. After the achievement of the three phases Extraction-Analysis-Scrambling, this one starts the emission of the generated scrambling requests through the speaker plugged into the RPi3. Since the RPi3 is beside the google home, this one listens and launches the scrambling requests, as if they were user requests. All this process creates noise, allowing to remedy the problem of profiling and linkage caused by Google Home.

4.4 Scrambling Mechanism Test

In order to test the functioning of PGG, we launch a voice request consisting of turning on the primary bulb in the living room at 8h00. This request is simultaneously listened to by both Google Home and PGG and this later generates a set of scrambling requests according to some strategy (giving four scrambling requests in this example). Table 2 depicts the features of both user request ur and generated scrambling requests sr_i. The dummy features are underlined in dashed lines. In particular, the two considered dummy devices ($Bulb_2$ and $window$) are virtually implemented in RPi3.

Table 2. Example of a user request and the corresponding generated scrambling requests

*Request	Features			
	Device	Action	Space	Time
ur	$Bulb_1$	$Turn\ on$	$Living\ room$	$08h00$
sr_1	$Bulb_2$	$Turn\ off$	$Garden$	$00h00$
sr_2	Fan	$Medium$	$Kitchen$	$08h14$
sr_3	$Window$	$Open$	$Hall$	$20h00$
sr_4	$Bulb_1$	$Turn\ on$	$Kitchen$	$12h00$

5 Discussion

In this section, we discuss the different works that focused on the privacy issues in IoT environments in general, cloud-based IoT apps, and SPAs.

5.1 Privacy in IoT Environments

Works in [5,7,18] give a presentation of privacy aspects in IoT context by discussing common privacy threats in IoT systems. Some effective solutions are cited allowing to reduce privacy issues within such systems. However, these solutions are not very practical according to the nature of the used smart devices which have limited energy and storage ability. Any IoT customer should have the required features to control his own information and define who can access it. Currently, some companies use a sort of agreement that allows certain services to access data as desired. Therefore, built-in tools to preserve the user's privacy are required to be built as an essential part of any product [7]. In addition, a countermeasure is proposed in [3] based on generating spoofed network traffic to hide real activities of devices. The authors show how machine learning can be exploited by passive attackers, emphasizing that if we use encryption techniques for transmissions, much information can be inferred without using advanced techniques. As an interesting solution for secured access in a smart environment, Kozlov et al. [14] propose a gateway that allows traffic filtering techniques and policies to prevent any unwanted access to the smart environment and minimize data forwarded on the outgoing in order to not leak sensitive data. Unfortunately, the architectures of some nowadays devices and the way they connect to the Internet prevent the intermediation with a gateway. Furthermore, the authors of [12] suggest to rethink access control and authentication of IoT devices in smart homes, by proposing an app that allows to set permissions for all the home members according to their ages, their characteristics, their neighbors and their relatives.

5.2 Privacy in SPAs for Smart Home Environments

Devices and apps operating in a smart home collect a huge amount of data and the majority of them are cloud-based, capable of disclosing user data for economic or political reasons. In [15], a privacy-preserving data analytics is proposed as a solution for enhancing the performance of cloud-based smart homes with community hierarchy based on a home controller for data hiding and minimization, in addition to a community broker for fulfilling data aggregation and separation. Nowadays, voice assistants are democratized by being embedded in SPAs or in smart devices (like smartphones and smart-TVs) allowing to interact with anyone and anything to favor usability. Such systems aim to receive user commands and perform them, however many issues could arise from malicious apps issuing voice commands, command injections from inaudible signals, and mangled voice attacks. Proposal of [10] focusses on user authentication requiring the user to wear a specific device (accelerometer) to receive the user voice and its body vibrating. The collected data is processed by a matching engine and sent to the voice assistant via Bluetooth, in order to ensure the user authentication. However, wearing additional things often disturbs the user as on the one hand we obligated him to wear electronic devices close to his head, and on the other hand, these devices may affect his health.

The works of [8,11] propose obfuscation techniques that prevent the voice assistant from listening and recording private conversations, by using ultrasound signals. These signals jam the assistant's microphone with inaudible obfuscation sound sent from the obfuscator, when listening to the user's hot-word lift the jamming. However, analyzing the user utterances for inferring the hot-word increases the time of responding to the user request. In addition, the authentication technique using Bluetooth makes another inconvenience of this approach where the request will be performed just when the user smartphone is beside.

A solution based on remote-controlled plugs or built-in mute buttons has been proposed [2] allowing to safely control the functioning of voice assistants. Nevertheless, the participants in the survey proposed in this work, find the latter solutions inconvenient because they degrade the usability of SPAs. Authors of [8] suggest hardware solutions for application layers of IoT architectures using signals in an environment containing a SPA. In fact, our approach is gone in that way since we propose noise based techniques allowing the obfuscation by performing dummy requests and speeches that introduce uncertainty about the true data. By this way, our proposed solution ensures a real time interaction between users and the SPA, while taking advantage of all the services the SPA provides. As the PGG aims to engage the user in the process of protecting his privacy since he is notified of any sensitive topic he discussed, home devices status and data leakage likelihood.

6   Conclusion

Smart home Personal Assistants (SPAs) are interesting IoT devices for home users, however, they suffer from profiling and linkage issues, mainly in the case of IoT device controlling. In this paper, we have proposed an efficient privacy guard system, called PGG, supporting all existing SPAs. PGG is adapted to any SPA, as long as the PGG and SPA are next to each other. In order to guard the user activities, PGG is based on a noise addition based mechanism that injects dummy requests according to some strategy. This scrambling mechanism adopts the engineering saying "too much information is equal to no information".

The main advantage of PGG is that it protects the user's privacy while being transparent. Indeed, no user request is rejected or lost by PGG, because all requests reach the SPA and the PGG in real time. Moreover, PGG does not store any activity of the user during its operation. In addition, the user notification mode is requested from the user, in order to allow him to control the storage of his activities.

In order to enhance the proposed approach, different scrambling strategies can be explored. Furthermore, in addition to handling smart home control, the PGG system can be expanded to other types of SPA commands (like useful information and broadcasting commands), that have also the profiling and linkage issues. Being a software system, PGG can also be installed in smart devices to guard the user from existing mobile assistants.

References

1. SpeechRecognition 3.8.1 (2020). https://pypi.org/project/SpeechRecognition/, https://ifttt.com/. Accessed 25 Aug 2020
2. Abdi, N., Ramokapane, K.M., Such, J.M.: More than smart speakers: security and privacy perceptions of smart home personal assistants. In: Symp. on Usable Privacy and Security. USENIX Association (2019)
3. Acar, A., et al.: Peek-a-boo: i see your smart home activities, even encrypted! arXiv preprint arXiv:1808.02741 (2018)
4. Ahmed, S., Chowdhury, A.R., Fawaz, K., Ramanathan, P.: Preech: a system for privacy-preserving speech transcription. In: {USENIX} Security Symposium, pp. 2703–2720 (2020)
5. AL-mawee, W., et al.: Privacy and security issues in IoT healthcare applications for the disabled users a survey (2012)
6. Alshohoumi, F., Sarrab, M., AlHamadani, A., Al-Abri, D.: Systematic review of existing IoT architectures security and privacy issues and concerns. Int. J. Adv. Comput. Sci. Appl **10**(7), 232–251 (2019)
7. Atlam, H.F., Wills, G.B.: IoT security, privacy, safety and ethics. In: Farsi, M., Daneshkhah, A., Hosseinian-Far, A., Jahankhani, H. (eds.) Digital Twin Technologies and Smart Cities. IT, pp. 123–149. Springer, Cham (2020). https://doi.org/10.1007/978-3-030-18732-3_8
8. Chandrasekaran, V., Linden, T., Fawaz, K., Mutlu, B., Banerjee, S.: Blackout and obfuscator: an exploration of the design space for privacy-preserving interventions for voice assistants. arXiv preprint arXiv:1812.00263 (2018)
9. Edu, J.S., Such, J.M., Suarez-Tangil, G.: Smart home personal assistants: a security and privacy review. arXiv preprint arXiv:1903.05593 (2019)
10. Feng, H., Fawaz, K., Shin, K.G.: Continuous authentication for voice assistants. In: 23rd Annual International Conference on Mobile Computing and Networking, pp. 343–355 (2017)
11. Gao, C., Chandrasekaran, V., Fawaz, K., Banerjee, S.: Traversing the quagmire that is privacy in your smart home. In: Workshop on IoT Security and Privacy, pp. 22–28 (2018)

12. He, W., et al.: Rethinking access control and authentication for the home internet of things (IoT). In: {USENIX} Security Symposium, pp. 255–272 (2018)
13. Inc., G.: Google Nest and Google Home device specifications (2020). https://support.google.com/googlenest/answer/7072284. Accessed 16 Aug 2020
14. Kozlov, D., Veijalainen, J., Ali, Y.: Security and privacy threats in IoT architectures. In: BODYNETS, pp. 256–262 (2012)
15. Lee, Y.T., Hsiao, W.H., Lin, Y.S., Chou, S.C.T.: Privacy-preserving data analytics in cloud-based smart home with community hierarchy. IEEE Trans. Consumer Electr. **63**(2), 200–207 (2017)
16. Mi, X., Qian, F., Zhang, Y., Wang, X.: An empirical characterization of IFTTT: ecosystem, usage, and performance. In: 2017 Internet Measurement Conference, pp. 398–404 (2017)
17. Sohn, M.N.: Security and privacy threats in IoT architectures, p. 71 (2017)
18. Ziegeldorf, J.H., Morchon, O.G., Wehrle, K.: Privacy in the internet of things: threats and challenges. Secur. Commun. Networks **7**(12), 2728–2742 (2014)

An Intelligent Agent-Based Industrial IoT Framework for Time-Critical Data Stream Processing

Ines Gharbi[1,2]($\boxtimes$), Kamel Barkaoui[1]($\boxtimes$), and Ben Ahmed Samir[2]($\boxtimes$)

[1] CEDRIC, Conservatoire National des Arts et Métiers, Paris, France
kamel.barkaoui@cnam.fr
[2] LIPSIC, Faculté des Sciences de Tunis,
Université de Tunis El Manar, Tunis, Tunisia
{ines.gharbi,samir.benahmed}@fst.utm.tn

Abstract. The Industrial Internet of Things (IIoT) intends to speed up digital manufacturing transformation. As a crucial role, Industrial IoT aims to improve the performance and reliability of the processing of massive time-critical data continually generated by heterogeneous smart objects. To resolve these challenges, Industrial IoT incorporates the Fog computing paradigm to support intelligence near the Edge level as an additional alternative to Cloud computing. However, a Fog node allows dealing with only limited data processing, storage, and communications. Indeed, a heavy load processing task requires multiple Fog nodes to achieve its execution and may need an intelligent dynamic pooling of Cloud resources. In this paper, we propose PIAF (A **P**rocessing **I**ntelligent **A**gent Running on **F**og Infrastructure). An intelligent agent-based IIoT framework that runs on the Fog infrastructure to distribute the processing of time-critical data streams. We outline its several components and their interactions. Then, for this purpose, we model the PIAF framework using the Time Petri Nets modeling.

Keywords: Industrial IoT · Multi-agent systems · Oriented service architecture · Smart objects · Bigdata stream · Fog computing · Cloud computing · Time Petri nets

1 Introduction

The Industrial Internet of Things (IIoT) is a subset of the IoT [1] that empowers the digital transformation of Industries. Hence, it leads to the implementation of the Industry 4.0 which is also called Smart Manufacturing, Digital Manufacturing, Factories of the Future, or the Factory of Things [16].

The IIoT makes this digital transformation possible by interconnecting a huge number of distributed, decentralized and heterogeneous objects endowed with advanced intelligence. Among the critical missions of the IIoT is to be able

© Springer Nature Switzerland AG 2021
S. Bouzefrane et al. (Eds.): MSPN 2020, LNCS 12605, pp. 195–208, 2021.
https://doi.org/10.1007/978-3-030-67550-9_13

to aggregate all time-sensitive data generated continuously from those hetero-geneous devices, remove data silos, and combine the rest to obtain useful and effective information [1].

Several works handle processing of data streams within the Cloud infras-tructure. Despite its powerful computing abilities, large storage capacity, and advanced BigData analysis, Cloud architecture presents various restrictions to process time-critical data. The centralized infrastructure of the Cloud, a gather-ing of massive data centers deployed worldwide requiring an Internet connection, is among the main issues of rapidly process decentralized data. Hence, establish-ing communication directly to devices increases time delay and leads to a later response. These delays may result in severe damage (fire, blackout, gas or water leak, equipment malfunction) to the industrial environment.

Those common traditional Cloud issues lead to the emergence of Fog comput-ing. Fog computing presents a distributed architecture of numerous small nodes. It is known as the Cloud near the ground [21]. Indeed, Fog processing, storage, and communication are performed on the Edge environment level approximated to the data source. Hence, it performs as middleware between those IIoT devices and the Cloud data centers. This infrastructure makes quick appropriate deci-sions to deal with unexpected industrial changes related to safety, maintenance, evolution, and service compatibility [1]. These abilities will reduce the time, latency, and cost required to transfer and process data in the Cloud [24].

Besides, Fog Computing enables different industrial devices to communicate with each other to supply several tasks. Accordingly, some complex tasks, which necessitate a large pool of resources, can be divided into multiple subtasks. Those assigned subtasks achieve their execution on multiple Fog nodes characterized by limited resources. In case of a lack of sufficient Fog node resources, they may require an intelligent dynamic pooling of Cloud capacities to complete their processes before their deadlines. The pooling function aims to determine the appropriate Cloud resource that can substitute the Fog node without violating Fog's requirements.

The system, enabling communication between those distributed Fog and Cloud nodes could be described as a complex, non-linear, interactive, decen-tralized, autonomous, self-intelligent, and self-healing one. This system can meet the similarity of objects' provided services, deal with critical changes, and adjust applications behavior in real-time [4].

To deal with these complex challenges, we propose PIAF (A **P**rocessing **I**ntelligent **A**gent Running on **F**og Infrastructure). PIAF Framework aims to maximize the distribution of time-critical data streams processing on the Fog infrastructure. This platform adopts the intelligent agent system paradigm to easily distribute the processing of time-critical data stream, generated from het-erogeneous and various smart objects (SO), between the Fog and the Cloud nodes. To support autonomous communications between agents, PIAF Frame-work deploys the Oriented Service Architecture (SOA).

The remainder of this study is organized as follows. In Sect. 2, we define some preliminary concepts to highlight the basic components of the conventional architecture of the IIoT. In Sect. 3, we discuss the related work. In Sect. 4, we present our PIAF framework. In Sect. 5, we model our proposed framework with the Time Petri Nets modeling framework. In Sect. 6, we conclude and enumerate future works.

2   Preliminaries

Every digital industrial transformation requires its own sets of devices, data, and communication technologies. This fact raises issues related to interoperability, complexity, and diversity in conceptual models that describe the structure, the functions, and the views of the systems [18]. Modelling an efficient architecture that describes the components of the system, as well as their interactions, is considered as an essential task to design Industrial IoT applications. IIoT architecture combines crucial building blocks including Edge Computing, Fog Computing, Cloud Computing and Business Value Environments [13,15,19] as described in Fig. 1.

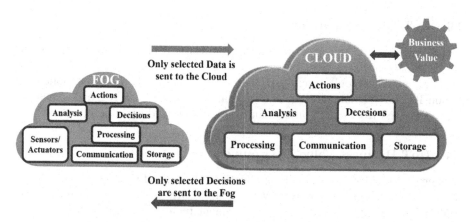

Fig. 1. Conventional industrial IoT architecture [13,15,19]

2.1   IIoT Edge Environment

IIoT Edge Environment describes the physical infrastructure including the IIoT devices. Those smart objects "SO" can be seen as a set of actuator and sensor nodes that can be connected to each other and to the Internet [8].

- **Sensor Node (SN):** This node includes data acquisition units (sensors, smart meters, RFID, and measurement systems) whose main missions are to generate heterogeneous big data and to detect events or variations. The received data will notify industrials about status change in the industrial environment and machines.

- **Actuator Node (AN):** This node includes actuators whose aim is to receive specific commands and to respond to an event request. For example, a relay can be applied as an actuator apt to close the faucet when detecting a water leak. Also, motors can be regarded as actuators able to execute several machines' commands. Moreover, a pick and place robot can be considered as an actuator providing continuous movements to change the product's positions.

2.2 IIoT Fog Environment

Fog Computing extends the Cloud computing abilities so that powerful resources are put on edge devices. Indeed, this IIoT component comprises the local network, communication, and storage infrastructure. It is responsible for managing critical operations near to the object via a gateway, a data hub, or a smart edge device. As a result, a small amount of data requires to be transferred to the Cloud such that industrial applications meet the requirements of low latency and reliability [8].

2.3 IIoT Cloud Environment

Cloud computing is known for its storage and computing capabilities. It encompasses the set of IT services (servers, storage, databases, network components, software, analysis tools, etc.) provided via the Internet. This component is responsible for the management of a very large volume of heterogeneous massive data generated from smart objects and the different industrial applications [8].

2.4 IIoT Business Value Environment

This environment defines all the applications deployed for users, and, includes all the forms of data generated by these applications. Among the most used applications to enhance industrial management includes Operational Efficiency, Energy Management, Predictive Maintenance, and Augmented Reality [14].

3 Related Work

Our main goal is to maximize distributed processing on Fog environment, a sub-layer of the IIoT conventional architecture.

Industrial IoT describes the networking of cyber-physical objects for data exchange. A cyber-physical system: i.e., an interconnection between physical covering sensors, actuators, machines, robots, etc., and software objects including communication, computing, storage, processing, analyzing, etc., [20]. This connectivity allows better management while maintaining security, reliability, low energy, equipment, and personals costs. The complexity of such a system is reduced to the converge of Information Technology (IT) and Operational Technology (OT) [22].

To resolve such complexity, a lot of research has emerged into the application of agents and agent-oriented services. Among motivations for agents' deployment to process distributed data stream as discussed in [2] are as follows: agents provide autonomous management of distributed processes. They can make critical decisions to deal with unpredictable events by reconfiguring the objectives to be achieved. Additionally, agents can provide interoperability between heterogeneous IIoT devices which ease their integration and communication.

To support communication between agents holding distinct profiles, researchers in [7] promote the use of service-oriented architecture (SOA).

SOA is a paradigm that aims to organize diverse entities that promote reuse, scalability, and interoperability, to identify relationships between them within a service-oriented environment, and to develop standards or specifications dealing with such an environment.

In literature, several works discuss the processing of data streams based on both MAS and SOA running on Cloud computing.

The authors in [10] propose a model for the automatic management of industrial processes based on multi-agent systems, and Cloud integration. This model enables real-time intelligent decisions to enhance control along the manufacturing process.

Yet, researchers in [12] declare that smart objects could still be a whole lot more intelligent and tackle far more complex tasks. This made to be possible when those systems move computation away from distant Cloud and toward the Fog. This approach reduces latency by minimizing data transfer to the faraway datacenters, and complexity by avoiding data stream processing close to the device.

Based on its advantages according to latency and computational capabilities, several authors exploit the efficacity of managing distributed processes on Fog infrastructure. The authors in [9] propose a cognitive IoT platform deployed on the Fog infrastructure. This platform defines the cognitive agent paradigm as a key enabler for embedded intelligence and provide PdM-as-a service based on SOA as a particular solution for predictive maintenance (PdM).

However, Fog nodes present a limited capacity for processing, storage, and communication. They are unable of holding sophisticated tasks that require more processing capabilities.

To the best of our knowledge, few researchers evaluate the profits of combined and continuous Fog-to-Cloud architectures. The authors in [3] propose a platform for healthcare critical task management. It deploys both the multi-agent and the SOA paradigms operating on both the Cloud and the Fog infrastructures.

In this work, we propose to design PIAF (A Processing Intelligent Agent Running on Fog Infrastructure) in the context of the Industrial IoT. An intelligent agent-based IIoT framework that runs on the Fog infrastructure to distribute the processing of time-critical data streams and attempts to minimize the dynamic pooling of Cloud resources.

4   PIAF Framework: Ecosystem Description

Since we aim to maximize the execution of time-critical tasks on the Fog infrastructure, we propose the PIAF: A Processing Intelligent Agent Running on Fog Infrastructure. PIAF is a framework that mediates intercommunications between two layers of the conventional IIoT architecture, which are the Fog Layer, and the Cloud Layer, exploring both intelligent agent systems and service-oriented architecture (as presented in Fig. 2).

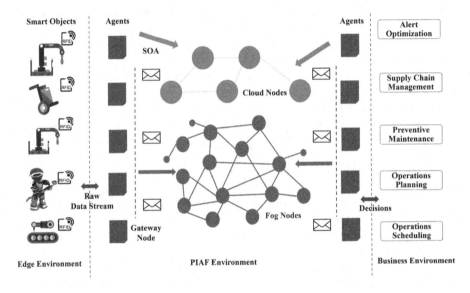

Fig. 2. A processing intelligent agent running on Fog infrastructure ecosystem

Fog node infrastructure is characterized by limited processing, communication, and storage resources. When demanding time-critical computing, the PIAF framework has two alternatives: *(i)* split the task into multiple sub-tasks that can be dispatched on multiple Fog nodes or *(ii)* , move execution from the Fog to the cloud infrastructure.

The big challenge is to find an available optimal computing resource allocation before exceeding the time limit authorized for starting the execution of a task. This resource is located in one of these three locations: *(i)* on the Fog infrastructure, *(ii)* on a substitutable cloud node having the same characteristics as the Fog node, *(iii)* on a cloud node with no optimal restriction.

Indeed, PIAF Framework is based on multi-agent systems running on Fog infrastructure to easily enable an efficient distribution process for the horizontal integration of all objects involved in the industry. The intelligent agent is held by an Information and Communication Technologies (ICT) infrastructure. It is viewed as a software programmed to provide efficient manipulation of complex critical-time Data Stream Management. This system is applied for receiving commands obtained through synchronization with the environment and with other system processes to make critical decisions in order to manage critical-time workflows. Those systems share communication across the service-oriented architecture [11].

For each process, an individual controller is synthesized that acts on locally available information obtained through synchronization with the environment and with other system processes.

4.1 Agent: Critical-Time Workflow Management

Massive raw gathered data streams from heterogeneous smart objects, including both critical and uncritical information, are viewed as inputs to the PIAF framework. The lifecycle of the critical-time data stream processing within the PIAF framework (as illustrated in Fig. 3) is proceeded from data aggregation time-critical tasks selected from the whole collected raw data, data distribution including three basic functionalities: splitting into sub-tasks, prioritization, allocating available resources, and finally data execution. In every step, traceability of events and data storage are taken into consideration.

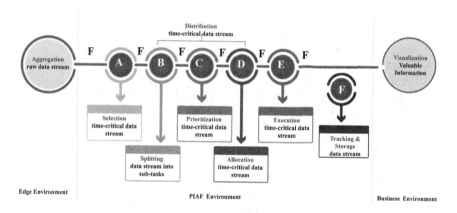

Fig. 3. PIAF: critical-time data stream processing workflow

Selection Time-Critical Data Stream. From all the gathered raw data, generated from several IIoT devices, this function aims to identify time-critical tasks by resolving the parameter identification problem [17]. In this paper, we consider the time-critical parameter (TCP) as a result of the problem of determining the optimal task parameters.

We consider $T = (T1, T2,..Ti,..Tn)$ the set of the time-critical tasks. Each task is characterized by a specific $TCP = (TCP1, TCP,..TCPi..TCPn)$.

Distributed Time-Critical Data Stream. A distributed decision-making data stream was developed to overcome the restrictions of centralized processing, where the whole data is required to be collected and transferred to one central location. In the PIAF framework model, the distribution functionality consists of performing three basic sub-steps.

1. **Splitting into Sub-Tasks:**
   Distributed systems allow the creating of sub-tasks, which they can be assigned to different resources at once with an estimated time to finish their execution. Considering that Fog nodes provide limited resources of processing capacity, a distributed task enables the simultaneous use of a massive amount of resources on the Fog infrastructure.

2. **Tasks Prioritization Management:** This function is responsible for arranging tasks according to the order of importance which is relative to their critical execution time and dependency. Dependencies are the connections between tasks that define the order in which operations should be performed. Each task may have multiple dependencies with other tasks. We consider 4 types of dependency [23]:

   - **Finish/Start (FS):** (End T1) $\ll$ (Start T2) where Task T1 must achieve before starting Task T2.
   - **Start/Start (SS):** (Start T1) $\ll$ (Start T2) where Task T1 must start before starting Task T2.
   - **Finish/Finish (FF):** (End T1) $\ll$ (End T2) where Task T1 must finish before ending Task T2.
   - **Start/Finish (SF):** (Start T1) $\ll$ (End T2) where Task T1 must start before ending Task T2.

3. **Searching Available Resources:**
   This function aims to identify the available resources before a required time slot where (TS $\geq$ TCPi). PIAF objective function focuses on finding primarily, an accessible Fog node resource. If there is no such resource able to manage a given task then PIAF lanchs research on the Cloud layer to identify a substitutable resource.

In order to realize an automated decision about the choice of resource availability, it is mandatory for each agent involved in the optimization strategy to start searching the adequate available resource on the cloud infrastructure. However, the agent is applied to resolve the Fog resource substitution problem.

Fog resource substitution refers to the problem of selecting an alternative resource installed on the Cloud that can replace the Fog node without violating the solicited requirements. An easier method to identify which cloud resource can be determined to substitute a specific Fog node is to check that they provide almost the same latency, cost, and dispatch agility.

Tracking and Storage. Storage operations aim to respond to the request of specific data throughout the entire process. PIAF Framework requires a local process to save task execution behaviors and parameters. Indeed, every distributed task is attached to a distributed tracker to mark their associated sub-tasks. Each task has several sub-tasks as a parameter and has a dynamic state which can be a READY state, a Waiting state, a Starting State, a Finishing State or an Error State.

4.2 Agent: Service Oriented Communication

The concept of service is frequently highlighted in publications about agent systems communication. SOA is a generic scheme used to establish interactions between agents with distinct profiles. The purpose of implementing SOA is to perform interoperability mechanisms between the distributed heterogeneous multi-agents using several gateways and protocols (MQTT...) as presented in Fig. 4.

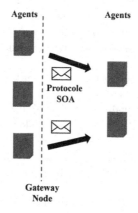

Fig. 4. PIAF: agent service oriented architecture

5   PIAF Framework: Time Petri Nets Modeling

A Petri net (PN), also known as a place/transition (PT) net, is a mathematical modeling language used to describe distributed and concurrent systems [5]. Time Petri nets (TPN for short), are obtained from PN by coupling each transition with a time interval [6]. TPNs are used here as a tool for modeling and analyzing time-critical data stream problems.

Definition 1. *(Time Petri nets (TPN))*
A TPN is a pair TPN = (PN, I_s), where:

- *PN is a set of 5-tuple PN = (P, T, pre, post, M_0) where:*
  - *P and T are disjoints, finite, non-empty sets of places and transitions, respectively.*
  - *Pre: P * T* **N** *is the pre-incidence or input function.*
  - *Post: T * P* **N** *is the post-incidence or output function.*
  - *M_0: is the initial distribution of tokens in places, called the initial marking.*
- *I_s is a function which associates with each transition t_i a static firing interval $Is(t_i)$. Each ti has a firing interval $[a_i, b_i]$ where $[a_i, b_i]$ specifies the minimal and maximal firing delays of ti. When t_i is newly enabled, $Is(t_i) = [a_i, b_i]$. Bounds of $I(t_i)$ decrease with time, until t_i is fired or disabled. t_i is firable, if $I(t_i) = 0$. It must fire immediately, when $I(t_i) = 0$. Firing a transition takes no time but leads to a new marking.*

We propose a modeling of PIAF interactions between Fog and Cloud resources based on Time Petri nets. We give semantics related to the net's components that include places, transitions, and evolution states.

Our PIAF Time Petri net is a directed bipartite graph that has two types of nodes, transitions, and places, represented in Fig. 5 as white rectangles and circles, respectively. The firing of transitions describes the occurrence of events related to the acquisition or the release of resources. While executing critical time tasks, the marking of places illustrates several states, namely:

- **Ready:** when the task is ready to be executed.
- **Start:** When the task starts its execution.
- **Waiting:** when the task wait for the availability of a resource during an allowed critical time (TCP) or when the task is dependent to a predecessor task.
- **Finish:** When the execution of the task is finished.
- **Error:** When an error occurs during the execution.

The main goal of our model is to maximize allocation resources in the Fog infrastructure rather than the Cloud infrastructure.

In our distributed framework, executing a critical time task may follow different scenarios:

- A task can be executed directly in a Fog node. In this case, the number of available resources in the Fog is not null.
- A task can be executed directly in a cloud node. In this case, the number of available resources in the Fog remains null even after the exemption of the critical time parameter (TCP) related to each task.
- A task execution will be delayed respecting its TCP. In this case, *(i)* the number of available resources in the Fog is null, *(ii)* a clock is triggered to inform about the remaining authorized time.

This leads to the following Definition 2.

Definition 2. *(Task Processing)*

  A Task Processing problem is a set of 7-tuple **TP = (T, RF, RC, TCP, PE, PEF, PEC)** *where:*

- ***T*** *: is a finite set of tasks.*
- ***RF*** *: is a finite set of Fog nodes resources.*
- ***RC*** *: is a finite set of cloud nodes resources.*
- ***TCP*** *: is a critical-time parameter where the task should start before its exhibition.*
- ***PE*** *: is the time that takes a task to be achieved.*
- ***PEF*** *: is the time when a Fog resource is released.*
- ***PEC*** *: is the time when a Cloud resource is released.*

A resource is considered available when no task is assigned or if the TCP of the requested task is upper than the time remaining to be free. We consider that if the execution of a task is shifted into the cloud infrastructure so it will be achieved there. The choice of the task allocation resource between Cloud and Fog resources is explained using the Time Petri nets model as illustrated in the Fig. 5.

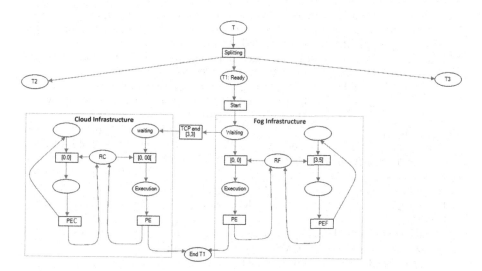

Fig. 5. PIAF framework: Tme Petri nets modeling

6   Conclusion

Intelligent agents perform to efficiently dispatch distributed tasks and resources in an autonomous way using service-oriented architecture.

In this paper, we propose PIAF framework which is an intelligent agent-based IIoT framework that runs on the Fog infrastructure to distribute the processing of time-critical data streams.

Our main contribution in this paper is to maximize the processing of critical-data tasks using Fog resources instead of Cloud resources. For this purpose, we apply the Multi-agent and SOA paradigms to improve the process, the communication, and the latency of data streams generated by all smart manufacturing objects. And, we use the Time Petri Nets to model the proposed framework.

There is no unique architecture that can be deployed to represent all industries' structures and behaviors. However, the use of this proposed framework could be an adequate solution to meet industrial fundamental needs, to enhance data stream processing. Hence, it can be implemented for many sets of industries providing diverse services and it will enable the Industrial Internet of any architecture IIo<*>(where '*' is considered as 'all' in computing).

Future research will aim at improving the specification of the PIAF framework and applying it in various industrial use cases.

References

1. Aazam, M., Zeadally, S., Harras, K.A.: Deploying fog computing in industrial internet of things and industry 4.0. IEEE Trans. Ind. Inform. **14**(10), 4674–4682 (2018)
2. Alkhabbas, F., Spalazzese, R., Davidsson, P.: An agent-based approach to realize emergent configurations in the internet of things. Electronics **9**, 1347 (2020). https://doi.org/10.3390/electronics9091347
3. Mutlag, A.A., et al.: MAFC: multi-agent fog computing model for healthcare critical tasks management. Sensors **20**(7), 1853 (2020)
4. Auliva, R.S., Sheu, R., Liang, D., Wang, W.: IIoT testbed: a DDS-based emulation tool for industrial IoT applications. In: 2018 International Conference on System Science and Engineering (ICSSE), pp. 1–4 (2018)
5. Barkaoui, K., Ayed, R.B.: Uniform verification of workflow soundness. Trans. Inst. Measur. Control **33**(1), 133–148 (2011). https://doi.org/10.1177/0142331208095676. https://doi.org/10.1177/0142331208095676
6. Barkaoui, K., Boucheneb, H., Hicheur, A.: Modelling and analysis of time-constrained flexible workflows with time recursive ecatnets. In: Bruni, R., Wolf, K. (eds.) Web Services and Formal Methods, pp. 19–36. Springer, Berlin, Heidelberg (2009)
7. Baumgärtel, H., Verbeet, R.: Service and agent based system architectures for industrie 4.0 systems. In: NOMS 2020–2020 IEEE/IFIP Network Operations and Management Symposium, pp. 1–6 (2020)
8. Caiza, G., Saeteros, M., Oñate, W., Garcia, M.V.: Fog computing at industrial level, architecture, latency, energy, and security: a review. Heliyon **6**(4), e03706 (2020). https://doi.org/10.1016/j.heliyon.2020.e03706. http://www.sciencedirect.com/science/article/pii/S240584402030551X

9. Foukalas, F.: Cognitive IoT platform for fog computing industrial applications. Comput. Electr. Eng. **87**, 106770 (2020). https://doi.org/10.1016/j.compeleceng.2020.106770. http://www.sciencedirect.com/science/article/pii/S004579062030625X

10. García Coria, J.A., Castellanos-Garzón, J.A., Corchado, J.M.: Intelligent business processes composition based on multi-agent systems. Expert Syst. Appl. **41**(4, Part 1), 1189–1205 (2014). https://doi.org/10.1016/j.eswa.2013.08.003. http://www.sciencedirect.com/science/article/pii/S0957417413006143

11. Giordano, A., Spezzano, G., Vinci, A.: Smart agents and fog computing for smart city applications. In: Alba, E., Chicano, F., Luque, G. (eds.) Smart Cities, pp. 137–146. Springer International Publishing, Cham (2016)

12. Greengard, S.: Ai on edge. Commun. ACM **63**(9), 18–20 (2020)

13. Guth, J., Breitenbücher, U., Falkenthal, M., Leymann, F., Reinfurt, L.: Comparison of IoT platform architectures: a field study based on a reference architecture. In: 2016 Cloudification of the Internet of Things (CIoT), pp. 1–6, November 2016. DOIurl10.1109/CIOT.2016.7872918

14. King, M.: The business value of industrial IoT. LHP Engineering Solutions, p. 40 (2017). https://cdn2.hubspot.net/hubfs/2512687/LHP%20Data%20Analytics%20-%20Business%20Value%20of%20IIoT%20-%20Automation%20Alley%2007122017.pdf?t=1500039830918

15. Lin, S.W., et al.: The industrial internet of things volume g1: reference architecture, industrial internet consortium. In: The Industrial Internet of Things Volume G1: Reference Architecture, Industrial Internet Consortium, pp. 117–122 (2017). IIC:PUB:G1:V1.80:20170131. www.iiconsortium.org/IIC_PUB_G1_V1.80_2017-01-31.pdf

16. Lu, Y.: Industry 4.0: a survey on technologies, applications and open research issues. J. Ind. Inf. Integr. **6**, 1–10 (2017). DOIurl10.1016/j.jii.2017.04.005. http://www.sciencedirect.com/science/article/pii/S2452414X17300043

17. Nyarko, E.K., Scitovski, R.: Solving the parameter identification problem of mathematical models using genetic algorithms. Appl. Math. Comput. **153**(3), 651–658 (2004). https://doi.org/10.1016/S0096-3003(03)00661-1. http://www.sciencedirect.com/science/article/pii/S0096300303006611

18. Perera, C., Liu, C.H., Jayawardena, S., Chen, M.: A survey on internet of things from industrial market perspective. IEEE Access **2**, 1660–1679 (2014). https://doi.org/10.1109/ACCESS.2015.2389854

19. Puri, K.: Industrial internet of things (IIoT) - conceptual architecture, July 2016. https://www.infosysblogs.com/data-analytics/2016/07/industrial_internet_of_things_.html

20. Sinha, D., Roy, R.: Reviewing cyber-physical system as a part of smart factory in industry 4.0. IEEE Eng. Manage. Rev. **48**(2), 103–117 (2020)

21. Stojmenovic, I.: Fog computing: a cloud to the ground support for smart things and machine-to-machine networks. In: 2014 Australasian Telecommunication Networks and Applications Conference (ATNAC), pp. 117–122, November 2014. https://doi.org/10.1109/ATNAC.2014.7020884

22. Stout, W.M.S.: Toward a multi-agent system architecture for insight cybersecurity in cyber-physical networks. In: 2018 International Carnahan Conference on Security Technology (ICCST), pp. 1–5, October 2018. https://doi.org/10.1109/CCST.2018.8585632

23. Tsinarakis, G.J., Spanoudakis, P.S., Arabatzis, G., Tsourveloudis, N.C., Doitsidis, L.: Implementation of a petri-net based digital twin for the development procedure of an electric vehicle. In: 2020 28th Mediterranean Conference on Control and Automation (MED), pp. 862–867, September 2020. https://doi.org/10.1109/MED48518.2020.9182784
24. Yu, R., Xue, G., Kilari, V.T., Zhang, X.: The fog of things paradigm: road toward on-demand internet of things. IEEE Commun. Mag. **56**(9), 48–54 (2018). https://doi.org/10.1109/MCOM.2018.1701140

Optimal Broadcasting Algorithm for VANET System

Ansam Ennaciri[1(✉)], Mohammed Erritali[1], Badreddine Cherkaoui[3], and Françoise Sailhan[2]

[1] TIAD Laboratory, Department of Computer Sciences, Faculty of Sciences and Techniques, Sultan Moulay Slimane University, Beni Mellal, Morocco
ennaciri.ansam@gmail.com, m.erritali@usms.ma
[2] Higher School of Technology, Chouaib Doukkali University, Sidi Bennour, Morocco
francoise.sailhan@lecnam.net
[3] Cedric Laboratory, CNAM- Paris, Paris, France
b.cherkaoui@ucd.ac.ma

Abstract. New and innovative approaches are expected to improve road safety and prevent road traffic incidents, based on the exchange of information between vehicles. Our aim is to respond to the need for rapid and reliable exchange of messages containing information on the state of vehicles. For this purpose, we propose an algorithm that prioritize the broadcasting of emergency messages and privilege long-distance communication so as to speed up the dissemination of warning messages without saturating the VANET.

Keywords: VANET · Broadcasting algorithms · Braking signals

1 Introduction

The main function of Vehicular Ad hoc NETwork (VANET) is to prevent road traffic incidents, leveraging a rapid and reliable exchange of messages vehicles. However, the high dynamics of VANETs, sometimes coupled with a high density of vehicles in urban areas, imposes several restrictions on the use of standard networking solutions used under static or low movement situations. The use of RoadSide-Units (RSU) and fixed infrastructure improves the message delivery and reduce the bandwidth usage by diminishing the need of multi-hop retransmissions; upon the reception of an emergency message, the RSU-based infrastructure may partially endorse the function of (i) disseminating alerts and (ii) displaying warning messages on dedicated information boards. Due to limited budget, RDU are often too few to cover the whole road network. Thus, VANET appear as a cost-effective alternative to RSU. Recent trends in the automotive industry lies in equipping vehicles with a VANET-enabled safety system, named on-Board Units (OBUs). Given the rapid renewal of the vehicle fleet in developing countries, more efforts have been conducted to enhance the messages spread, considering their relative priorities. In this respect, some solutions reduce the probability of collisions during the message spread across the network, by adapting the signal strength [3–7] or

© Springer Nature Switzerland AG 2021
S. Bouzefrane et al. (Eds.): MSPN 2020, LNCS 12605, pp. 209–222, 2021.
https://doi.org/10.1007/978-3-030-67550-9_14

leveraging directional antennas [1, 2]. Nonetheless, lowering the signal strength reduces the network connectivity/reachability [8–12]. Directional antennas perform poorly if the antenna get misaligned during an accident. The proposed algorithms control the message transmission [13–15] depending on the environmental conditions (presence of fading and multipath propagation caused by the re-reflection of signals from obstacles).

In this article, we propose a novel dissemination strategy that prioritizes time-sensitive messages that relate to an accident. We first evaluate the distance that a message should travel to alert nearby vehicles and avoid an accident (Sect. 3). Based on this distance, we prioritize warning messages. In addition, we propose a strategy that prevents the saturation of the transmission channel, by privileging long-distance communication to the detriment of many short distance transmissions (Sect. 4) so as to speed up the dissemination of broadcasted messages (Sect. 5).

2 Related Works

Like any network using competitive CSMA/CA access technology, VANET is extremely sensitive to the number of users and the volume of traffic that is carried. The IEEE 802.11p standard prioritizes some messages, using the so-called CCH channel. In this paper, we analyze the methods of prioritizing traffic on the main channel. There are two situations in which a node is unable to transmit a message. In the first case, the node, which attempts to access the transmission medium, detects that the channel is occupied. A temporization is then started, followed by a new access attempt. In the second case, several nodes simultaneously attempt to transfer data, which leads to a collision followed by a retry. In order to prevent such overload/collision, the following approaches have been proposed:

Broadcasting Based on Environmental Information - The basic idea is to tune the transfer of messages, based on a knowledge on neighboring nodes. Information about neighboring nodes is added to the packet header and the packet is broadcasted over one or two hops, which leads to an excessive overload.

Broadcasting Based on Network Clustering - This approach is widely used with MANET. Network clustering is the process of dividing the nodes into clusters. Clusters maintenance is done in two ways:

- Based on the control of periodically broadcasted messages over the network.
- By listening to data traffic. Algorithms based on this principle include On Demand Multicast Routing Protocol (ODMPR), Mobility-Centric Data Dissemination Algorithm for Vehicular Networks (MDDV), Dynamic Backbone-Assisted MAC (DBA-MAC) [10].

Sending Based on Information on Traffic Parameters – Protocols operate based on some information related to the neighboring nodes, their direction of travel and speed. Usually, the network congestion is limited by restricting the transmission to a small number of hops (typically one or two hops) and by merging the packets during their relaying. The merging is done when the incoming packets e.g., follow the same direction of travel. Protocols include Optimized Adaptive Probabilistic Scattering (OAPB), Optimized Adaptive Probabilistic Scattering and Deterministic Scattering (OAPB/DB), Automatic Scattering, Distributed Vehicular Scattering (DV-CAST), Density Dependent Reliable Scattering in Vehicular Ad Hoc Networks (DECA) [10, 16, 17].

Broadcasting Based on Location Information - Location-based broadcast methods rely on the information from satellite navigation systems such as GPS or GLONASS. The message source indicates in the message the geographical area wherein the message should be distributed. Upon the reception of a message, a node forwards the incoming message towards the desired area. Note that such approaches do not perform well in absence of positioning (tunnels). Location-aware protocols include Ad-Hoc Multi-Hop Broadcast (AMB), Distributed Robust Geocast (DRG), Edge Aware Epidemic Protocol (EAEP), Position Aware Reliable Broadcast Protocol (POCA), Smart Broadcast (SB), Urban Multi-Hop Broadcast (UMB) [10, 14, 16].

Distance-Aware Broadcasting - The decision on whether to retransmit the message is made based on the distance with the message source. The nodes, at the greatest distance, retransmit the incoming message quickly while others delay their retransmissions. As a result, a small number of retransmissions is needed to cover a large area. Such protocols include: direct retransmission (CTR), MobySpace, optimized alarm message broadcasting (ODAM), fast broadcast (FB), vehicle assisted data transmission (VADD) [10, 16].

Probabilistic Diffusion – protocols rely on probabilistic functions to control the transmission delay; the same transmission probability is applied to all the traffic or is parametrized depending on the message content, the number of neighbors, the number of duplicates received so far etc. Such protocols include e.g. Position Based Adaptive Broadcasting (PAB), Receive Estimate Alarm Routing (REAR) [18, 19].

3   Techniques for Improving the Resilience of the VANET Network

The network resilience depends of the quantity of message drops due to e.g. noise, interferences, reverberation or collisions. In particular, the probability that the message delivery fails, which is denoted p_{fail}, corresponds to the cumulated probability of failure during message delivery (p_{col}) and during access to the channel (p_{acc}). Thus, the probability of success of the transmission process, denoted P_{tr} verifies:

$$P_{tr} = \left(1 - p_{fail}\right) = (1 - (p_{col} + p_{acc})) \tag{1}$$

In turn, the probability of success of the transmission depends on the number of nodes N in communication range and the frequency of generated messages f_{br}. The following notation reflects the dependence:

$$P_{tr} \rightarrow max_{Ua}|N, f_{br} \tag{2}$$

The probability of success may be increased by diminishing the volume of relayed traffic, by devising an efficient relaying algorithm or by decreasing the message coverage (a.k.a time to live). In addition, it is necessary to prioritize critical messages.

4   Calculation of the Information Distance

The main objective of our emergency system is to inform road users that are nearby, about accidents. To this end, it is necessary to infer the distance that the warning message should travel and to set accordingly a proper TTL for the warning/alter messages. Similarly, the frequency of dissemination of safety information messages needs to be parametrized. These parameters should be sufficient to enable a vehicle travelling at high speed to avoid an accident.

4.1   Limitation of Information Distance

It is assumed that the location of each node is determined by the coordinates given by the GPS system. Let consider an accident (see Fig. 1) in which the vehicle V1 collides with an obstacle and, stops abruptly, i.e., $v1 = 0$. In order to avoid another accident, the second vehicle V2, which is travelling at a speed of $v2$, should have enough time to stop.

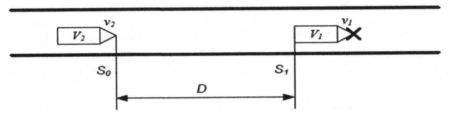

Fig. 1. Notification distance

Assuming that the driver of V2 is successfully warned of the danger, the distance that the V2 vehicle has time to travel, depends of (i) the driving speed $v2$, (ii) the driver reaction time t_r and (ii) the braking distance, which in turn depends on the acceleration/deceleration a2 of the vehicle. Taking into account the above parameters, we may deduce the average time t_{stop} during which the driver must be warned and the distance, D_{stop} which the vehicle will travel from the moment of warning:

$$\overline{t_{stop}} = t_r + t_{br} \tag{3}$$

$$\overline{D_{stop}} = v_2 t_r + S_{br} \tag{4}$$

Where t_{br} is the braking time, S_{br} is the distance travelled by the car in t_{br}, t_r is the reaction time of the driver. To determine the values of t_{br} and S_{br}, we assume that the braking of the V2 vehicle occurs with a constant acceleration a2, then we use the following uniform deceleration equations:

$$S_{br} = S_0 + v_0 t_{br} - \frac{a t_{br}^2}{2} \tag{5}$$

$$v = v_0 - a t_{br} \tag{6}$$

Where v0 is the speed of the V2 vehicle, at the time the warning report is received. Substituting these values in Eqs. (7) and (8), the braking time and the braking distance are:

$$t_{br} = \frac{v_0}{a} \qquad (7)$$

$$S_{br} = v_0 t_{br} - \frac{a t_{br}^2}{2} \qquad (8)$$

Overall:

$$\overline{t_{stop}} = t_r + \frac{v_0}{a'} \qquad (9)$$

$$\overline{D_{stop}} = v_2 t_r + v_0 t_{br} - \frac{a t_{br}^2}{2} \qquad (10)$$

Taking into account ISO 611:2003 standard [20], relating to the vehicle braking, the driver's reaction time varies from 0.4 to 1.6 s, depending on e.g. her/his psycho-physiological characteristics, her/his condition, her/his experience. Acceleration at uniform idle speed depends strongly on the quality of the braking system and the road surface [21]. Thus, still according to ISO611:2003(en) [20], on dry surfaces and drum brakes, it is 6 m/s^2. For a winter road, this value is reduced up to 6 times. Therefore, taking into account the worst-case scenario, we assume that a = 1 m/s^2.

Overall, we obtain $\overline{t_{stop}}$ = 22.2 s, $\overline{D_{stop}}$ = 282 m for a vehicle moving at 80 km/h. Since the V2 vehicle must stop well in advance, the minimum information distance must be $D_{inf}^{min} > \overline{D_{stop}}$.

5 Relays Dimensioning and Parameterization

5.1 Estimation of the Number of Relays

In order to ensure that the warning message travels the required distance, it should be considered that setting the TTL value too low will result in a premature packet drop, i.e. before they reach the required information distance.

$$TTL > t_{inf}^{max} >= t_{inf}^{min} \qquad (11)$$

$$with : \overline{t_{stop}} = t_r + \frac{v_0}{a'} \qquad (12)$$

- t_{inf}^{max} = The time of the arrival of the braking message at the node concerned.
- $t_{inf}^{min} = \overline{t_{stop}}$

So, to avoid saturating the channel, the TTL must be minimized as much as possible, while keeping it higher than t_{inf}^{max}.

Furthermore, to avoid broadcasting when the node is too far from the accident, the TTL must be as small as possible.

$$D_{inf}^{max} > D_{inf}^{min} = \overline{D_{stop}} \tag{13}$$

D_{inf}^{max} = Maximum distance to which the braking message must reach the driver.

We calculate the probability of receiving the message as a function of the distance, using the model introduced by Nakagami [28].

In order to assess the distance of distribution of broadcast messages, many factors are considered, e.g. vehicle density, location and ground conditions, which affect the occurrence of reflected signals. In [22, 27, 28], it is proposed to use the analysis apparatus obtained in [22] which, taking into account the above factors, allows the cumulative probability distribution function CDF (Cumulative Distribution Function) of the message transmission distance to be evaluated as follows:

$$F_R(a) = 1 - P(\gamma(a) > \psi) \tag{14}$$

Where R is the interaction distance; $P(\gamma(a) > \psi)$ is the probability that the Signal-to-NoiseRatio (SNR), is greater than the threshold value required for proper message reception.

By substituting the probability density function of the Nakagami [28] model in the expression (14), it is possible to calculate the CDF under different signal propagation conditions, depending on the location of the transmission. In this case, the mean value of the information distance can be obtained from (14) as:

$$E[R] = \int_0^\infty (1 - F_R(a))da \tag{15}$$

5.2 Algorithm for Delay Level Control

The proposed broadcasting algorithm corresponds to probabilistic and parametric methods. We propose to use the SINR (Signal-to-interference-plus-noise ratio) to control the propagation. The proposed algorithm determines a delay for transmitting the incoming messages; the delay value varies according to the SINR of the received message. When the message is delayed, the node is placed in a promiscuous mode and listens to any emitted message. If a duplicate message is sniffed, the delayed message is deleted.

In addition, the algorithm limits the message lifetime. The working principle of the algorithm is detailed in Fig. 2.

Originally, the node is in the free state (1). The node leaves this state upon reception (2) or emission (6) of a message on the channel. If a new message arrives, the delay is defined based on the related SINR value, which is distributed according to the exponential law (3).

This setting of the delay interval gives priority to messages with lowest SINR levels, because the source of these messages is either far away or are located in the deepest fading zone. If no duplicate message is received during the delay interval, the current message is sent (4). Otherwise (i.e. if a duplicate message is received), then the original

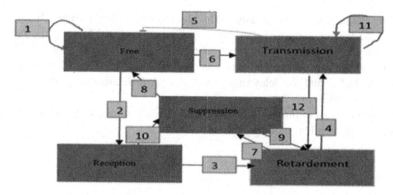

Fig. 2. Diagram of node state transitions

message is deleted. In the following cases of duplicate messages, they are all deleted immediately (10).

Once the deletion interval is elapsed, the message is removed from the delay buffer (7). If the delay buffer is empty, the node switches to the "free" state (8). Otherwise, the node expects the timer to expire to treat the next message (9). After all messages have been sent using the transmit queue (11), the node returns to the free state (5) or switches to the waiting state (12).

5.3 Choosing a Delay

A critical feature of the proposed algorithm is the parametrization of the delay, which is based on the SINR value obtained from the physical layer. The delay is set so as maximize reliability rather than based on the distance as is the case in [22, 23]. Thus, priority is not given to nodes that are far from the source but to nodes for which there is a degradation in the probability of successful delivery:

$$Delay = \left(\frac{1}{1 + SINR} \right) * TTL + cte \tag{16}$$

$$SINR = \frac{Signal}{Interferance + Noise} \tag{17}$$

6   Proposed Algorithm

6.1   Lifetime Limit and Duplication Control

Let analyze the proposed algorithm (Fig. 2). A buffer is needed to store the incoming messages. If the incoming packet has been broadcasted, the packet is processed. Otherwise, the packet follows standard mechanism regulated by IEEE 802.11p.

During the period of low channel load, the buffer is mainly empty. If no data is available, the packet is immediately processed, i.e., the signal level of the incoming packet is used to determine the corresponding time delay value. A flag is used in the buffer structure to indicate if a duplicate message has been received. Then, the packet is placed in the buffer and the delay timer set is started. A detailed block diagram of this algorithm is shown in Fig. 3.

The intended goal of this algorithm is to keep packets with a TTL below a threshold TTL max $= t_{inf}^{max}$, while removing duplicate packets.

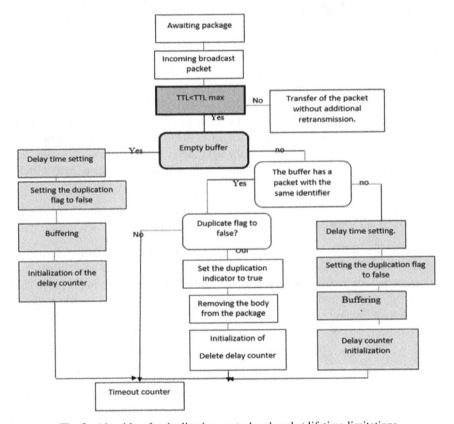

Fig. 3. Algorithm for duplication control and packet lifetime limitations

7 Experiments

In order to evaluate the performance associated with our solution, we have carried out a series of simulations.

7.1 Simulation Environment and Parameters

Relying in the NS-2 simulation tool (v-2.35), we evaluate the effectiveness of our proposed method. Table 1 summarizes the simulation parameters. We consider the road network of the city of Béni Mellal, Marocco (Fig. 4), which is quite complex and contains many branched structures. Such an urban area is characterized by a high level of interferences and by some multipath propagations of the radio waves. Situation gets worse at road intersections due to the high density of vehicles and to crossing of vehicles that lead to an increase of the number of collisions and, consequently, a decrease in the probability of successful message delivery. Relying on the so-called SUMO simulator (Simulation of Urban MObility), we simulate the vehicle mobility, considering the road network of Béni Mellal.

Table 1. Simulation parameters

Parameters	Values
Number of vehicles	200
Simulation time	200 s
Data rate	0.25
Packet size	1000
Traffic model	FTP
Routing protocol	AODV
Number of receivers	1, 2, 3, 4
Number of senders	1
IEEE standard	802.11p

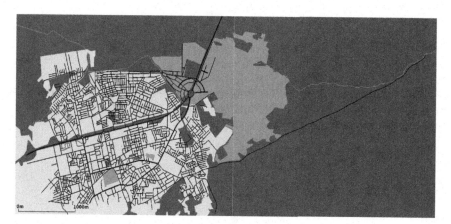

Fig. 4. Map of Béni Mellal city

7.2 Experimental Results

In Figs. 5 and 6, we plot the delay for several vehicles that are indexed by a number that reflects their distance to the source. One can see that with a basic/naïve solution, the delay is low when the node is far away. As visible in Fig. 5, the delay at node 46 is very high compared to node 80. With our approach, the message dissemination is favored with the closest nodes, based on the SINR.

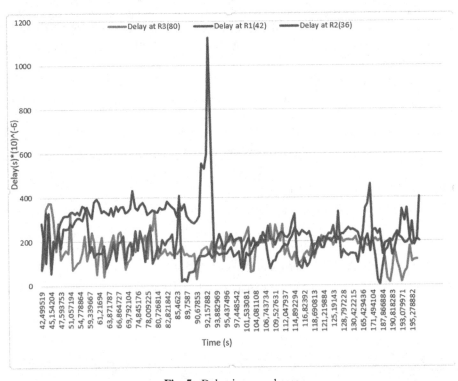

Fig. 5. Delay in normal case

Figures 7 and resp. 8 show the influence of the normal and resp. our improved protocol on the packet loss ratio. As expected, ratio of packet loss of our approach is considerably lower compared to the ordinary protocol.

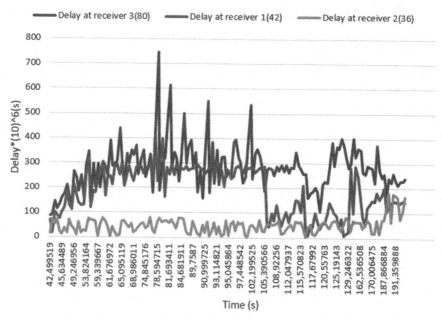

Fig. 6. Delay in improved case

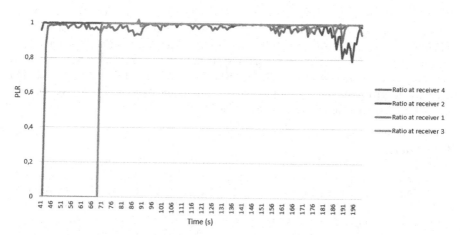

Fig. 7. Packet loss ratio in normal case

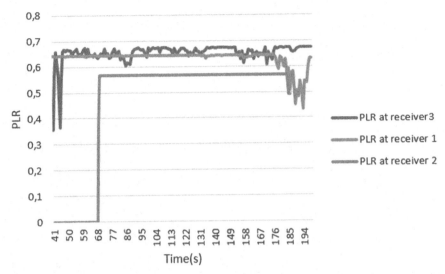

Fig. 8. Packet loss ratio in improved case

8 Conclusion

Excessive message transfer easily overload VANET: e.g. uncontrolled message broadcasting over several hops may lead to a message storm. With these regards, our aim is to limit the message dissemination to a small area and to keep to a minimum the amount of collisions, without leveraging a positioning system. In these regards, we have proposed to enhance de dissemination of warning messages over a VANET. The proposed design rational is to give preference to long-distance communication. To do so, we forward rapidly the message characterized by the lowest SINR.

References

1. Hadded, M., Zagrouba, R., Laouiti, A., Muhlethaler, P., Saidane, L.A.: An optimal strategy for collision-free slots allocations in vehicular ad-hoc networks. In: Laouiti, A., Qayyum, A., Mohamad Saad, M.N. (eds.) Vehicular Ad-hoc Networks for Smart Cities. AISC, vol. 306, pp. 15–30. Springer, Singapore (2015). https://doi.org/10.1007/978-981-287-158-9_2
2. Zhang, G., et al.: Multicast capacity for VANETs with directional antenna and delay constraint. IEEE J. Sel. Areas Commun. **30**(4), 818–833 (2012)
3. Caizzone, G., Giacomazzi, P., Musumeci, L., Verticale, G.: A power control algorithm with high channel availability for vehicular ad hoc networks. In: IEEE International Conference on Communications, ICC 2005, vol. 5, pp. 3171–3176 (2005)
4. Lei, G., Liu, F., Wang, P.: Power adjustment based congestion control in vehicular ad-hoc networks. In: 2014 4th International Conference on Artificial Intelligence with Applications in Engineering and Technology (ICAIET), pp. 280–285 (2014)
5. Rubio-Loyola, J., Galeana-Zapien, H., Aguirre-Gracia, F.: Towards intelligent tuning of frequency and transmission power adjustment in beacon-based ad-hoc networks. In: Proceedings of the 4th International Conference on Vehicle Technology and Intelligent Transport Systems - Volume 1, Funchal, Madeira, Portugal, pp. 648–656 (2018)

6. Khan, M.I.: Network parameters impact on dynamic transmission power control in vehicular ad hoc networks. Int. J. Next-Gener. Netw. (IJNGN) **5**(3), 1–22 (2003)
7. Sulistyo, S., Alam, S.: Distributed channel and power level selection in VANET based on SINR using game model. Int. J. Commun. Netw. Inf. Secur. (IJCNIS) **9**(3), 432–438 (2017)
8. Li, X., Nguyen, T., Martin, R.: Using adaptive range control to maximize 1-hop broadcast coverage in dense wireless networks. In: IEEE SECON, Santa Clara, CA, pp. 397–405, October 2004
9. Kwon, J.-H., Kwon, C., Kim, E.-J.: Neighbor Mobility-based clustering scheme for vehicular ad hoc networks. In: 2015 International Conference on Platform Technology and Service, pp. 31–32 (2015)
10. Najafzadeh, S., Ithnin, N.B., Razak, S.A.: Broadcasting in connected and fragmented vehicular ad hoc networks. Int. J. Veh. Technol. 249–258 (2013)
11. Yang, P., Wang, J., Zhang, Y., Tang, Z., Song, S.: Clustering algorithm in VANETs: a survey. In: 2015 IEEE 9th International Conference on Anti-counterfeiting, Security, and Identification (ASID), pp. 166–170, September 2015
12. Hande, R.S., Muddana, A.: Comprehensive survey on clustering-based efficient data dissemination algorithms for VANET. In: 2016 International Conference on Signal Processing, Communication, Power and Embedded System (SCOPES), pp. 629–632 (2016)
13. Cooper, C., Franklin, D., Ros, M., Safaei, F., Abolhasan, M.: A Comparative survey of VANET clustering techniques. IEEE Commun. Surv. Tutorials **19**(1), 657–681 (2017)
14. Nakorn, N., Rojviboonchai, K.: POCA: position-aware reliable broadcasting in VANET. In: Proceedings of the Asia-Pacific Conference of Information Processing (APCIP 2010), Nanchang, China, pp. 420–428 (2010)
15. Wisitpongphan, N., Tonguz, O.K.: Broadcast storm mitigation techniques in vehicular ad hoc networks. IEEE Wireless Commun. **14**(6), 84–94 (2007)
16. Nakorn, N.N., Rojviboonchai, K.: DECA: density-aware reliable broadcasting in vehicular ad hoc networks. In: Proceedings of the 7th Annual International Conference on Electrical Engineering/Electronics, Computer, Telecommunications and Information Technology, ECTI-CON, pp. 598–602 (2010)
17. Tonguz, O.K., Wisitpongphan, N., Bai, F.: DV-CAST: a distributed vehicular broadcast protocol for vehicular ad hoc networks. IEEE Wireless Commun. **17**(2), 47–57 (2010)
18. Jiang, H., Guo, H., Chen, L.: Chen reliable and efficient alarm message routing in VANET. In: 2008 The 28th International Conference on Distributed Computing Systems Workshops, pp. 186–191 (2008)
19. Yang, Y.-T., Chou, L.-D.: Position-based adaptive broadcast for inter-vehicle communications. In: ICC Workshops-2008 IEEE International Conference on Communications Workshops, pp. 410–414 (2008)
20. https://www.iso.org/obp/ui/#iso:std:iso:611:ed-4:v1:fr
21. Pyykonen, P., Kauvo, K., Viitanen, J., Eloranta, P.: Vehicle ITS station for C2X communication. In: 2014 IEEE 10th International Conference on Intelligent Computer Communication and Processing (ICCP), pp. 211–214 (2014)
22. Miorandi, D., Altman, E.: Connectivity in one-dimensional ad hoc networks: a queueing theoretical approach. Wireless Netw. **12**(5), 573–587 (2006)
23. Korkmaz, G., Ekici, E.: Urban multihop broadcast protocol for intervehicle communication systems. In: ACM VANET 2004, pp. 76–85, October 2004
24. Mutalik, P., Patil, V.C.: A survey on vehicular ad-hoc network [VANET's] protocols for improving safety in urban cities. In: 2017 International Conference On Smart Technologies For Smart Nation (SmartTechCon), pp. 840–845 (2017)
25. Bako, B., Weber, M.: Efficient information dissemination in VANETs, InTech, pp. 45–64 (2011)

26. Zhao, J., Cao, G.: VADD: vehicle-assisted data delivery in vehicular ad hoc networks. IEEE Trans. Veh. Technol. **57**(3), 1910–1922 (2008)
27. Behnad, A., Nader-Esfahani, S.: Probability of node to base station connectivity in one-dimensional ad hoc networks. IEEE Commun. Lett. **14**(7), 650–652 (2010)
28. Li, G.-S., Wang, W.-L., Yao, X.-W.: An adaptive and opportunistic broadcast protocol for vehicular ad hoc networks. Int. J. Autom. Comput. **9**(4), 378–387 (2012)
29. Vavoulas, A., Harilaos, G., Sandalidis, H., Varoutas, D.: Node isolation probability for serial ultraviolet UV-C multi-hop networks. J. Opt. Commun. Netw. **3**(9), 750–757 (2011)
30. Xie, X., Huang, B., Yang, S., Lv, T.: Adaptive multi-channel MAC protocol for dense VANET with directional antennas. In: 2009 6th IEEE Consumer Communications and Networking Conference. 10–13 January 2009, pp. 1–5 (2009)

A Reaction-Diffusion and Gür Game Based Routing Algorithm for Wireless Sensor Networks

Shu-Yuan Wu[1]([✉]), Theodore Brown[2], and Hsien-Tseng Wang[3]

[1] Graduate Center, City University of New York, New York, NY 10016, USA
swu2@gradcenter.cuny.edu
[2] Queens College, City University of New York, Queens, NY 11367, USA
tbrown@qc.cuny.edu
[3] Lehman College, City University of New York, Bronx, NY 10468, USA
hsientseng.wang@lehman.cuny.edu

Abstract. In this paper, we propose an energy-efficient, cluster-based routing algorithm to address the issue of energy constraints in wireless sensor networks. There are two components in the proposed model, the first supports the development of clusters and the second helps decide which of the sensors will sleep. Together they improve the lifetime of the clusters. Biologically inspired activator-inhibitor mechanism is employed to form clusters and select cluster heads based on the activator concentration where each sensor is associated with a pair of activator and inhibitor concentration values. In each cluster, a Gür game is applied to determine the set of active sensor nodes while inactive sensor nodes turn to sleep mode for conserving energy. The activator–inhibitor system is known to provide the mechanism for autonomous biological pattern formation, such as spots on mammals' coats, through interactions between molecules and their diffusion rates. The Gür game is a self-organized artificial game associating voters in the game with finite state automata and a moderator with a reward function. Typically in wireless sensor networks, the base station is considered as the moderator and sensor nodes as voters in the Gür game. To further maximize the lifetime of the network, in our proposed routing algorithm, each cluster is then associated with a Gür game to determine the number of active sensor nodes where the cluster head is regarded as the moderator and the cluster members as voters. Finally, we present preliminary results on the comparison between the proposed routing algorithm and LEACH, a well-known distributed clustering protocol used in wireless sensor networks that shows our method works better than LEACH.

Keywords: Gür game · Reaction-diffusion · Wireless sensor networks · LEACH

1 Introduction

Wireless Sensor Networks (WSNs) have been utilized in applications such as military, health care monitoring, transportation, environment monitoring, surveillance, etc. Typically, a WSN is deployed in an application field with a set of base

© Springer Nature Switzerland AG 2021
S. Bouzefrane et al. (Eds.): MSPN 2020, LNCS 12605, pp. 223–234, 2021.
https://doi.org/10.1007/978-3-030-67550-9_15

stations and autonomous computation agents that are built into micro-sized and cost-effective sensor nodes. Data transmission and routing are standard operations between sensor nodes and base stations or sensor nodes themselves in the network. These operations consume energy in the form of electricity sourced from the battery. There are different limitations imposed on a WSN, such as energy, processing capability of sensor nodes, storage space and so on. Consequently, the lifetime of a WSN highly depends on the aggregated effect of energy consumption and other constraints in the network.

One of the main concerns in WSNs is the energy consumption due to data transmission, routing, sensing circuitry, internal processing of sensor nodes, which directly impact the network lifetime. Comprehensive surveys on energy-efficient routing algorithms have been conducted, such as in [7]. Generally, data communication or sensing activities of sensor nodes incur the most of energy consumption. To maximize the network lifetime, we focus on reducing sensing activities by dynamically setting some sensor nodes idle and still achieving the same objective of sensing quality and quantity by the remaining active sensor nodes. Concurrently, this strategy would also decrease the volume of required data transmission, and contribute to the conservation of energy.

The reaction-diffusion model [16] proposed by Alan Turing in 1952 is a well-known mathematical model that addresses the development of biological structures or patterns autonomously in a system of chemical substances, called morphogens that interact and diffuse through cells. Specifically, the reaction-diffusion model considers two types of interacting morphogens, which can establish chemical gradients through short-range activation and long-range inhibition. Since then, Turing's reaction-diffusion model has inspired many subsequent studies for modeling pattern formation on mammals' coats, veins on a leaf and many other biological patterns. These mathematical models, such as activator-inhibitor models, are now referred as reaction-diffusion models in general, which calculate the concentration of two chemical substances at a given time based on the diffusion, reaction, removal and basic production of two interacting chemical substances [6]. Applications of the reaction-diffusion model to WSNs include distributed cluster head election [18] and coordination of active and idle sensor nodes [9] based on the activator concentration. As we shall see in the next section, research has shown that reaction-diffusion models are capable of modeling autonomous coordination of nodes, and can be resilient to the disruption and failure of nodes.

The Gür game, a self-organized artificial game associating voters in the game with finite state automata and a moderator with a reward function, was introduced by Tsetlin [13] in 1973 and further studies by Tung et al. [14,15], etc. In 2003, Iyer and Kleinrock [4] presented that the base station can adjust the number of active sensors in wireless sensor networks efficiently using the Gür game. Since then, the Gür game has been applied to WSNs to achieve self-organizing, battery life control of sensor nodes, optimal Quality of Service (QoS) and so on. Typically the base station is considered as the moderator and sensor nodes as voters in the Gür game.

In this paper, we propose a cluster-based routing algorithm to maximize the lifetime of a WSN. We first employ the Gierer-Meinhardt activator-inhibitor model to select cluster heads and organize sensors into dynamic clusters autonomously through an activation-inhibition process. On this basis, we then apply the Gür game to each cluster. Each cluster head is modeled as a moderator in the Gür game configuration, and member nodes are modeled as finite state automata. Ultimately, each cluster head would determine the number of active sensor nodes in the cluster while inactive sensor nodes turn to sleep mode to save energy. Specifically, our approach takes advantage of both the reaction-diffusion mechanism and the Gür game without the presence of the base station and global knowledge of sensor locations in the networks for autonomous dynamic clustering and determination of active sensor nodes to tackle the energy consumption issue in the network.

The paper is organized as follows: Sect. 2 presents related works on the Gür game paradigm and reaction-diffusion models in WSNs. Section 3 proposes our clustering-based routing algorithm using the Gierer-Meinhardt activator-inhibitor model and the Gür game. Section 4 shows the experiment setup and the simulation results. The paper concludes with observations and future works in Sect. 5.

2   Related Work

The Gür game was introduced by Tsetlin [13] and further studied in [14,15]. A Gür game usually involves two types of players: a moderator and a set of voters with selective actions to facilitate rounds of the game. In each round, the moderator asks all voters to vote yes or no simultaneously. Then it accumulates the fraction f of yes votes. The feedback from the moderator to voters is either a reward or a penalty based on a generated reward function $r(f)$; only the moderator knows the details of $r(f)$. The boundary of the reward function $r(f)$ is assumed: $0 \leq r(f) \leq 1$. At the end of each round, each voter is either rewarded or penalized one unit independently. The outcome is subject to the discretion of the moderator who utilizes $r(f)$ and $1 - r(f)$ as values for reward or penalty respectively regardless of individual votes. Each voter continues to the next round and casts a new vote based on the reward it receives in the current round. As the number of rounds grows, approximately f^* voters appear to vote yes regardless the number of participating voters. f^* is where the maximum value of the reward function occurs. It is up to the moderator's decision to select the reward function, which can be uni-modal, discontinuous, or multi-modal function, etc. As an example, an exponential-based reward function is shown in Fig. 1 where the reward function has its maximum 0.9 at the desired proportion of players who vote yes, or $f^* = 0.3$.

Tsetlin [13] further formulated the Gür game by modeling each voter with an automaton $L_{2,2n}$ of $2n$ states. In other words, each vote assumes a memory size of n, as shown in Fig. 2.

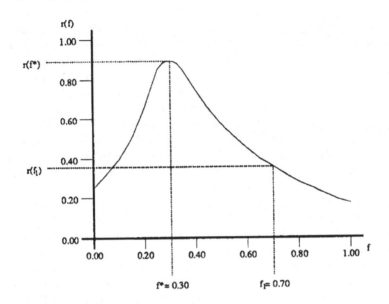

Fig. 1. A typical reward function. Figure extracted from [14].

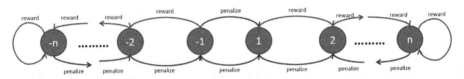

Fig. 2. Automata design of $L_{2,2n}$. Figure redrawn from [13].

If its current state is a negative numbered state, the automaton gives output of A_0; otherwise A_1 is given. If an automaton is rewarded, it moves from state i to $i+1$ if i is positive or from i to $i-1$ if i is negative. If the automaton is penalized, it moves from state i to $i-1$ if i is positive or from i to $i+1$ if i is negative.

The theory and practice of Gür game have been applied to WSNs to achieve self-organizing, battery life control of sensor nodes, and optimal Quality of Service (QoS). Iyer and Kleinrock [4] used the Gür game to allow the base station to adjust the resolution (the number of active sensors) of wireless sensor networks. This model defines its own QoS control measure, instead of focusing on the coverage and lifetime of active sensors. Tsai and Wang [12] sought to present an enhanced Gür game-based QoS control scheme to balance power consumption in the model by Iyer and Kleinrock's model [4]. Nayer and Ali [8] sought to cover maximum number of regions with minimum number of nodes using the dominating sets and the Gür game. Tsai and Wang [11] combined the Gür game-based scheme presented by Iyer and Kleinrock [4] and Nayer and Ali [8] to take both the coverage and the number of active sensors into consideration. They divide the target field into a number of small regions and assign an ID to each region. Each region is covered by one or more sensors. Each sensor knows its covered region IDs. Active sensors transmit the covered region IDs and collected data to the base station. Ayers and Liang [1] proposed a new QoS control algorithm, Gureen game which improves the Gür game to further prolong the lifetime of wireless sensor networks compared to the original algorithm of Gur Game based QoS control [4]. Liu et al. [5] proposed a distributed QoI-aware energy-management scheme for WSNs based on the framework of the Gür Game, which satisfies the QoI (Quality-of-Information) requirements.

In 1952, Alan M. Turing [16] suggested that a chemical mechanism can address the main phenomena of morphogenesis. Turing presented that concentration of two interacting chemical substances, called morphogens can generate biological patterns. He employed a mathematical model to show that if morphogens react and diffuse in an appropriate way, a spatial pattern of morphogen concentrations can arise from an initial uniform distribution in an assemblage cell under the assumption that morphogens can react with one another and diffuse through cells. Since then, Turing's model has inspired many models for pattern formation on mammals' coats, veins on a leaf and many biological patterns. These mathematical models, such as activator-inhibitor models, are now referred as reaction-diffusion models, which calculate the concentration of two chemical substances at a given time based on the diffusion, reaction, removal and basic production of two interacting chemical substances [6].

Activator-inhibitor models, a type of reaction-diffusion, describe competition of two chemical substances over space and time. An activator, short-range auto-catalytic substance tends to self-enhance the process in its vicinity. Long-range inhibition tends to inhibit the activation. In certain circumstances, the interaction between short-range activation and long-range inhibition can lead to the formation of asymmetric spatial patterns, such as spots and stripes on mammals' coats.

Gierer-Meinhardt activator-inhibitor model [2] is one of the most widely used activator-inhibitor models, depicts pattern formation in the following reaction–diffusion equations:

$$\frac{\partial a}{\partial t} = D_a \nabla^2 a + \frac{\rho_a a^2}{h} - \mu_a a + \sigma_a \tag{1}$$

$$\frac{\partial h}{\partial t} = D_h \nabla^2 h + \rho_h a^2 - \mu_h h + \sigma_h \tag{2}$$

where a and h are the concentration values of the activator and the inhibitor, ∇^2 is the Laplace operator. D_a and D_h are the diffusion rates, μ_a and μ_h the removal rates, ρ_a, ρ_h the reaction coefficients, and σ_a, σ_h the basic production terms.

To the best of our knowledge, there are very few researches on applying activator-inhibitor mechanisms to autonomous organization of sensor nodes. Neglia and Reina [9] configured a uniform random dense sensor network to study and compare two methodologies of coordination mechanism of sensor nodes' sensing activities. Ideally, sensor nodes shall organize themselves autonomously and control their sensing circuitry which incurs the major energy consumption. The first method considered is the activator-inhibitor-based communication mechanism. Each sensor node stores and broadcasts its activator and inhibitor values, which are based on the activator and inhibitor values collected from its neighbors. If a sensor node maintains an activator value that is higher than a given threshold and also the highest one among neighbors, this sensor node becomes active and turns on its sensing circuitry to collect data. The second method is the probabilistic-based mechanism. Each sensor node independently activates its sensing circuitry with a pre-determined probability. There is no broadcasting (i.e. communication) needed in this method. The simulation in [9] showed that the activator-inhibitor mechanism is able to preserve more energy for sensing activities.

Yamamoto et al. [18] evaluated three methods with respect to their functionalities and performance in distributed cluster-head selection algorithms. Three methods being considered are the Gierer and Meinhardt activator-inhibitor model, the activator–substrate depleted model, and the Gray–Scott model. Their experiment results show a tournament between the stability of network patterns and the ability to recover upon disruption. Specifically, for a method that is more stable with rare failure, it recovers slower from disruption and vice versa. For instance, The Gierer-Meinhardt model is more stable, but slower to recover from disruptions. The activator–substrate model is neutral that sits between the above two extremities.

3   Routing Algorithm in the Framework of Reaction-Diffusion Mechanism and Gür Game

With a clear objective of maximizing the lifetime of a wireless sensor network, we design a routing algorithm to tackle two important tasks of a wireless sensor network deployment, which are both critical in controlling energy consumption in the network. The Gierer-Meinhardt activator-inhibitor model, which is one of the most widely used reaction diffusion models, is adapted to the selection of cluster heads and the dynamic cluster formation. Furthermore, each cluster is configured as a Gür game whose moderator is the cluster head, and cluster members are voters. For each iteration, active sensor nodes can be determined autonomously based on the outcome of each game round.

To illustrate our proposed method, we set up a wireless sensor network as follows: N wireless sensor nodes are randomly deployed in high density in an area A. The distance d that each sensor node can transmit is bounded by the radio transmission range, r. For each sensor, its sensing activity consumes the most energy. The network is configured as a cluster-based wireless sensor network where each sensor node connects to the closest cluster head. A cluster head gathers, fuses, and transmits the data collected from its member nodes to the base station.

In the rest of this section, we present details of adapting the Gierer-Meinhardt activator-inhibitor model and the Gür Game to our proposed methodology.

3.1 Reaction-Diffusion

In our approach, the Gierer-Meinhardt activator-inhibitor model is used to determine the cluster heads and form clusters dynamically in a wireless sensor network. Each sensor i stores its own concentration values of activator and inhibitor, a_i and h_i respectively. The pair (a_i, h_i) is broadcasted every τ seconds. Each sensor i updates its a_i and h_i based on the following discrete equation system using the concentration values of activator and inhibitor collected from its 1-hop neighbors [9].

$$a_i(t_{k+1}) = a_i(t_k) + [\frac{9D_a}{4r^2} \sum_{j \in N_i} (a_j(t_{k+1}) - a_i(t_k)) + \frac{\rho_a a_i^2}{h_i} - \mu_a a_i + \sigma_a]\tau \quad (3)$$

$$h_i(t_{k+1}) = h_i(t_k) + [\frac{9D_h}{4r^2} \sum_{j \in N_i} (h_j(t_{k+1}) - h_i(t_k)) + \rho_h a_i^2 - \mu_h h_i + \sigma_h]\tau \quad (4)$$

where $t_{k+1} = t_k + \tau$, $a_j(t)$ and $h_j(t)$ denote the concentration values of sensor i's 1-hop neighbor j at time t. D_a and D_h are the diffusion rates, r the transmission range, μ_a and μ_h the removal rates, ρ_a, ρ_h the reaction coefficients, and σ_a, σ_h the basic production terms. Cluster heads are then selected based on the concentration value a_i. A sensor node is selected as the cluster head if its a_i is larger than a threshold in the neighborhood. In each cluster, we only set a certain number of sensors active in each time step based on the Gür Game, which will be described below. Each sensor i is associated with a game state value s_i, along with the concentration values a_i and h_i. Values of a_i, h_i, and s_i all get updated for each time step and game round.

3.2 Gür Game

With respect to the $L_{2,2n}$ automaton illustrated in Fig. 2, we established the state transition rules [17] for each node in a given cluster as follows:

if an automaton is rewarded **then**
    if its current state, $i = n$ or $-n$ **then**
        stay in the current state
    else if $1 \leq$ current state, $i < n$ **then**
        next state $= i + 1$
    else if $-n <$ current state, $i \leq -1$ **then**
        next state $= i - 1$
    end if
else

```
if current state, i = −1 then
    next state = 1
else if current state, i = 1 then
    next state = −1
else if current state, i > 1 then
    next state = i − 1
else if current state, i < −1 then
    next state = i + 1
    end if
end if
```

The above rule considers a single automaton only. While the analysis of multiple automata is beyond the scope of this paper, we summarize the asymptotic behaviors of the Gür game below, which have been proven or shown by simulations by Tung and Kleinrock [14,15].

1. Suppose that each automaton has only two states. As the number of automata, N and time, $t \to \infty$, $f(t) \to 1/2$.
2. For any number of N, the system will spend a desired proportion of time in optimal configurations when the number of states for each automaton is high enough.
3. Given a fixed memory size of n, an increasing number of automata of N will lead the system to spend more time on $f \approx 1/2$.

The Gür game is applied to each cluster with the cluster heads as moderators. The sensor nodes with the positive numbered states become active sensing nodes. Otherwise, they are in a sleep mode, which perform neither sensing nor data transmission.

4   Simulation Results

In this section, we present preliminary simulation results that are conducted in a Matlab simulator we developed based on a LEACH simulator [19]. While we do not formulate our proposed algorithm as an optimization problem, we are still interested in studying the feasibility of fusing two autonomous and self-organizing methodologies to tackle the energy consumption problem. As a result, we attempt to compare our experiment results on the network lifetime between the our proposed algorithm and LEACH. Heinzelman et al. [3] proposed the Low Energy Adaptive Clustering Hierarchy (LEACH) routing protocol to minimize energy consumption in a wireless sensor network so that the network lifetime increases significantly. LEACH achieves this by reducing the necessary number of communication messages sent by sensor nodes and in turn decreasing the energy dissipation of nodes. In LEACH, all sensor nodes organize into dynamic clusters autonomously. A node n generates a $[0, 1]$ bounded random number m and compares it with the preset cluster-head selection threshold $T(n)$, defined as follows:

$$T(n) = \begin{cases} p/(1 - p(r \bmod \frac{1}{p})) & \text{if } n \in G \\ 0 & \text{otherwise} \end{cases} \tag{5}$$

where p is a preset fractions of nodes that would become cluster heads, r is the current round, and G is the set of nodes that have been cluster heads in the last $\frac{1}{p}$ rounds. A node is acknowledged as a cluster head if $m < T(n)$. Simulations performed in [3] showed that LEACH reduces communication energy significantly, and the first node death time is prolonged. Since its introduction, LEACH has been studied and enhanced extensively [10]. Moreover, our proposed algorithm is of the same essence of dynamic cluster formation as LEACH.

We consider a field of 100 m × 100 m where 100 sensor nodes are deployed randomly with the base-station placed in the coordinates (50, 200), as shown in the Fig. 3.

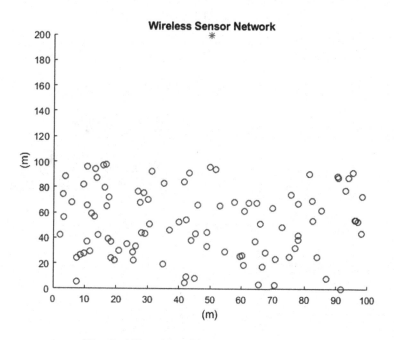

Fig. 3. 100-node and base station network.

The parameters for the simulation in our proposed model is summarized in the Table 1. We use the same energy dissipation setup for both LEACH and the proposed model.

In order to assess the feasibility of fusing activator-inhibitor mechanism and the Gür game on lifetime in wireless sensor networks, we compare the first node death, and the number of alive sensor nodes and active cluster heads of the proposed model and LEACH where $p = 0.05$ is adapted for LEACH.

Table 1. Simulation parameters for the proposed model.

Activator-inhibitor mechanism	
D_a	0.000222273
D_h	0.00580619
μ_a	0.75
μ_h	0.8
σ_a	0.25
σ_h	0.25
ρ_a	0.5
ρ_h	0.5
Gür Game	
Number of states	6
$r(f) =$	$0.2 + 0.6 * exp(-800 * (f - 0.6)^2)$

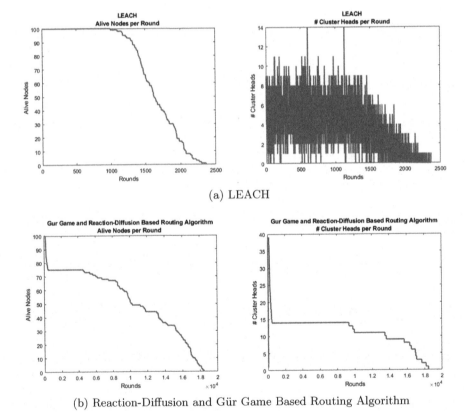

(a) LEACH

(b) Reaction-Diffusion and Gür Game Based Routing Algorithm

Fig. 4. Simulation results: the number of alive sensor nodes and cluster heads over time in LEACH and the proposed algorithm.

The simulation results shows that our proposed algorithm can have longer network lifetime than LEACH does. However, the first node death in the proposed algorithm occurs earlier than the first node death in LEACH. Furthermore, the number of active cluster heads becomes quite static after the first node death in our proposed algorithm, while the number of active cluster heads in LEACH varies over time.

5 Conclusions

In this paper, we present a activator-inhibitor and Gür game based routing algorithm that reduces the energy consumption of a WSN to maximize the network lifetime. The proposed algorithm is distributive and requires neither control information from the base station nor the architecture of the entire network. The Gierer-Meinhardt activator-inhibitor model [2] is employed to determine cluster heads and form clusters autonomously and dynamically. In each cluster, the Gür game is utilized to determine the active and idle sensor nodes so that only the active nodes transmit sensing data to its cluster head. Consequently, cluster heads relay the aggregated data to the base station.

Our simulation results show that the proposed routing algorithm prolongs the network lifetime compared to LEACH although the first node death in our algorithm comes earlier than in LEACH. The number of cluster heads in the proposed algorithm does not change frequently after the first node death. We believe that it is worth of additional efforts to explore more scenarios of fusing the two methodologies we have selected.

References

1. Ayers, M., Liang, Y.: Gureen game: an energy-efficient QoS control scheme for wireless sensor networks. In: 2011 International Green Computing Conference and Workshops (IGCC), pp. 1–8. IEEE (2011)
2. Gierer, A., Meinhardt, H.: A theory of biological pattern formation. Kybernetik **12**(1), 30–39 (1972)
3. Heinzelman, W.R., Chandrakasan, A., Balakrishnan, H.: Energy-efficient communication protocol for wireless microsensor networks. In: Proceedings of the 33rd Annual Hawaii International Conference on System Sciences, p. 10. IEEE (2000)
4. Iyer, R., Kleinrock, L.: QoS control for sensor networks. In: IEEE International Conference on Communications. ICC 2003, vol. 1, pp. 517–521. IEEE (2003)
5. Liu, C., Hui, P., Branch, J., Yang, B.: QoI-aware energy management for wireless sensor networks. In: 2011 IEEE International Conference on Pervasive Computing and Communications Workshops (PERCOM Workshops), pp. 8–13. IEEE (2011)
6. Murray, J.: II. Spatial Models and Biomedical Applications. Springer, New York (2003). https://doi.org/10.1007/b98869
7. Nakas, C., Kandris, D., Visvardis, G.: Energy efficient routing in wireless sensor networks: a comprehensive survey. Algorithms **13**(3), 72 (2020)
8. Nayer, S.I., Ali, H.H.: A dynamic energy-aware algorithm for self-optimizing wireless sensor networks. In: Hummel, K.A., Sterbenz, J.P.G. (eds.) IWSOS 2008. LNCS, vol. 5343, pp. 262–268. Springer, Heidelberg (2008). https://doi.org/10.1007/978-3-540-92157-8_23

9. Neglia, G., Reina, G.: Evaluating activator-inhibitor mechanisms for sensors coordination. In: 2007 2nd Bio-Inspired Models of Network, Information and Computing Systems, pp. 129–133. IEEE (2007)

10. Singh, S.K., Kumar, P., Singh, J.P.: A survey on successors of leach protocol. IEEE Access **5**, 4298–4328 (2017)

11. Tsai, R.G., Wang, H.L.: A coverage-aware QoS control in wireless sensor networks. In: 2010 International Conference on Communications and Mobile Computing (CMC), vol. 3, pp. 192–196. IEEE (2010)

12. Tsai, R.-G., Wang, H.-L.: Shuffle: an enhanced QoS control by balancing energy consumption in wireless sensor networks. In: Bellavista, P., Chang, R.-S., Chao, H.-C., Lin, S.-F., Sloot, P.M.A. (eds.) GPC 2010. LNCS, vol. 6104, pp. 603–611. Springer, Heidelberg (2010). https://doi.org/10.1007/978-3-642-13067-0_62

13. Tsetlin, M.: Automaton theory and modeling of biological systems: by ML Tsetlin. Translated by Scitran (Scientific Translation Service), vol. 102. Academic Press (1973)

14. Tung, B., Kleinrock, L.: Distributed control methods. In: Proceedings the 2nd International Symposium on High Performance Distributed Computing, pp. 206–215. IEEE (1993)

15. Tung, B., Kleinrock, L.: Using finite state automata to produce self-optimization and self-control. IEEE Trans. Parallel Distrib. Syst. **7**(4), 439–448 (1996)

16. Turing, A.M.: The chemical basis of morphogenesis. Philos. Trans. R. Soc. Lond. Ser. B Biol. Sci. **237**(64), 37–72 (1952)

17. Wu, S.-Y., Brown, T.: Opinion formation using the Gür game. In: Zhang, L., Song, X., Wu, Y. (eds.) AsiaSim/SCS AutumnSim -2016. CCIS, vol. 646, pp. 368–377. Springer, Singapore (2016). https://doi.org/10.1007/978-981-10-2672-0_38

18. Yamamoto, L., Miorandi, D., Collet, P., Banzhaf, W.: Recovery properties of distributed cluster head election using reaction-diffusion. Swarm Intell. **5**(3–4), 225–255 (2011)

19. Zattas, A.: Leach simulator, matlab central file exchange (2020). https://www.mathworks.com/matlabcentral/fileexchange/66574-leach

Low Complexity Neural Network Based Digital Predistortion for Memory Power Amplifiers

Meryem M. Benosman[1,2]($\boxtimes$), Hmaeid Shaiek[2], Yassin Bendimerad[1,3], Rafik Zayani[2,4], Daniel Roviras[2]($\boxtimes$), and Fethi T. Bendimerad[1]

[1] LTT Laboratory, University of Tlemcen, Tlemcen, Algeria
`meryemmamia.benosman@univ-tlemcen.dz`
[2] CEDRIC Laboratory, Conservatoire National des Arts et des Métiers, Paris, France
[3] Electrical and Electronic Engineering Department, University of Bechar, Bechar, Algeria
[4] Innov'COM/Sup'Com, Carthage University, Tunis, Tunisia

Abstract. Digital Predistortion (DPD) is an effective technique for Power Amplifier (PA) non-linear distortion and memory effects compensation. Different topoligies of DPD are presented in the literature. In this paper, we propose a mimetic neural network based DPD for Hammerstein power amplifier for OFDM signal with a reduction of Peak to Average Power Ration (PAPR) by Selective Mapping (SLM) method. This proposed model is compared with Real Valued Multilayer Perceptron (R-MLP). Simulation results show that the mimetic-R-MLP manifests more efficiency for PA linearization and for memory effect reduction in terms of Error Vector Magnitude (EVM) by a gain of 2 dB. It outperforms the R-MLP in terms of Mean Squared Error (MSE) for the convergence of the Neural Network (NN) and its complexity is 23% lower. The results in terms of Power Spectral Density (DSP) show also that our model compensates efficiently the out of band distortion (OOB) of the PA.

Keywords: Digital predistortion · Mimetic architecture · MLP · Neural network · OFDM · PA

1 Introduction

Upcoming 5G wireless communication systems are expected to support a wide range of services with increased data rates and reduced energy consumption. A key issue for 5G and beyond wireless systems acceptance will be a reduced footprint on CO_2 emissions. Indeed, information and communications technologies sector (ICT) currently consumes 3% of the world-wide energy and generates about 2% of the world-wide CO_2 emissions [1]. One main concern for 5G systems is to reduce energy consumption and increase energy efficiency. For 5G and

This work is supported by the Patenariat Huber Curien (PHC) Tasilli project: ATOME5+ 19MDU2014.

beyond wireless systems, Multiple-Input Multiple-Output (MIMO) systems are a key technology for data rate improvement. In this context, a wireless access point consists in several RF transmission chains. Knowing that the most important part (50–80%) of the total power budget is actually consumed by the PA in each RF chain, it is of paramount importance to increase energy efficiency of the PA device.

PA are non-linear devices where power efficiency is maximized when the device is operated near its saturation region. On the other hand, transmitted signals in 5G systems are multi-carrier signals based on the well known Orthogonal Frequency Division Multiplexing waveform with Cyclic Prefix (CP-OFDM) [2]. Envelope of CP-OFDM signals exhibits high peaks that are characterized by the Peak to Average Power Ratio (PAPR). The conjunction of a non-linear device operated near saturation with a high PAPR signal generates severe degradations over the transmitted signal [3]. These effects are twofold, first we have out of band (OOB) degradation through spectral regrowth. Due to spectral regrowth, the non-linear amplified signal will interfere with adjacent wireless systems. A frequency gap can be necessary between two adjacent wireless systems but this will decrease spectral efficiency. The second effect of the non-linear device is the in band (IB) distortion creating increased error vector magnitude (EVM) and higher bit error rate (BER). Furthermore, the above effects are emphasized if the amplified signal has a high PAPR.

To decrease IB and OOB effects two techniques are currently employed: PAPR reduction of the transmitted signal and PA linearization. Among all existing linearization techniques this paper will focus on predistortion techniques applied on the digital baseband signal called digital predistortion (DPD). PAPR reduction lies out of the scope of the paper and we will concentrate our study of DPD using neural networks (NN) for non-linear PA with memory effects. Memory effects have to be taken into account because of the large OFDM signal bandwidth. For modelling PA memory effects we have used an Hammerstein model [4] with an embedded Saleh PA model [5]. NN based DPD have been studied in past years [6,7]. The most studied NN architectures are based on multilayer perceptron (MLP). In this paper we adapt the architecture of the NN to the Hammerstein model and compare a classical fully connected MLP to a mimetic architecture, taking into account the Hammerstein structure. Performance in terms of complexity, OOB and EVM will be presented, showing the very good behavior of the mimetic architecture.

The remainder of this paper is organized as follows. Section 2 presents the system model with the Hammerstein HPA model (Saleh model used in the paper) and the PAPR reduction technique used. In Sect. 3 we present the two NN architectures based on MLP: fully connected MLP and mimetic MLP architecture. Performances in terms of power spectral density (PSD for the OOB effect) and EVM (for IB effects) together with computational complexity are presented in Sect. 4. Finally, the conclusion of this paper is given in Sect. 5.

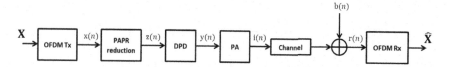

Fig. 1. CP-OFDM transceiver in presence of PA, PAPR reduction and DPD.

2   System Model

Figure 1, shows a CP-OFDM transmission scheme in presence of power amplifier (PA). CP-OFDM is an orthogonal multicarrier system, which transmitter is based on the Inverse Fast Fourier Transform (IFFT). The time domain signal $x(n)$ at the output of CP-OFDM modulator is given by:

$$x(n) = \frac{1}{\sqrt{N}} \sum_{k=0}^{N-1} X(k) e^{\frac{j2\pi kn}{N}}, \ n = 0, 1, \ldots, N-1 \qquad (1)$$

where $\mathbf{X} = [X(0), X(1), \ldots, X(N-1)]$ is a vector of complex M-QAM symbols, k is the subcarrier index and N is the total number of subcarriers.

For high number of subcarrier N, the CP-OFDM signal tends to a complex random process, with Gaussian and independent real and imaginary parts. The modulus of $x(n)$ has a Rayleigh distribution, with a non constant envelop characterized by what's commonly called in the literature: Peak to Average Power Ratio (PAPR). The PAPR of the CP-OFDM symbol is defined as follows:

$$PAPR = 10 log_{10} \left(\frac{\max\limits_{0 \leq n \leq N-1} \left\{ |x(n)|^2 \right\}}{\mathbb{E} \left\{ |x(n)|^2 \right\}} \right) \qquad (2)$$

where $\mathbb{E}\{.\}$ is the statistical expectation operator. PAPR is a random variable characterizing the signal dynamics. Commonly, PAPR is represented by the Complementary Cumulative Distribution Function (CCDF). The CCDF is the probability that the PAPR is greater than a fixed PAPR, called γ_0.

$$CCDF_{PAPR}(\gamma_0) = Pr\left(PAPR > \gamma_0\right) \qquad (3)$$

As the PAPR of signal $x(n)$ is high, it should be reduced before high power amplification in order to avoid signal distortion. For this purpose, many PAPR reduction techniques have been proposed in literature for CP-OFDM and for other post-OFDM waveforms. Consequently, numerous surveys have been published on this issue [8,9]. As PAPR reduction is out of the scope of this paper, we will only give here some insights on the technique we have used: SeLected Mapping (SLM) [10]. A block diagram of SLM technique is shown in Fig. 2.

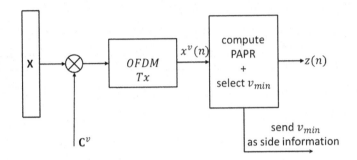

Fig. 2. Block diagram of SLM technique for reducing the PAPR.

Firstly, we generate V complex phase rotation vectors $\mathbf{C}^v$, for $0 \leq v \leq V - 1$, of length N as:

$$\mathbf{C}^v = \begin{cases} (1, ..., 1)^\mathsf{T}, & v = 0, \\ (C_0^v, ..., C_{N-1}^v)^\mathsf{T}, & 1 \leq v \leq V - 1. \end{cases} \tag{4}$$

where, C_n^v is the nth element of $\mathbf{C}^v$ defined as

$$C_n^v = e^{j\psi_n} \in \mathbb{C}, \ 0 \leq v \leq V - 1, \ 0 \leq n \leq N - 1 \tag{5}$$

where, ψ_n is a uniformly distributed phase between 0 and 2π. The frequency-domain input symbols $\mathbf{X}$ with N tones, are phase rotated by V phase rotations vectors $\{\mathbf{C}^v\}_{v=0}^{V-1}$, having a size of N

$$\mathbf{X}^v = \mathbf{X} \odot \mathbf{C}^v, \ 0 \leq v \leq V - 1 \tag{6}$$

where, $\odot$ denotes carrier-wise point-to-point multiplication.

By applying a modulation operation on $\{\mathbf{X}^v\}_{v=0}^{V-1}$, we obtain the V time-domain signal patterns $\{x^v(n)\}_{v=0}^{V-1}$. The target of the SLM optimization problem is to identify the signal $x^{v_{min}}(n)$ that has the least PAPR so that

$$v_{min} = \underset{0 \leq v \leq V-1}{\arg \min} \Big[PAPR(x^v(n)) \Big], 0 \leq n \leq N \tag{7}$$

The index of the optimal phase rotation vector, v_{min} is sent to the receiver as side information (SI) comprising of $\log_2(V)$ bits.

After PAPR reduction a linearization of PA conversion characteristics will be performed. Many techniques for pre-distorting the signal to be amplified have been proposed in the literature. The interested reader could refer to some overview papers as [11]. The approach considered in our work is based on Digital Pre-Distortion (DPD), by using Neural Network (NN). The NN chosen is based on MultiLayer Perceptron (MLP). More details on the NN architectures and the adaptation algorithms will be given in Sect. 3.

An indirect approach, as shown in Fig. 3, has been used for training the NN. With this approach, a DPD is found for the nonlinear device by minimizing the error between the DPD output and the PA input signal and is then copied to be used as a DPD. During the training step, the following Means Square Errors are minimized:

$$MSE_{\Re} = \mathbb{E}\left\{|\Re(y(n)) - \Re(\hat{y}(n))|^2\right\}$$

$$MSE_{\Im} = \mathbb{E}\left\{|\Im(y(n)) - \Im(\hat{y}(n))|^2\right\}$$
(8)

were $\Re(.)$ and $\Im(.)$ stand for real and imaginary parts of the signal

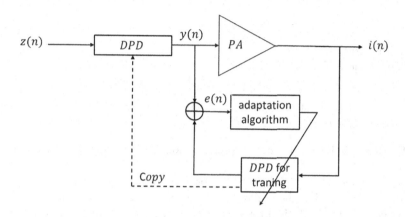

Fig. 3. Indirect learning architecture for DPD.

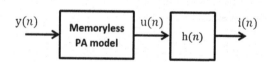

Fig. 4. Hammerstein model for a PA with memory.

In practice in order to avoid working near to the saturation point of the power amplifier (PA), the power of signal $y(n)$, at the PA input, is adjusted at a given Input Back-Off (IBO), from the saturation power P_{sat}. This IBO is defined as follows:

$$\text{IBO} = 10\log_{10}\left(\frac{P_{sat}}{P_y}\right)$$
(9)

where P_y is the average power of the signal to be applied at the input of the PA.

The PA models can be classified into two categories: memoryless PA models and those with memory [13]. As CP-OFDM signals have wide-band, the frequency dependency of the PA characteristics becomes important, giving rise to the so-called memory effects in the response of the PA. The most well-known PA models with memory are the Wiener and the Hammerstein one [13]. In our study the Hammerstein model will be used. This model can be represented by a memoryless PA followed by a linear filter, as shown by Fig. 4.

The memoryless amplified signal $u(n)$ can be written as

$$u(n) = F_a(\rho) \exp(jF_p(\rho)) \exp(j\varphi) \tag{10}$$

where

- ρ is the modulus of $y(n)$,
- $F_a(\rho)$ is the AM/AM characteristic of the memoryless PA,
- $F_p(\rho)$ is the AM/PM characteristic of the memoryless PA.

Many memoryless PA models have been proposed in the literature, among them we can mention:

- SEL, for Soft Envelop Limiter, used to model a perfectly linearised PA with saturation,
- Rapp, for modelling Solid State Power Amplifier,
- Saleh, for modelling the behavior of Travelling Wave Tube Amplifiers,
- Polynomial, for analytical purposes and also for modelling real life measured PA.

In our work, we have chosen a Saleh model [12]. This PA model has been mainly used in several works dealing with the impact of nonlinearities in OFDM systems [6]. According to this model, the AM/AM and AM/PM conversion characteristics can be expressed as follows:

$$F_a(\rho) = \frac{\alpha_a \rho}{1 + \beta_a \rho^2}$$

$$F_p(\rho) = \frac{\alpha_p \rho^2}{1 + \beta_p \rho^2} \tag{11}$$

were α_a and β_a are the parameters to decide the nonlinear amplitude distortion level, and α_p and β_p are phase displacements.

In Figs. 5 and 6, we plot the AM/AM and AM/PM characteristics of the Saleh model with $\alpha_a = 2$, $\beta_a = 1$, $\alpha_p = 4$ and $\beta_p = 9$.

Finally, the signal $i(n)$ at the output of the PA block, taking into account memory effects, is given by:

$$i(n) = u(n) * h(n) \tag{12}$$

where $*$ stands for the convolution product and $h(n)$ is the impulse response of the PA memory filter.

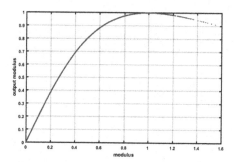

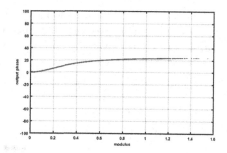

Fig. 5. AM/AM characteristics of Saleh PA model.

Fig. 6. AM/PM characteristics of Saleh HPA model.

At the receiver side, the performances of the transmission scheme will be assessed in terms of EVM between the complex transmitted symbols and the received ones. The EVM measurement is done on baseband signals. It is therefore necessary to demodulate the signal, by a Fast Fourier Transform (FFT), to recover the I and Q signals. The EVM criterion is defined as:

$$EVM = 10\log_{10}\left(\sqrt{\frac{\mathbb{E}\left\{\left|X(k) - \hat{X}(k)\right|^2\right\}}{\mathbb{E}\left\{|X(k)|^2\right\}}}\right) \tag{13}$$

where, $X(k)$ and $\hat{X}(k)$ are respectively the complex M-QAM transmitted and received symbols over subcarrier k, $k = 1..N$.

3 Neural Network-Based DPD Architectures

Neural Networks (NN) are general function approximations that can be applied to solve almost any machine learning (ML) problems. They attempt to learn a complex mapping from a given input space to another output space. NN have proven their efficiency in modeling non-linear systems such as Power amplifiers. They show also capacity to mitigate PA nonlinear distortion by inverting the PA characteristic via the so called NN-based DPD technique. The multilayer perceptron (MLP) architecture represents an attractive NN structure to compensate for AM/AM and AM/PM distortions [14]. It relies on the input/output relationship of the PA signals and is independent from the origin of the distortions. The complex-valued MLP(C-MLP) topology represents the most basic NN structure proposed to emulate DPD characteristics [15]. The main drawback of this architecture is the cumbersome complex operations resulting in complex weight matrices. To address this issue, the polar MLP (P-MLP) was proposed in [16]. It employs simultaneously two neural networks that deal separately with the amplitude and the phase responses. However, the two NN branches in parallel can converge in different instants, resulting in overtraining or undertraining problem [17]. To this end the real-valued MLP(R-MLP) or Cartesian MLP was introduced which uses the in-phase and quadrature components of the input signal [14]. By this way, the simultaneous convergence issue is resolved. Figure 7 represents the R-MLP structure.

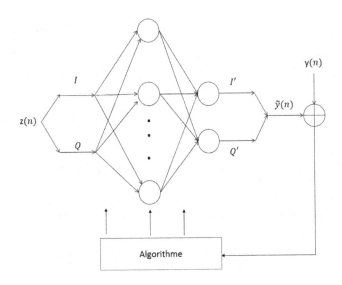

Fig. 7. MLP structure.

The paper proposes and compares two R-MLP structures, presented in Figs. 8 and 9, for DPD modeling. The two architectures take into consideration the PA memory effects. These ones are incorporated using additional buffers at the MLP input layer to account for the previous samples. The back propagation-learning algorithm is used for both architectures to effectively train the MLP neural network. After each forward pass through the network, back propagation performs a backward pass while adjusting the NN's parameters (weights and biases). This learning algorithm makes the MLP very suitable for PA and DPD behavioral modeling [18]. The architecture 1, shown in Fig. 8, contains one input layer, one output layer and one hidden layer. This architecture is fully connected, that is, each input is connected with all the neurons of the hidden layer. The activation function for the hidden layer is the hyperbolic tangent function which is a non-linear function defined by:

$$f(n) = \frac{e^n - e^{-n}}{e^n + e^{-n}} \tag{14}$$

Successively, the output layer uses the following linear activation function:

$$f(n) = n \tag{15}$$

The second architecture, shown in Fig. 9, is a mimetic architecture with an input layer, two hidden layers and an output layer. The input layer and the first hidden layer are no more than a FIR filter in charge of compensating for PA memory. The linear function, given by Eq. 15, is the activation function of the first hidden layer and the output layer, while the hyperbolic tangent function, given by Eq. 14, is the activation function of the second hidden layer. The advantage of this architecture is that it is not completely connected and therefore less complex than the first architecture [19]. For the Hammerstein PA model, the mimetic architecture consists of inverting the FIR filter with 2 linear neurons of the first hidden layer and then inverting the PA non-linearity, with the second hidden layer.

The setting of the number of the hidden layers to 1, in this first proposed architecture, is mainly motivated by the universal approximation theorem, which states that only one hidden layer, with a monotonic bounded and non-constant activation function like hyperbolic tangent function, is sufficient to accurately approximate any nonlinear function [20]. However, this theorem does not insure that the single hidden layer MLP topology is the best and the optimal structure in terms of NN performance criteria like learning time, ease of implementation and the generalization capability [21]. To this end, we have extended the use of the R-MLP to two hidden layers in the second architecture. In addition to the compensation for the effects of nonlinearity of the PA model, the complexity is considered to be the key parameter in the definition of our second structure of MLP neural networks.

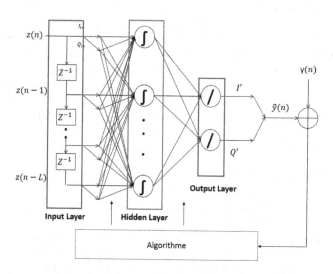

Fig. 8. Architecture 1: Fully connected architecture.

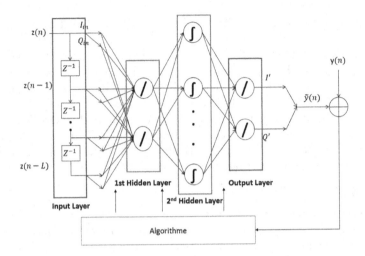

Fig. 9. Architecture 2: Mimetic architecture.

4   Simulation Results

The performances of the two NN architectures are evaluated in terms of EVM, MSE, PSD and complexity. For simulations, we considered the system model presented in section (Sect. 2), with the following parameters: The OFDM modulator uses 128 sub-carriers with 64 activated tones. Each sub-carrier of the OFDM symbol is modulated using a $16 - QAM$ alphabet. To reduce the PAPR of the OFDM signal we use the SLM method with 4 phase vectors. By using the SLM algorithm, the PAPR of the time domain signal is reduced by about 5.5 dB. Next, two different NN based DPD techniques (architectures 1 and 2 of Figs. 8 and 9) are used. Finally, the IBO is adjusted to 9 dB, before amplification using the Hammerstein PA memory model. This model integrates the Saleh PA model and a 2nd order FIR filter with 3 taps ($h = [0.7692, 0.1538, 0.0769]$) for memory effect. The performance of the proposed NN architectures are tested and compared.

EVM. This metric shows the ability of the NN architectures to compensate the IB distortions. It is used to find the optimal parameters for each architecture. To this end, the EVM is calculated by varying the number of neurons in the hidden layer (the 2nd one for architecture 2) from 5 to 29 neurons and the delays of the input layer from 2 to 12. Table 1 and 2 give the EVM results of architecture 1 and 2 respectively. It is clear that both architectures exhibit the best performance with 20 neurons and a delay equal to 12. In terms of EVM, the 2nd architecture outperforms the first one by a gain of 1.9 dB.

Table 1. EVM for architecture 1.

Architecture 1									
NN	5	8	11	14	17	20	23	26	29
L 2	−26.7080	−26.7685	−28.2459	−27.2470	−28.0809	−28.6506	−28.4801	−28.6389	−27.5018
4	−18.9687	−30.0934	−30.7194	−30.8000	−32.0393	−31.9383	−32.1121	−32.5964	−33.5577
6	−23.3207	−29.2637	−30.4050	−31.5621	−32.0150	−32.1873	−32.6012	−33.0532	−33.9788
8	−29.2418	−30.4146	−31.3905	−31.8556	−29.6720	−33.1815	−31.5881	−31.8794	−33.1815
10	−23.5642	−28.8883	−31.1528	−31.1660	−30.9355	−32.8365	−31.8019	−32.9242	−31.4654
12	−22.0144	−31.1849	−32.5831	−30.0112	−32.7602	−34.0035	−33.9383	−33.2987	−33.7231

Table 2. EVM for architecture 2.

Architecture 2									
NN	5	8	11	14	17	20	23	26	29
L 2	−20.9007	−28.0421	−28.8611	−28.8290	−29.0693	−29.0503	−29.1217	−29.0996	−29.0632
4	−22.0709	−30.3681	−34.4262	−34.7913	−35.1514	−34.8413	−35.4390	−35.2956	−32.7934
6	−23.5401	−32.5729	−32.6386	−35.1871	−35.6785	−35.6808	−34.3486	−33.8395	−34.6910
8	−22.0765	−31.3947	−34.9377	−34.9430	−34.9829	−35.2378	−34.5353	−33.4848	−34.0092
10	−30.1637	−33.0369	−34.3699	−34.7963	−34.9769	−35.1675	−34.9960	−35.3396	−35.1908
12	−21.5337	−32.4907	−34.9785	−34.9367	−35.3465	−35.9364	−34.4962	−35.7447	−35.3659

MSE. The MSE measures the convergence of the Neural Network according to the mean square error given by Eq. 9. It is clear from Fig. 10 that architecture 1 converges after 20 iterations approximately and the second one after 100 iterations. Nevertheless it can be seen that architecture 2 achieves the best performance in terms of MSE after convergence.

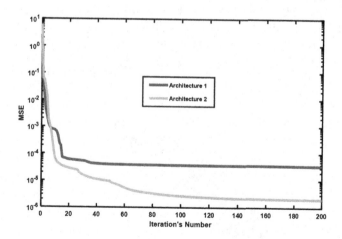

Fig. 10. NN convergence.

PSD. The Power Spectral Density measures the neural network's capability for compensation of the OOB distortions. Figure 11 illustrates the PSD of the signal at the output the PA without DPD and using architecture 1 and 2. From Fig. 11, it can be seen that the two NN based DPD compensate for the OBO distortions and correct the memory efficiently the memory effects over the useful signal bandwidth. Performances of the two architectures, in terms of PSD, are almost the same and very close to the PSD achieved by a perfect linear PA.

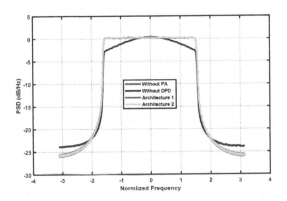

Fig. 11. PSD at the PA output using:(1) ideal PA, (2) NL PA without DPD, (3) NL PA with DPD 1, (4) NL PA with DPD 2.

AM/AM and AM/PM Characteristics. The Hammerstein Model exhibits non linear characteristics and strong memory effects, corresponding to high dispersion over the AM/AM and AM/PM PA conversion characteristics. The two proposed R-MLP architectures do well in linearizing the PA characteristics, by reducing both memory and non linear effects. From Fig. 12 and Fig. 13 it can be seen also that architecture 2 outperforms architecture 1, in terms of PA linearization, confirming the advantage of the proposed architecture.

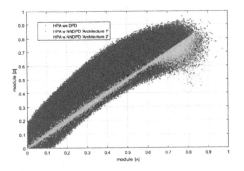

Fig. 12. AM/AM characteristic.

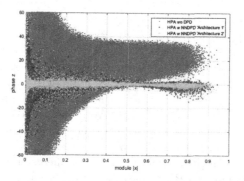

Fig. 13. AM/PM characteristic.

Complexity. It is important to compare the neural network's architectures in terms of complexity. This criterion is assessed in terms of the number of real multiplication (RM) involved in the NN structure. For the two architectures the complexities are given by the following equations:

$$Architecture1 : RM1 = 2(I_1 + 1)H_{11} + H_{11}O_1 \tag{16}$$

$$Architecture2 : RM2 = 2(I_2 + 1)H_{21} + H_{21}H_{22} + H_{22}O_2 \tag{17}$$

- I_1, I_2: Number of Inputs of architecture 1 and 2 respectively
- H_{11}: Number of neurones in the 1st hidden layer of architecture 1
- H_{21}: Number of neurones in the 1st hidden layer of architecture 2
- H_{22}: Number of neurones in the 2nd hidden layer of architecture 2
- O_1, O_2: Number of neurones in the output layer of architecture 1 and 2 respectively.

Table 3 gives the number of real multiplication for each architecture. It is well shown that the architecture 2 is significantly less complex than architecture 1 with only 132 multiplications, corresponding to a more than 76% gain, in terms of complexity.

Table 3. Complexity.

Architectures	Number of multiplications	Best performance EVM
1	560	-34.0035
2	132	-35.9364

5   Conclusion

This paper investigates a NN-based digital predistortion for the compensation of PA impairment in an OFDM systems. The considered PA is a Hammerstein model. The proposed solution is modeled by a mimetic-R-MLP that aims at realizing the memory predistortion by a linear network and the predistortion of the memoryless nonlinearities (AM/AM and AM/PM) with a nonlinear neural network. We carried out a comparative study of the proposed mimetic-R-MLP and the classical R-MLP, which deals with the two problems as a whole and compensate jointly the nonlinear distortions and memory effects. The simulation results show that the mimetic-R-MLP provides slight improvement in linearization performance, about 1.9 dB in terms of EVM, compared to the classical R-MLP. Most importantly, the computational complexity of the proposed mimetic-R-MLP is much lower than the R-MLP with an approximate gain of 76.4%.

As mentioned earlier, PAPR reduction together with DPD is primordial in order to enhance both linearity and efficiency. In the future, we intend to study technology and opportunities offered by advanced machine/deep learning to deal jointly with PAPR reduction and DPD, improving the transmitter's performance in presence of hardware imperfections. The intended machine/deep learning techniques are Autoencoder, LSTM,... accompanied with meta-learning and reinforcement-learning methods.

References

1. Fettweis, G., Zimmermann, E.: ICT energy consumption trends and challenges. In: 11th International Symposium on Wireless Personal Multimedia Communications (WPMC 2008)
2. Zaidi, A.A., et al.: Waveform and numerology to support 5G services and requirements. IEEE Commun. Mag. **54**(11), 90–98 (2016)
3. Shaiek, H., Zayani, R., Medjahdi, Y., Roviras, D.: Analytical analysis of SER for beyond 5G post-OFDM Waveforms. In: Presence of High-Power Amplifiers. IEEE Access, vol. 7, no. 1, pp. 29441–29452, December 2019. https://doi.org/10.1109/ACCESS.2019.2900977
4. Gilabert, P.-L., Montoro, G., Bertran, E.: On the Wiener and Hammerstein models for power amplifier predistortion. In: Asia-Pacific Microwave Conference Proceedings (2005)
5. Shammasi, M.-M., Safavi, M.: Performance of a predistorter based on Saleh model for OFDM systems. In: HPA nonlinearity, 14th International Conference on Advanced Communication Technology (ICACT) (2012)
6. Zayani, R., Bouallegue, R. Roviras, D.: Adaptive predistortions based on neural networks associated with Levenberg-Marquardt algorithm for satellite down links. EURASIP J. Wirel. Commun. Netw. **2008** (2008). Article ID 132729, 15 pages
7. Tarver, C., Jiang, L., Sefidi, A., Cavallaro, J.-R.: Neural network DPD via back-propagation through a neural network model of the PA. In: 53rd Asilomar Conference on Signals, Systems, and Computers (2019)
8. Jiang, T., Wu, Y.: An overview: peak-to-average power ratio reduction techniques for OFDM signals. IEEE Trans. Broadcast. **2**(54), 257–268 (2008)

9. Wunder, G.: The PAPR problem in OFDM transmission. IEEE Signal Process. Mag. **30**, 130–144 (2013)
10. Bauml, R.R.-W.-R., Fischer, F.-H., Huber, J.-B.: Reducing the peak-to-average power ratio of multicarrier modulation by selected mapping. IEEE Electron. Lett. **32**(22), 2056–2057 (1996)
11. Katz, A., Wood, J., Chokola, D.: The evolution of PA linearization. IEEE Microw. Mag. **17**(2), 32–40 (2016)
12. Saleh, A.-A.: Frequency-independent and frequency-dependent nonlinear models of TWT amplifiers. IEEE-J-COM **29**(11), 1715–1720 (1981)
13. Kenington, P.: High-Linearity RF Amplifier Design. Artech House, Boston (1999)
14. Rawat, M., Ghannouchi, F.M.: A mutual distortion and impairment compensator for wideband direct-conversion transmitters using neural networks. IEEE Trans. Broadcast. **58**(2), 168–177 (2012)
15. Ibukahla, M., et al.: Neural networks for modeling nonlinear memoryless communication channels. IEEE Trans. Commun. **45**(7), 768–771 (1997)
16. Benvenuto, N., Piazza, F., Uncini, A.: A neural network approach to data predistortion with memory. In: Digital Radio Systems. Proceedings of ICC 1993-IEEE International Conference on Communications, vol. 1. IEEE (1993)
17. Wang, D., et al.: Augmented real-valued time-delay neural network for compensation of distortions and impairments. IEEE Trans. Neural Netw. Learn. Syst. **30**(1), 242–254 (2018)
18. Wood, J., et al.: Envelope-domain time series (ET) behavioral model of a Doherty RF power amplifier for system design. IEEE Trans. Microwave Theory Tech. **54**(8), 3163–3172 (2006)
19. Belkacem, O.-B., Zayani, R., Ammari, M-L., Bouallegue, R., Roviras, D.,: Neural network equalization for frequency selective nonlinear MIMO channels. In: 2012 IEEE Symposium on Computers and Communications (ISCC), pp. 000018–000022, July 2012
20. Funahashi, K.-I.: On the approximate realization of continuous mappings by neural networks. Neural Netw. **2**(3), 183–192 (1989)
21. Mkadem, F., Boumaiza, S.: Physically inspired neural network model for RF power amplifier behavioral modeling and digital predistortion. IEEE Trans. Microwave Theory Tech. **59**(4), 913–923 (2011)

Author Index

Printed in the United States
By Bookmasters